WRITER: Robert Kirkm[an]
ARTIST: Sean Phillip[s]
COLORIST: June Chun[g]
LETTERER: VC's Rus Woo[ton]
ASSISTANT EDITOR: Lauren Sankovitch
EDITOR: Bill Rosemann
SENIOR EDITOR: Ralph Macchio

COVER ARTIST: Arthur Suydam

COLLECTION EDITOR: Mark D. Beazley
ASSISTANT EDITORS: Nelson Ribeiro & Alex Starbuck
EDITOR, SPECIAL PROJECTS: Jennifer Grünwald
SENIOR EDITOR, SPECIAL PROJECTS: Jeff Youngquist
SENIOR VICE PRESIDENT OF SALES: David Gabriel
SVP OF BRAND PLANNING & COMMUNICATIONS: Michael Pasciullo
PRODUCTION: Jerry Kalinowski

EDITOR IN CHIEF: Axel Alonso
CHIEF CREATIVE OFFICER: Joe Quesada
PUBLISHER: Dan Buckley
EXECUTIVE PRODUCER: Alan Fine

MARVEL ZOMBIES 2. Contains material originally published in magazine form as MARVEL ZOMBIES 2 #1-5. Second printing 2012. ISBN# 978-0-7851-2546-4. Published by MARVEL WORLDWIDE, INC., a subsidiary of MARVEL ENTERTAINMENT, LLC. OFFICE OF PUBLICATION: 135 West 50th Street, New York, NY 10020. Copyright © 2008 and 2009 Marvel Characters, Inc. All rights reserved. $15.99 per copy in the U.S. and $17.99 in Canada (GST #R127032852); Canadian Agreement #40668537. All characters featured in this issue and the distinctive names and likenesses thereof, and all related indicia are trademarks of Marvel Characters, Inc. No similarity between any of the names, characters, persons, and/or institutions in this magazine with those of any living or dead person or institution is intended, and any such similarity which may exist is purely coincidental. Printed in the U.S.A. ALAN FINE, EVP - Office of the President, Marvel Worldwide, Inc. and EVP & CMO Marvel Characters B.V.; DAN BUCKLEY, Publisher & President - Print, Animation & Digital Divisions; JOE QUESADA, Chief Creative Officer; DAVID BOGART, SVP of Business Affairs & Talent Management; TOM BREVOORT, SVP of Publishing; C.B. CEBULSKI, SVP of Creator & Content Development; DAVID GABRIEL, SVP of Publishing Sales & Circulation; MICHAEL PASCIULLO, SVP of Brand Planning & Communications; JIM O'KEEFE, VP of Operations & Logistics; DAN CARR, Executive Director of Publishing Technology; SUSAN CRESPI, Editorial Operations Manager; ALEX MORALES, Publishing Operations Manager; STAN LEE, Chairman Emeritus. For information regarding advertising in Marvel Comics or on Marvel.com, please contact John Dokes, SVP Integrated Sales and Marketing, at jdokes@marvel.com. For Marvel subscription inquiries, please call 800-217-9158. jdokes@marvel.com. For Marvel subscription inquiries, please call 800-217-9158. Manufactured between 2/6/12 and 2/28/12 by QUAD/GRAPHICS, DUBUQUE, IA, USA.

098765432

IT STARTED WITH A FLASH IN THE SKY, AND A RIPPLE THROUGH THE CLOUDS. THE HUNGER IS WHAT BROUGHT IT HERE — AND FEED IT DID, UNTIL THE MARVEL HEROES WERE NO MORE.

THEY WERE REPLACED BY SOULLESS MONSTERS, DRIVEN ONLY BY AN INSATIABLE HUNGER FOR HUMAN FLESH.

AFTER THEY RAN OUT OF FOOD, MISTER FANTASTIC DEVISED A PLAN TO LURE HIS COUNTERPART FROM ANOTHER DIMENSION INTO A DEADLY TRAP. THANKS TO MAGNETO, WHO HAD MANAGED TO STAY UNINFECTED, REED'S PLAN FAILED, LEAVING HIM AND THE REST OF THE FANTASTIC FOUR STRANDED IN ANOTHER DIMENSION.

MAGNETO HAS DESTROYED THE MACHINE THAT ALLOWED THEIR PASSAGE INTO ANOTHER DIMENSION — AN ACTION HE PAID FOR WITH HIS LIFE.

THE SILVER SURFER APPEARED IN THE SKIES FOLLOWED SHORTLY AFTER BY THE ARRIVAL OF GALACTUS. IT WAS LITTLE MORE THAN AN OBSTACLE FOR THE MONSTERS THE MARVEL HEROES HAD BECOME.

DEVOURING THE SILVER SURFER AND GALACTUS PROVIDED THE GHOULS WITH COSMIC POWERS AND COSMIC HUNGER. WITH NO FOOD LEFT ON EARTH, THEY SET THEIR SIGHTS FOR THE STARS, FOR SPACE — AND THE UNIVERSE WAS NEVER THE SAME AGAIN.

THIS IS NO WORLD OF MARVEL HEROES.

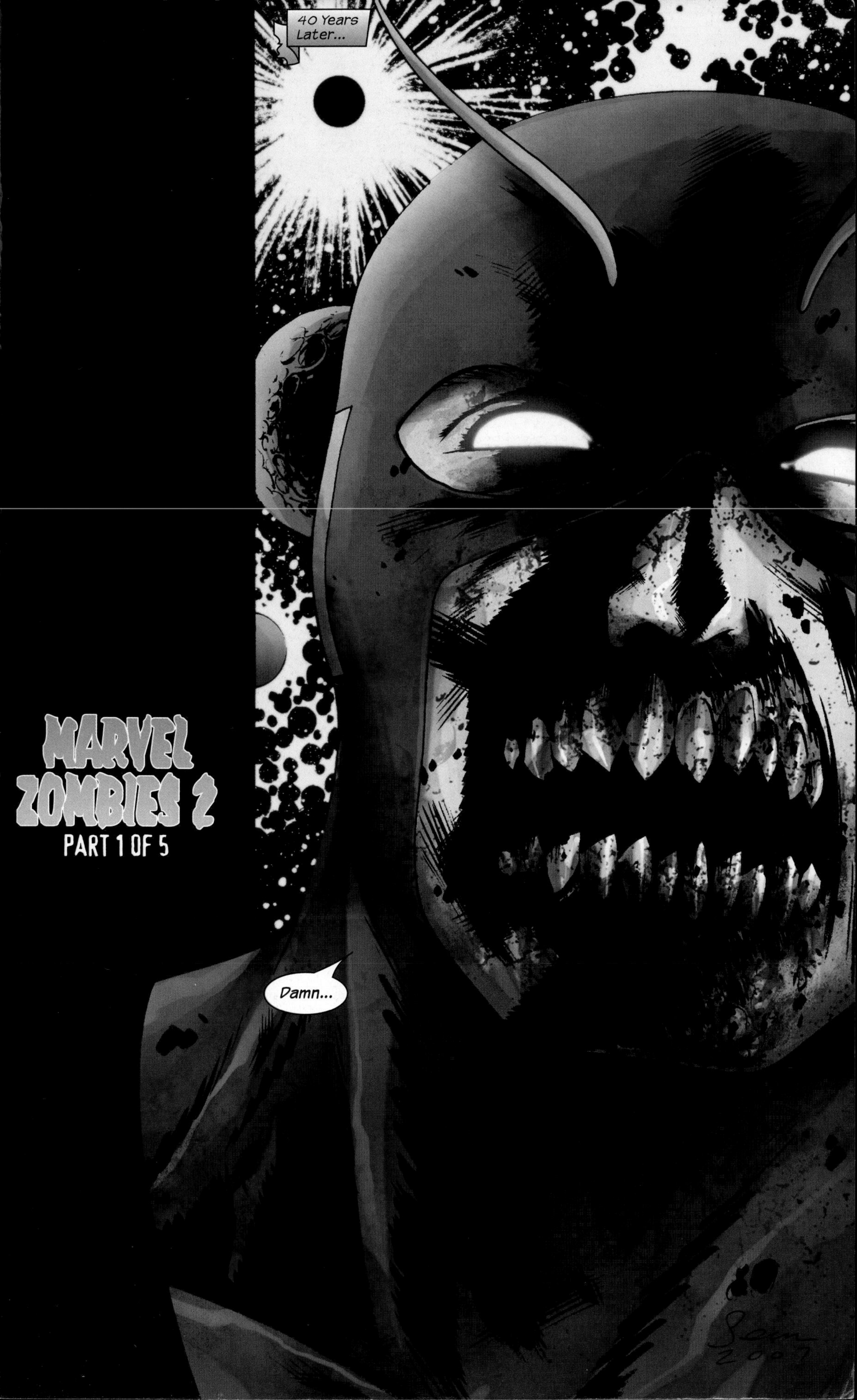
40 Years Later...
MARVEL ZOMBIES 2
PART 1 OF 5
Damn...

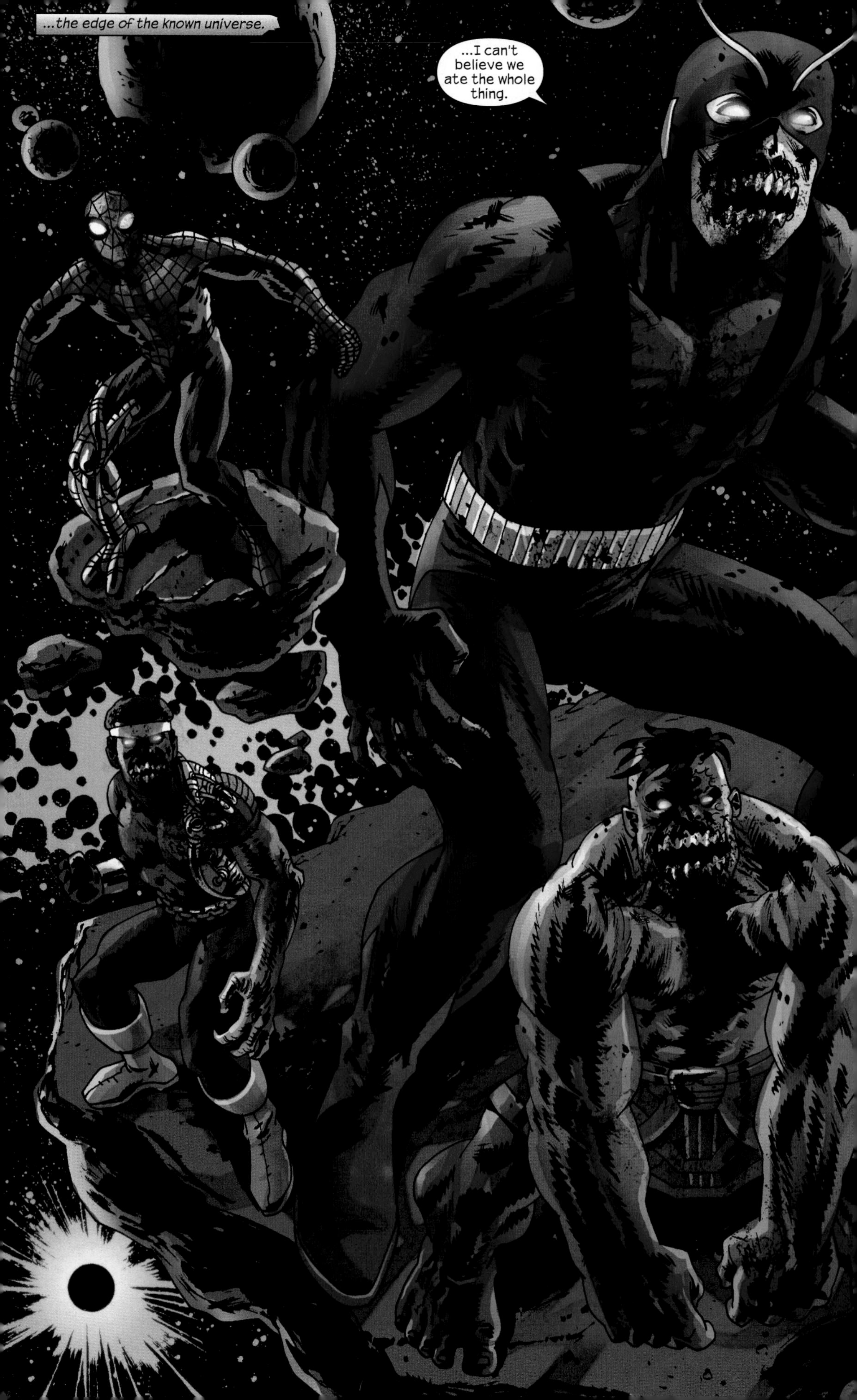
...the edge of the known universe.
...I can't believe we ate the whole thing.

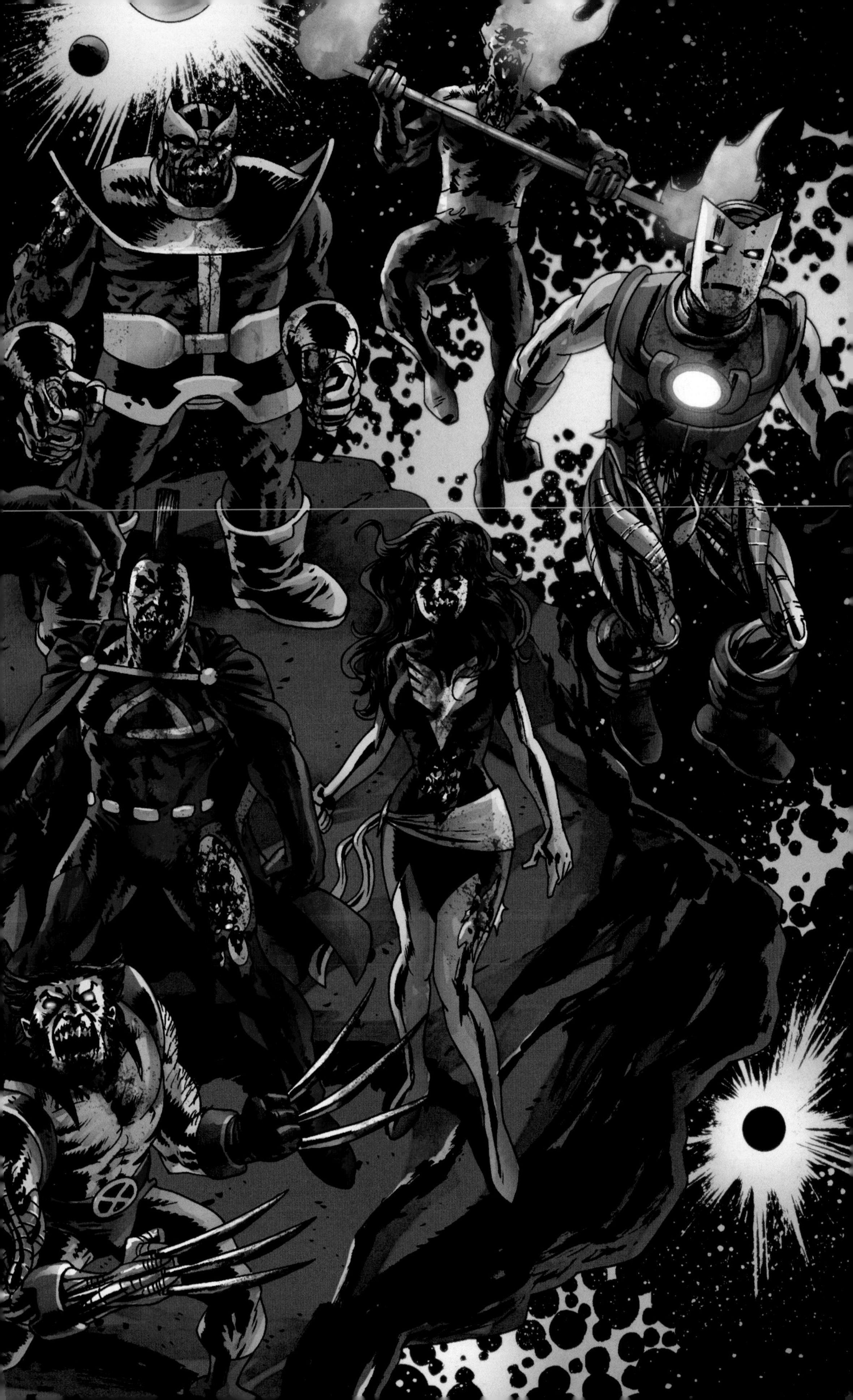

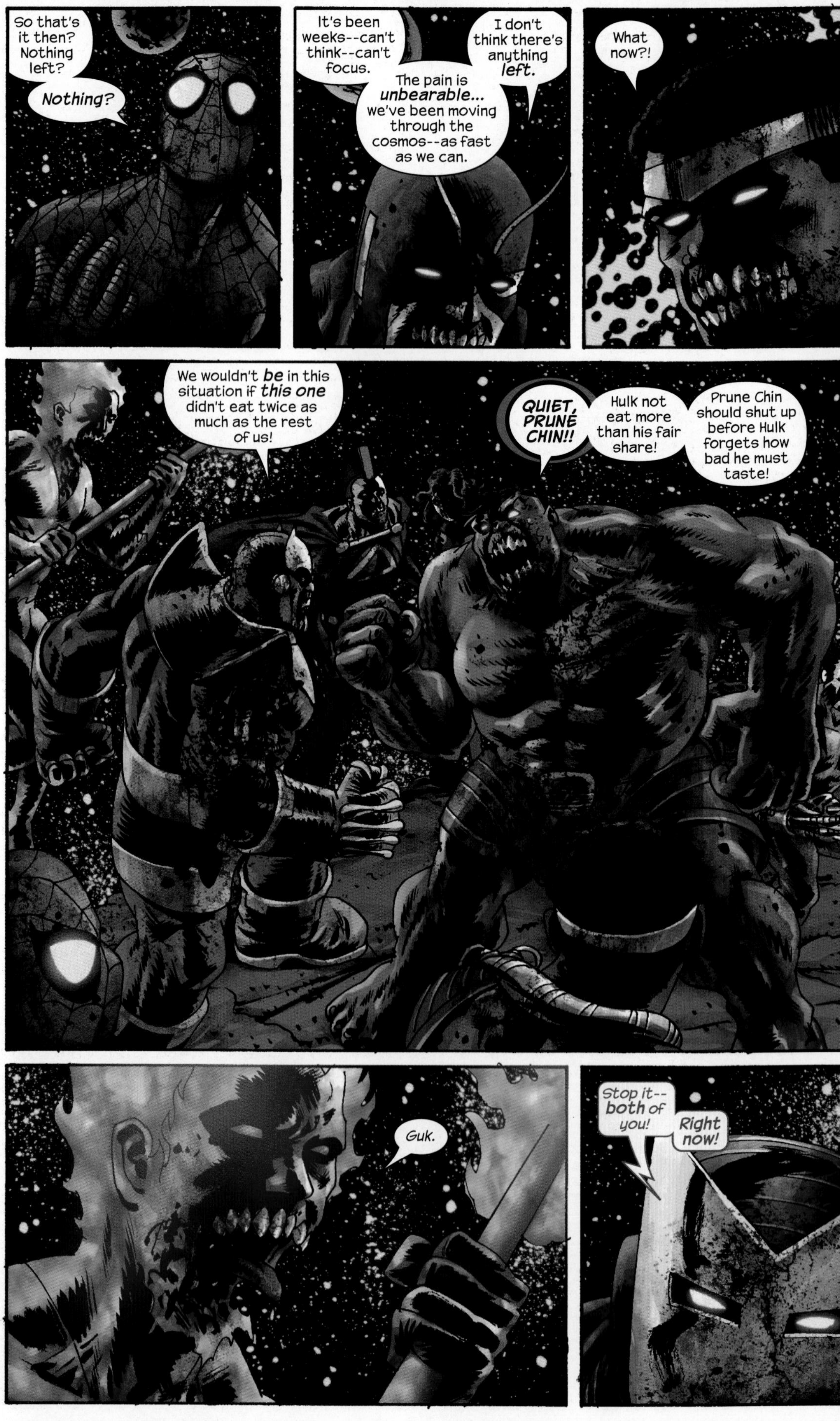
So that's it then? Nothing left?
Nothing?
It's been weeks--can't think--can't focus.
The pain is unbearable... we've been moving through the cosmos--as fast as we can.
I don't think there's anything left.
What now?!
We wouldn't be in this situation if this one didn't eat twice as much as the rest of us!
QUIET, PRUNE CHIN!!
Hulk not eat more than his fair share!
Prune Chin should shut up before Hulk forgets how bad he must taste!
Guk.
Stop it--both of you!
Right now!

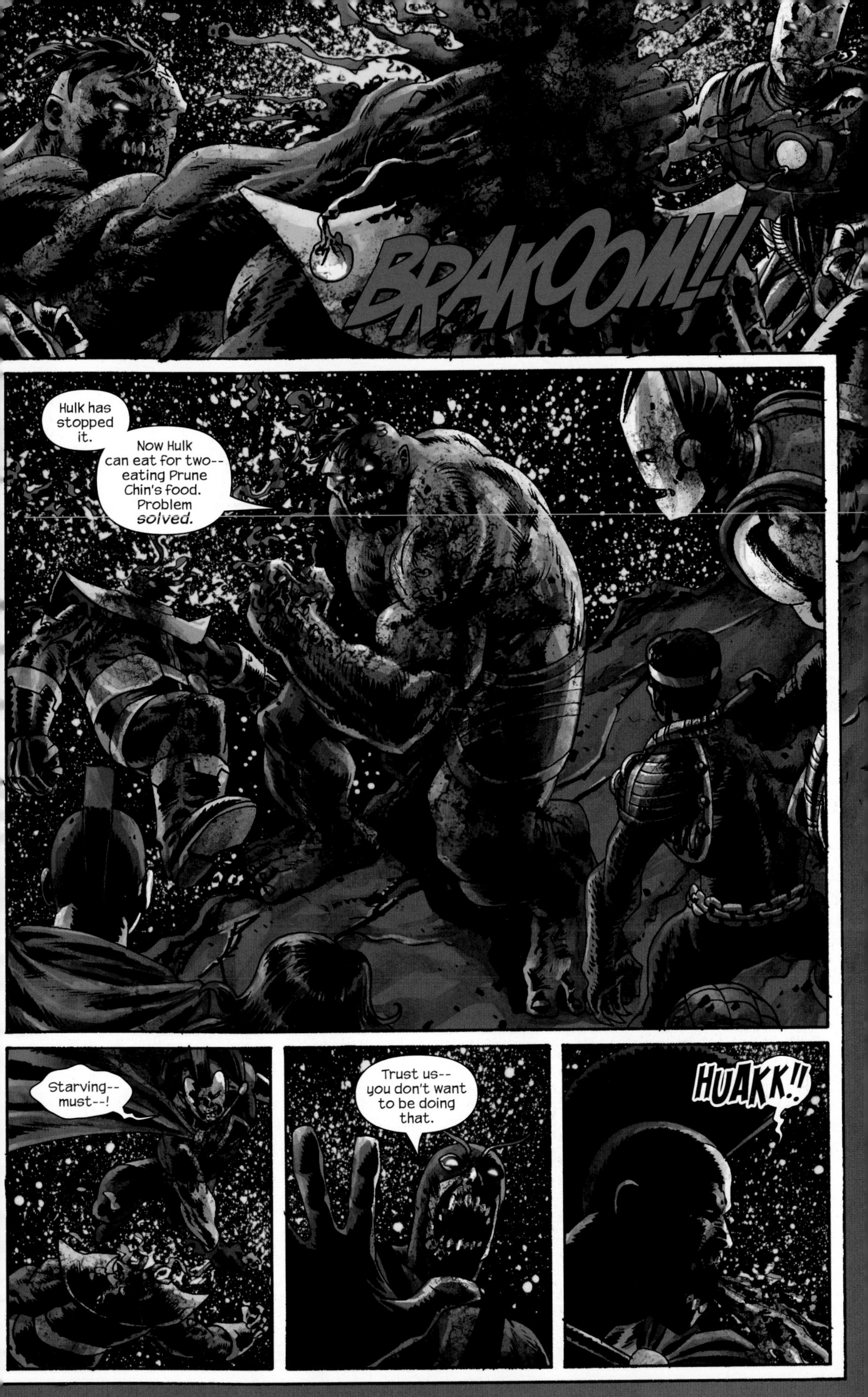
BRAKOOM!!
Hulk has stopped it.
Now Hulk can eat for two-- eating Prune Chin's food. Problem solved.
Starving-- must--!
Trust us-- you don't want to be doing that.
HUAKK!!

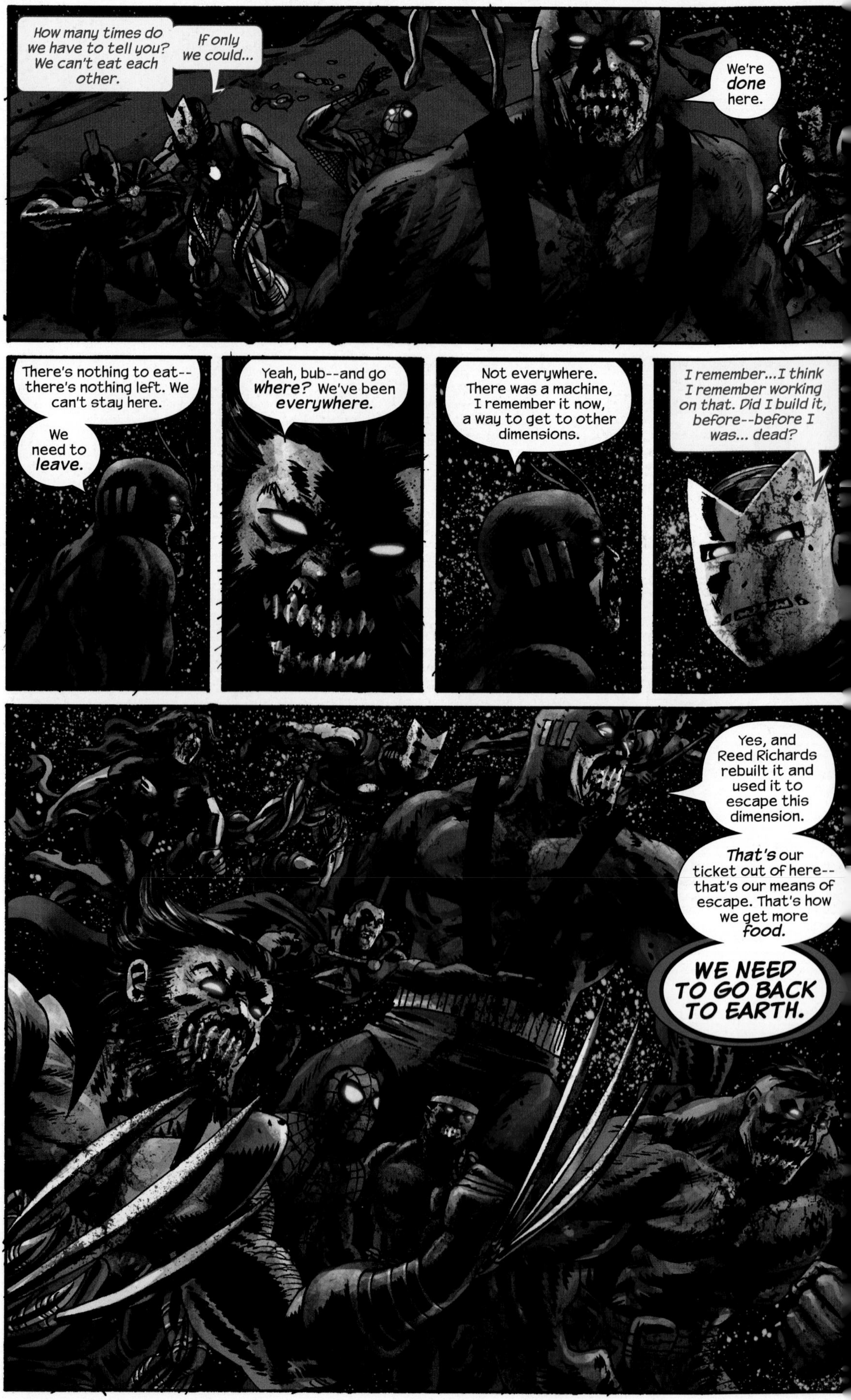
How many times do we have to tell you? We can't eat each other.
If only we could...
We're done here.
There's nothing to eat--there's nothing left. We can't stay here.
We need to leave.
Yeah, bub--and go where? We've been everywhere.
Not everywhere. There was a machine, I remember it now, a way to get to other dimensions.
I remember...I think I remember working on that. Did I build it, before--before I was... dead?
Yes, and Reed Richards rebuilt it and used it to escape this dimension.
That's our ticket out of here--that's our means of escape. That's how we get more food.
WE NEED TO GO BACK TO EARTH.

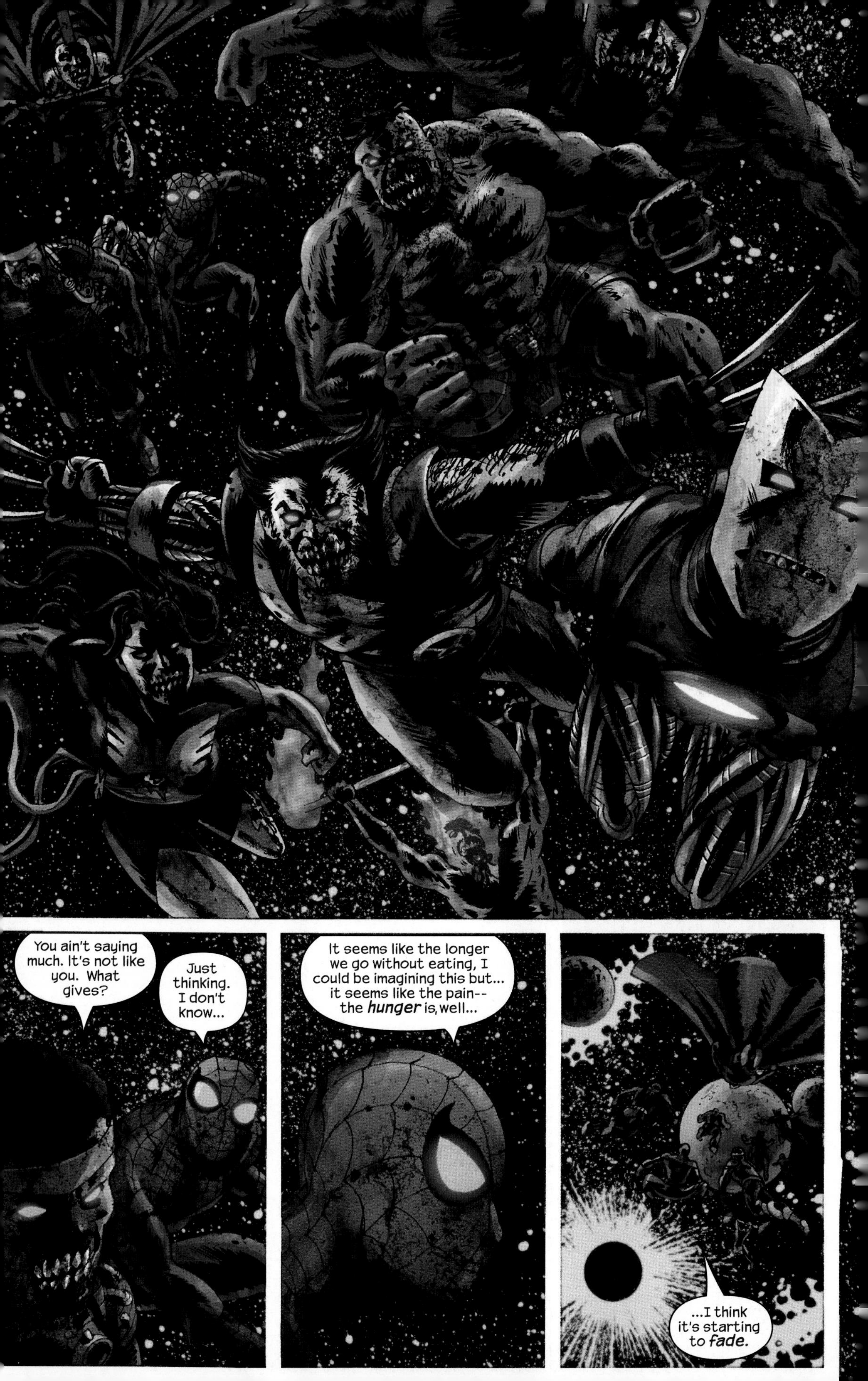
You ain't saying much. It's not like you. What gives?
Just thinking. I don't know...
It seems like the longer we go without eating, I could be imagining this but... it seems like the pain-- the *hunger* is, well...
...I think it's starting to *fade*.

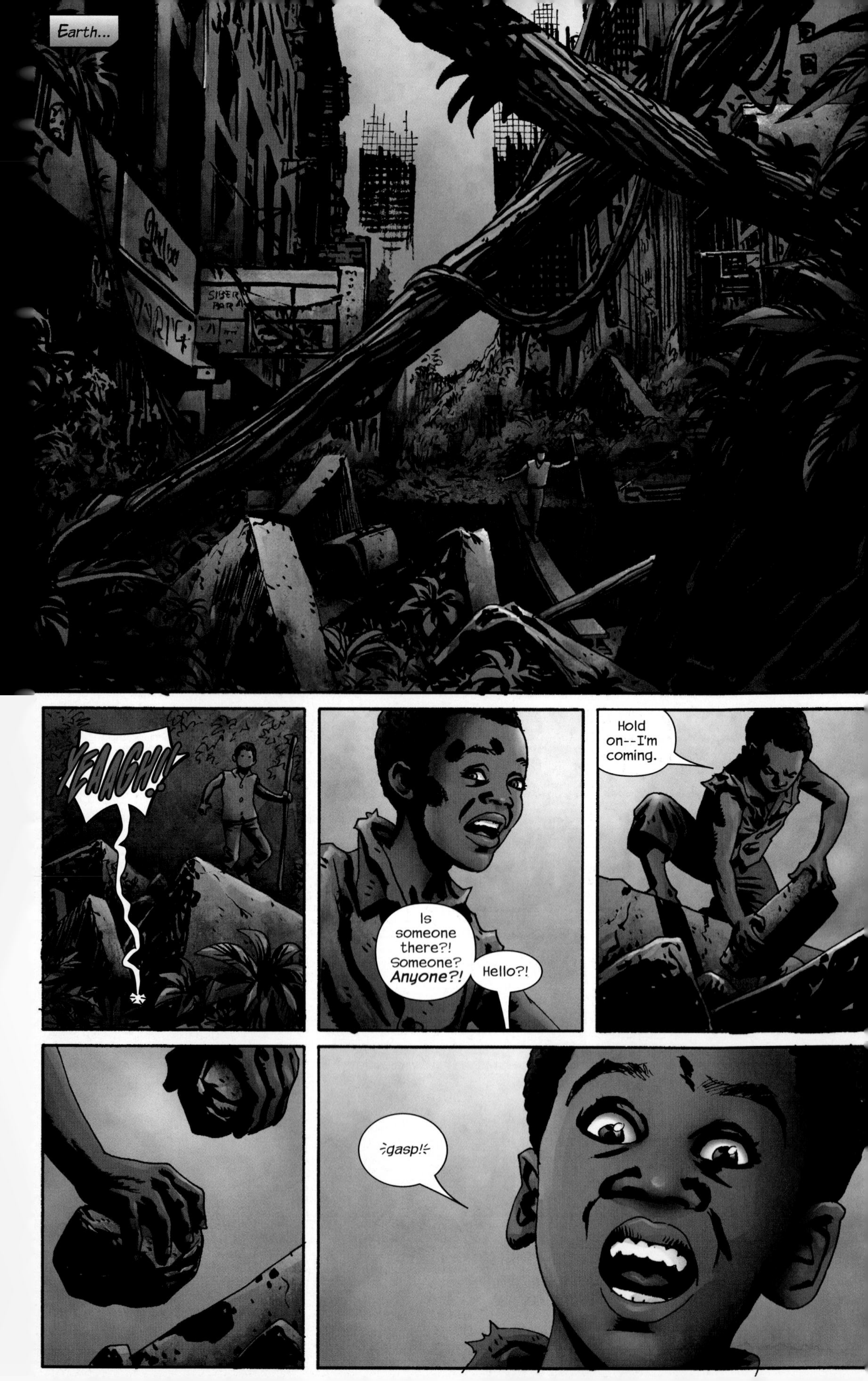
Earth...
YEAAGH!!
Is someone there?! Someone? Anyone?!
Hello?!
Hold on--I'm coming.
gasp!

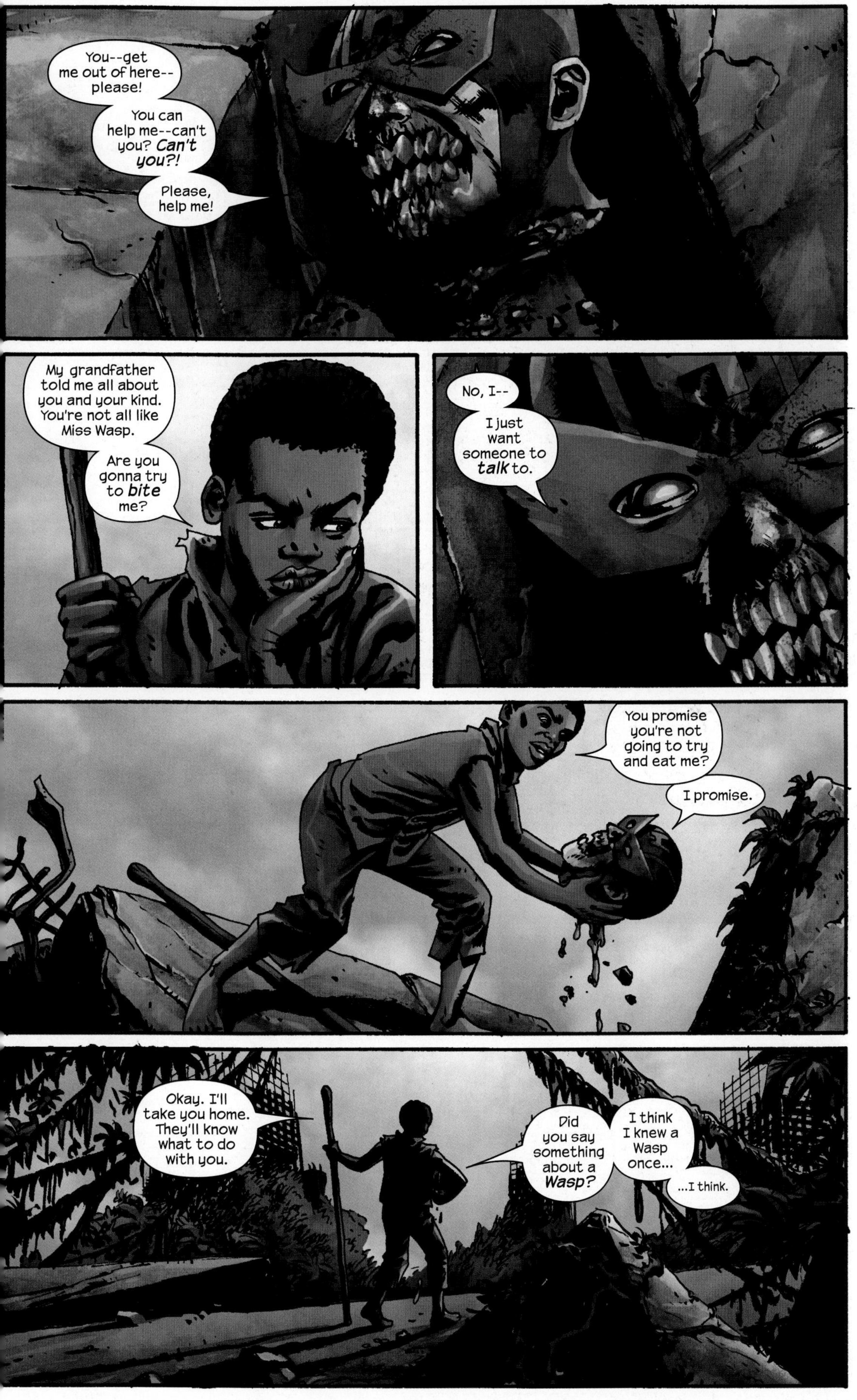
You--get me out of here-- please!
You can help me--can't you? Can't you?!
Please, help me!
My grandfather told me all about you and your kind. You're not all like Miss Wasp.
Are you gonna try to bite me?
No, I--
I just want someone to talk to.
You promise you're not going to try and eat me?
I promise.
Okay. I'll take you home. They'll know what to do with you.
Did you say something about a Wasp?
I think I knew a Wasp once...
...I think.

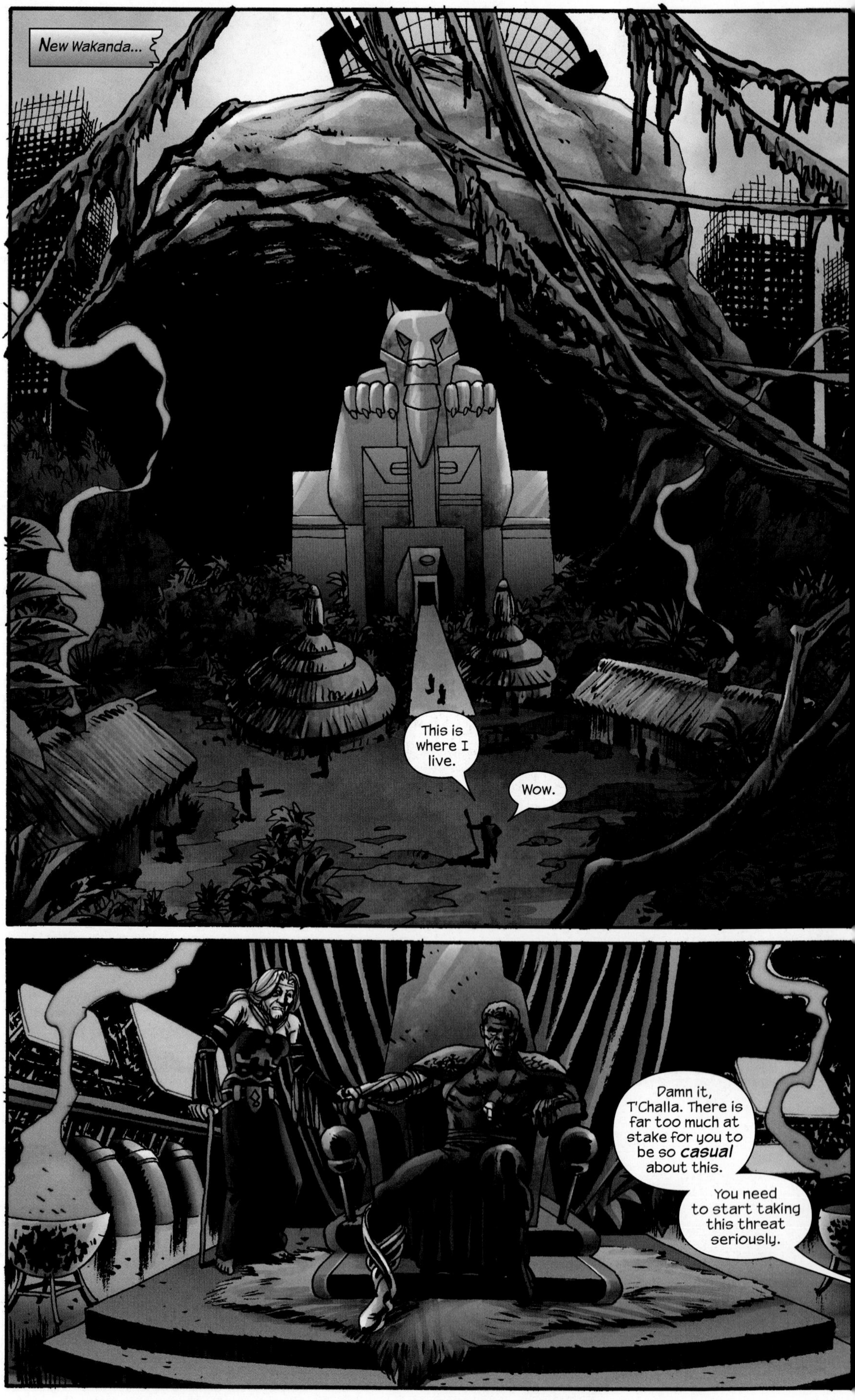

New Wakanda...
This is where I live.
Wow.
Damn it, T'Challa. There is far too much at stake for you to be so *casual* about this.
You need to start taking this threat seriously.

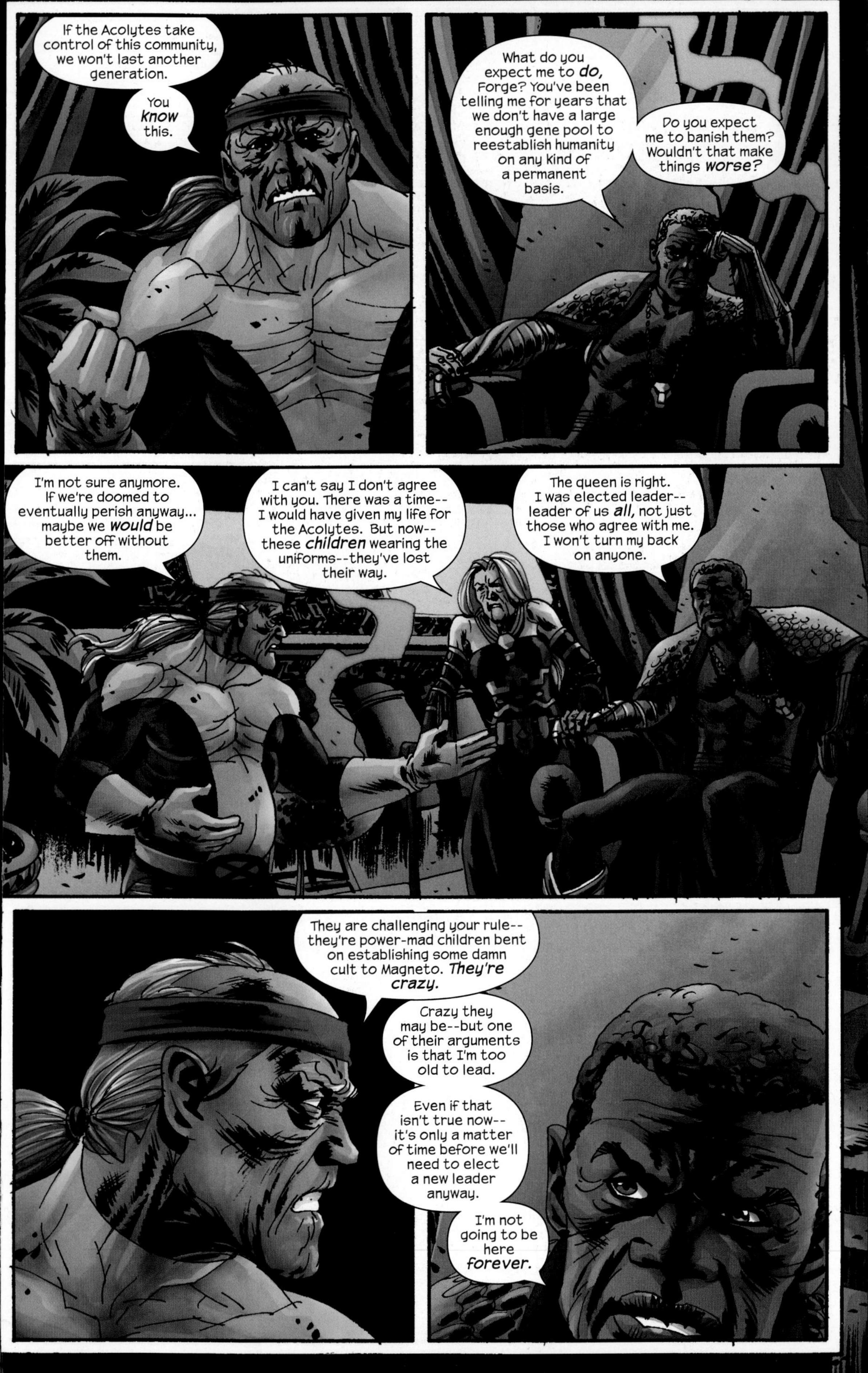

If the Acolytes take control of this community, we won't last another generation.
You *know* this.
What do you expect me to *do,* Forge? You've been telling me for years that we don't have a large enough gene pool to reestablish humanity on any kind of a permanent basis.
Do you expect me to banish them? Wouldn't that make things *worse?*
I'm not sure anymore. If we're doomed to eventually perish anyway... maybe we *would* be better off without them.
I can't say I don't agree with you. There was a time--I would have given my life for the Acolytes. But now--these *children* wearing the uniforms--they've lost their way.
The queen is right. I was elected leader--leader of us *all,* not just those who agree with me. I won't turn my back on anyone.
They are challenging your rule--they're power-mad children bent on establishing some damn cult to Magneto. *They're crazy.*
Crazy they may be--but one of their arguments is that I'm too old to lead.
Even if that isn't true now--it's only a matter of time before we'll need to elect a new leader anyway.
I'm not going to be here *forever.*

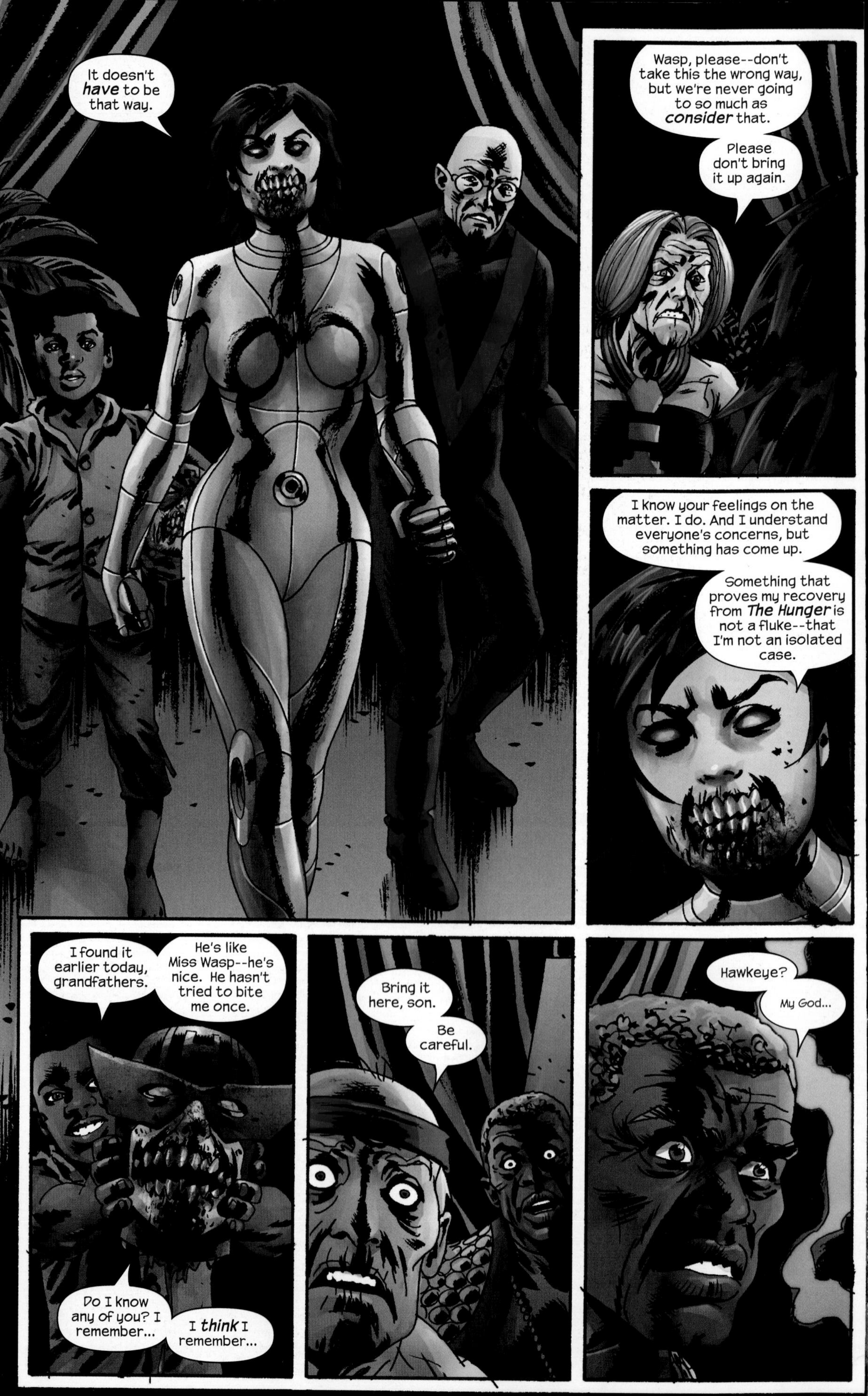
It doesn't *have* to be that way.
Wasp, please--don't take this the wrong way, but we're never going to so much as *consider* that.
Please don't bring it up again.
I know your feelings on the matter. I do. And I understand everyone's concerns, but something has come up.
Something that proves my recovery from *The Hunger* is not a fluke--that I'm not an isolated case.
I found it earlier today, grandfathers.
He's like Miss Wasp--he's nice. He hasn't tried to bite me once.
Do I know any of you? I remember...
I *think* I remember...
Bring it here, son.
Be careful.
Hawkeye?
My God...

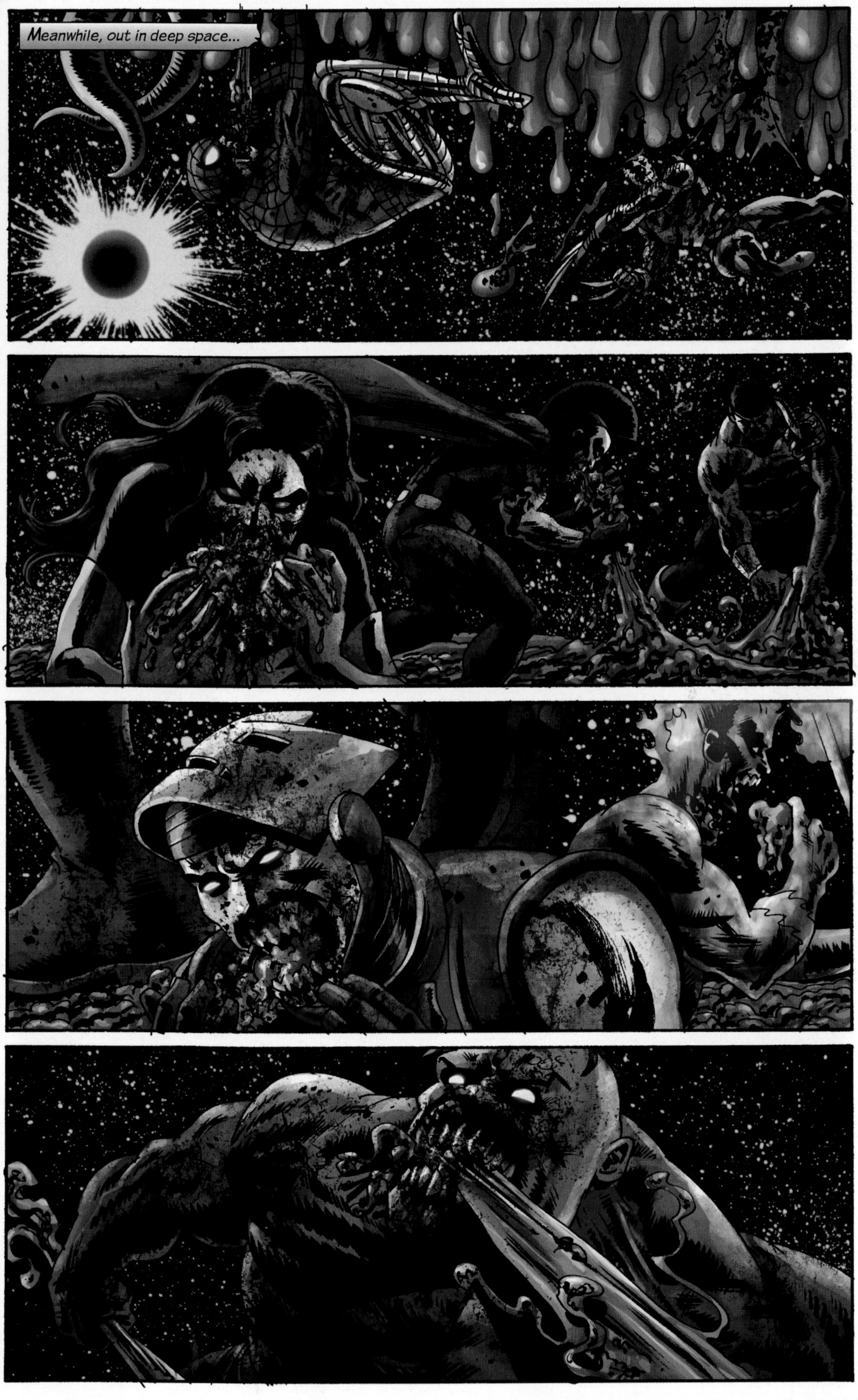
Meanwhile, out in deep space...

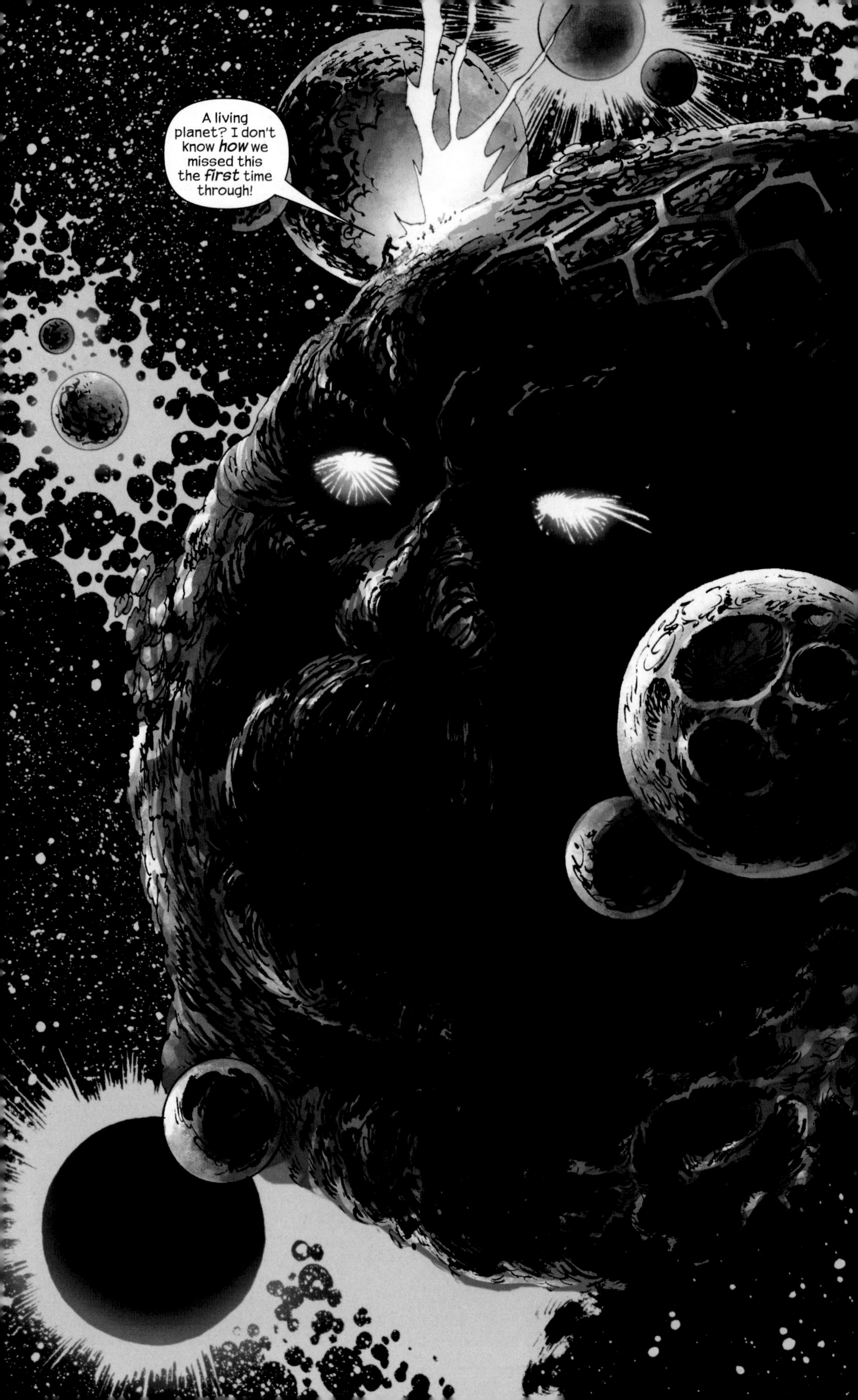
A living planet? I don't know *how* we missed this the *first* time through!

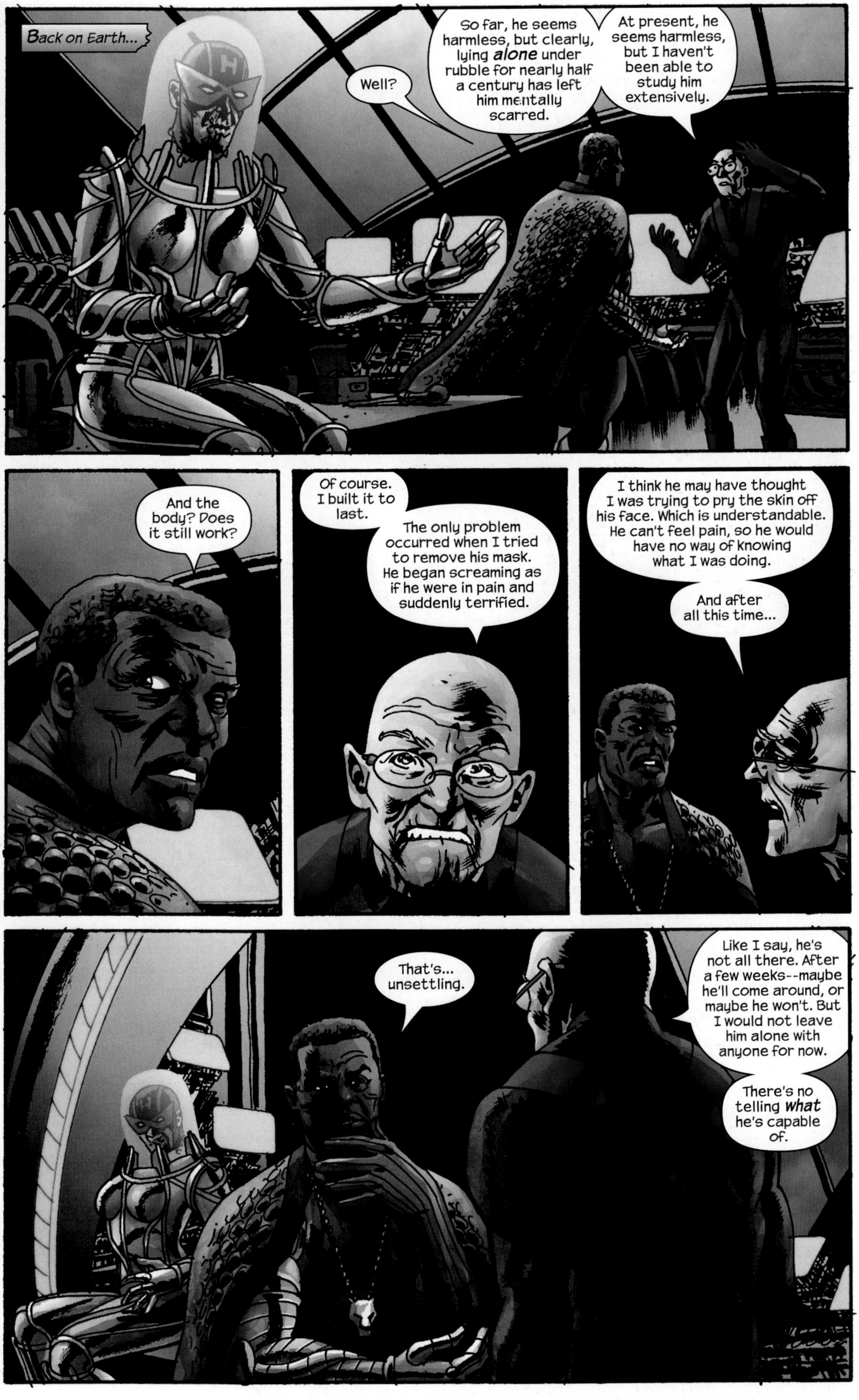
Back on Earth...
Well?
So far, he seems harmless, but clearly, lying *alone* under rubble for nearly half a century has left him mentally scarred.
At present, he seems harmless, but I haven't been able to study him extensively.
And the body? Does it still work?
Of course. I built it to last.
The only problem occurred when I tried to remove his mask. He began screaming as if he were in pain and suddenly terrified.
I think he may have thought I was trying to pry the skin off his face. Which is understandable. He can't feel pain, so he would have no way of knowing what I was doing.
And after all this time...
That's... unsettling.
Like I say, he's not all there. After a few weeks--maybe he'll come around, or maybe he won't. But I would not leave him alone with anyone for now.
There's no telling *what* he's capable of.

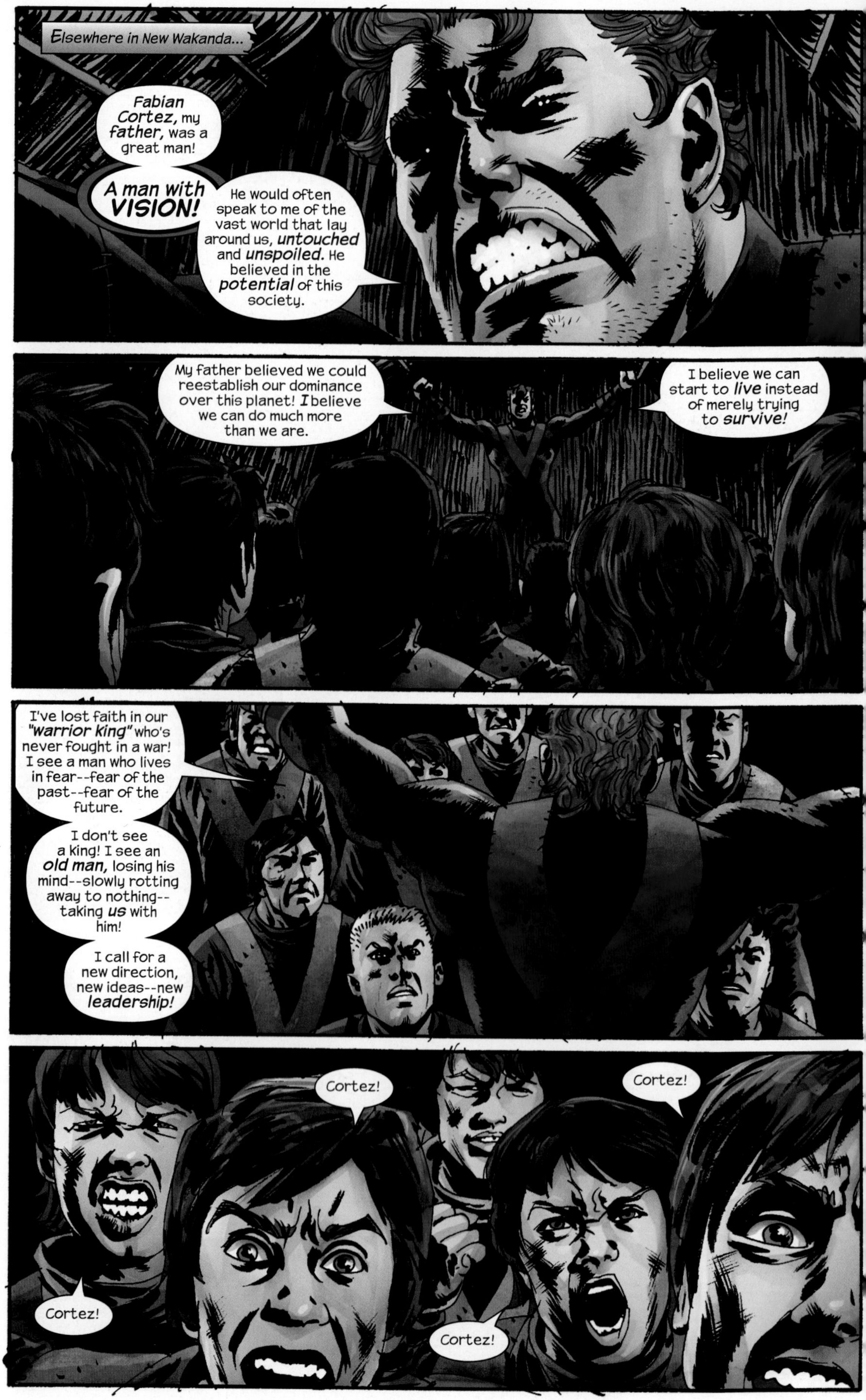
Elsewhere in New Wakanda...
Fabian Cortez, my father, was a great man!
A man with VISION!
He would often speak to me of the vast world that lay around us, untouched and unspoiled. He believed in the potential of this society.
My father believed we could reestablish our dominance over this planet! I believe we can do much more than we are.
I believe we can start to live instead of merely trying to survive!
I've lost faith in our "warrior king" who's never fought in a war! I see a man who lives in fear--fear of the past--fear of the future.
I don't see a king! I see an old man, losing his mind--slowly rotting away to nothing--taking us with him!
I call for a new direction, new ideas--new leadership!
Cortez!
Cortez!
Cortez!
Cortez!

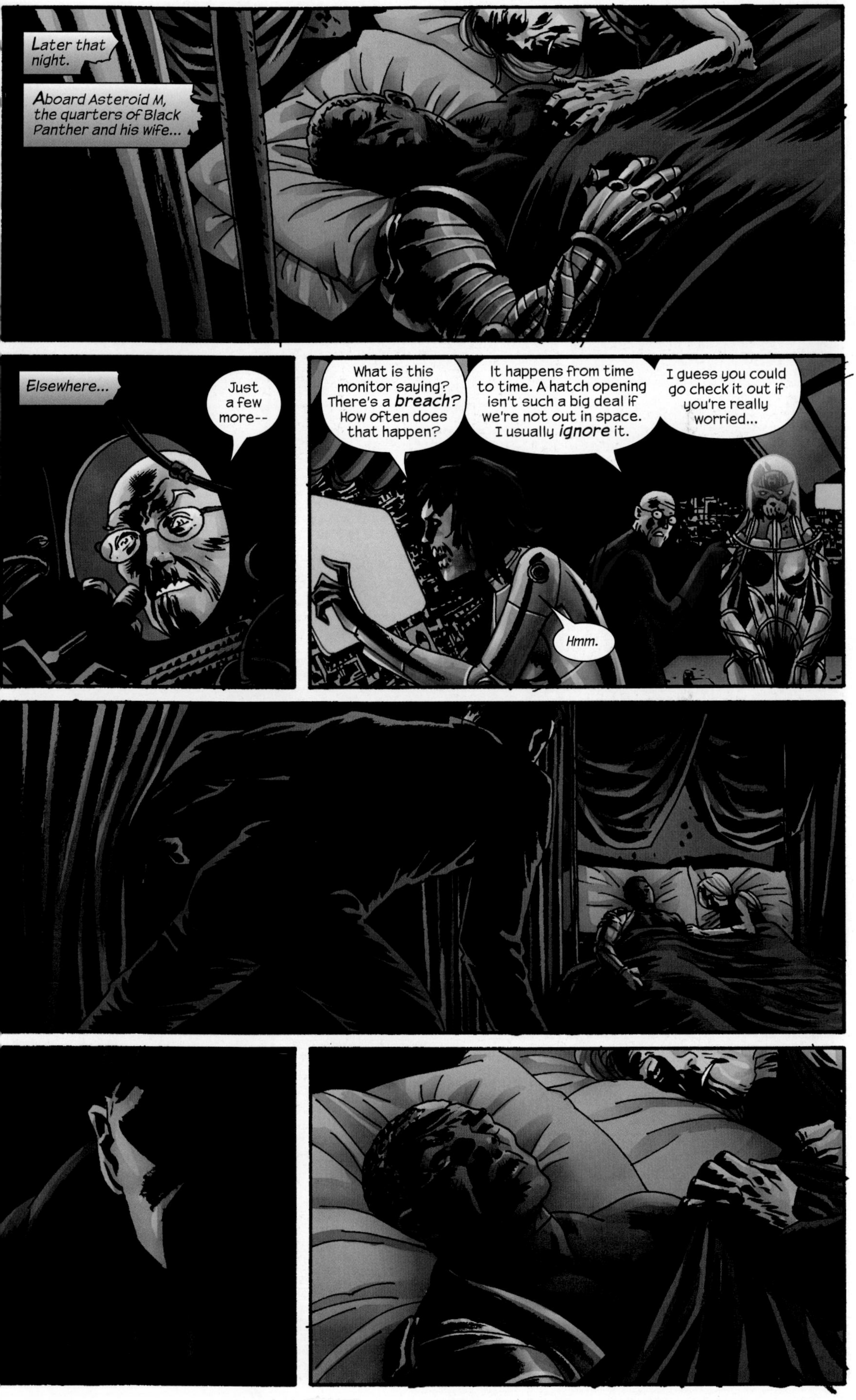
Later that night.
Aboard Asteroid M, the quarters of Black Panther and his wife...
Elsewhere...
Just a few more--
What is this monitor saying? There's a breach? How often does that happen?
It happens from time to time. A hatch opening isn't such a big deal if we're not out in space. I usually ignore it.
I guess you could check it out if you're really worried...
Hmm.

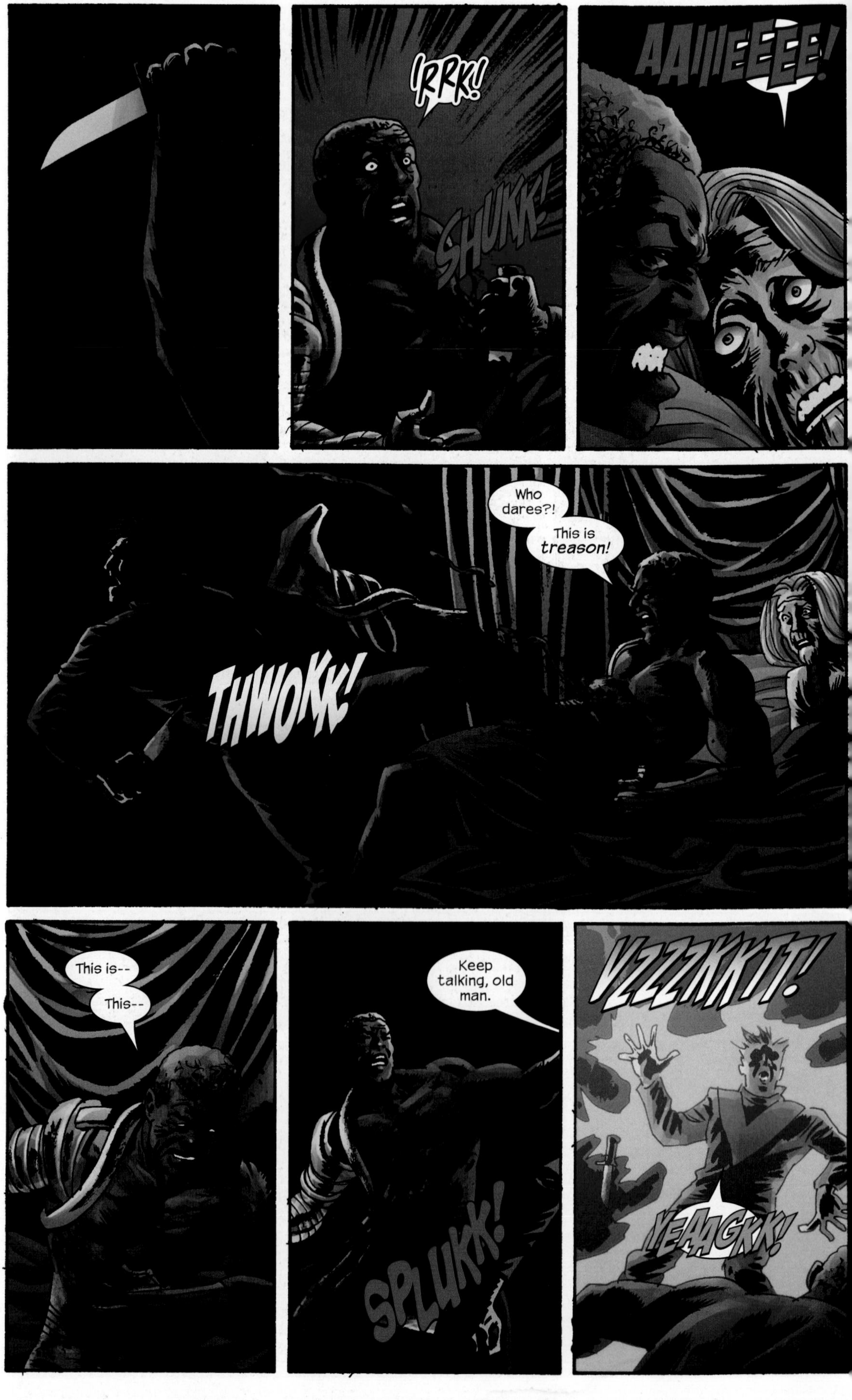

!RRK!
SHUKK!
AAIIIEEEE!
Who dares?!
This is treason!
THWOKK!
This is--
This--
Keep talking, old man.
SPLUKK!
VZZZKKTT!
YEAAGKK!

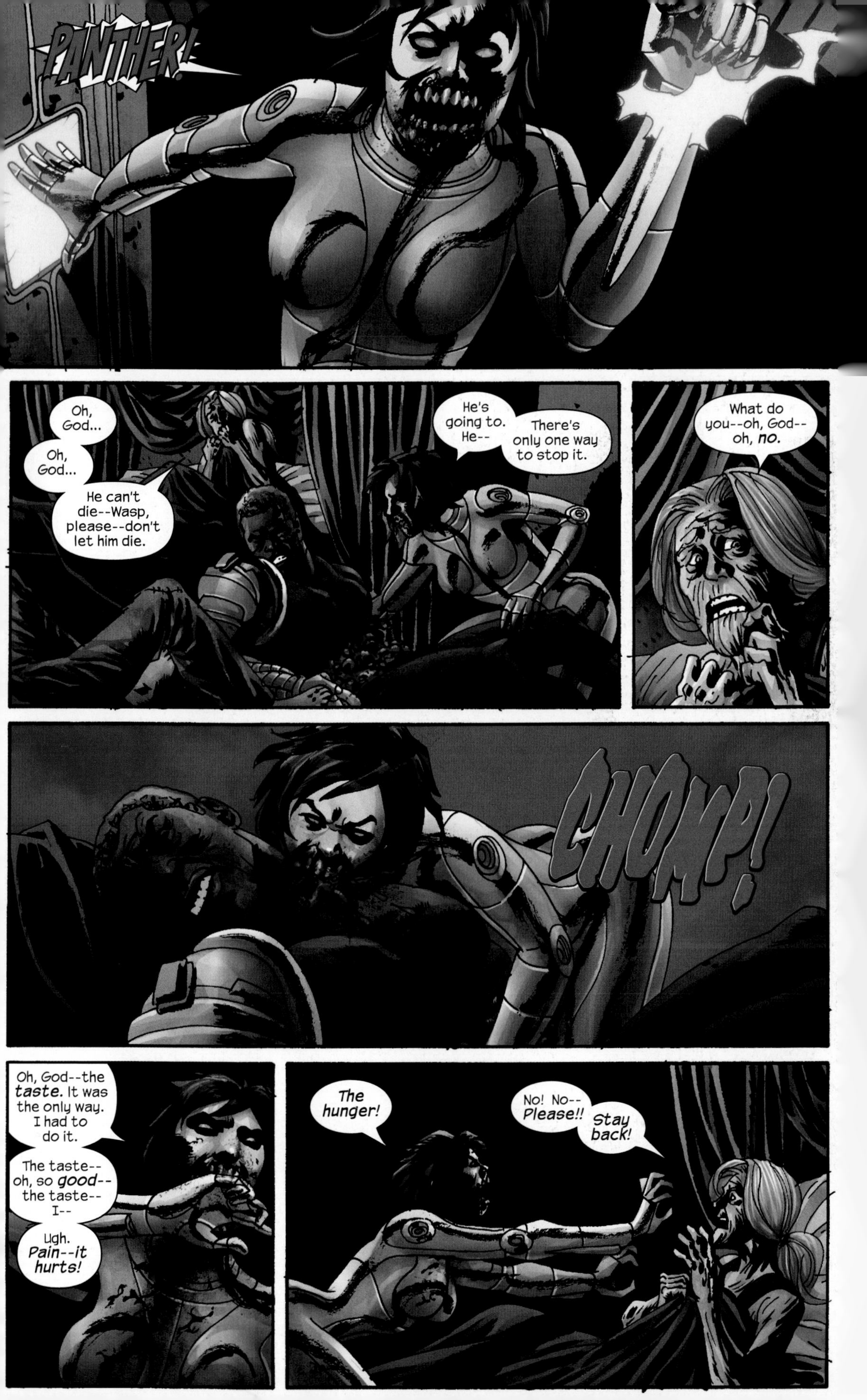
PANTHER!
Oh, God...
Oh, God...
He can't die--Wasp, please--don't let him die.
He's going to. He--
There's only one way to stop it.
What do you--oh, God--oh, *no.*
CHOMP!
Oh, God--the *taste.* It was the only way. I had to do it.
The taste--oh, so *good*--the taste--I--
Ugh. *Pain--it hurts!*
The hunger!
No! No--*Please!!*
Stay back!

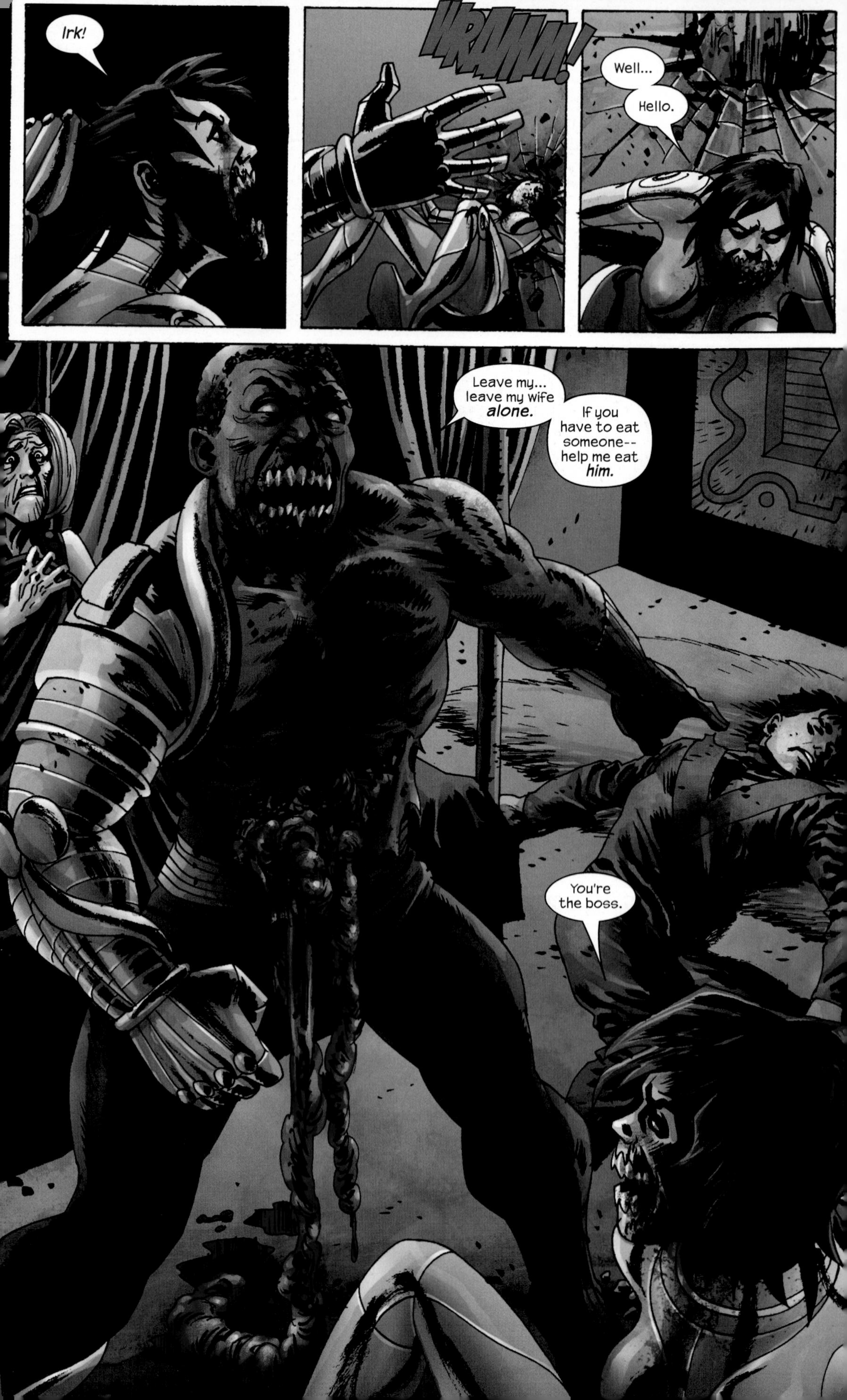
Irk!
VRAMM!
Well...
Hello.
Leave my... leave my wife alone.
If you have to eat someone-- help me eat him.
You're the boss.

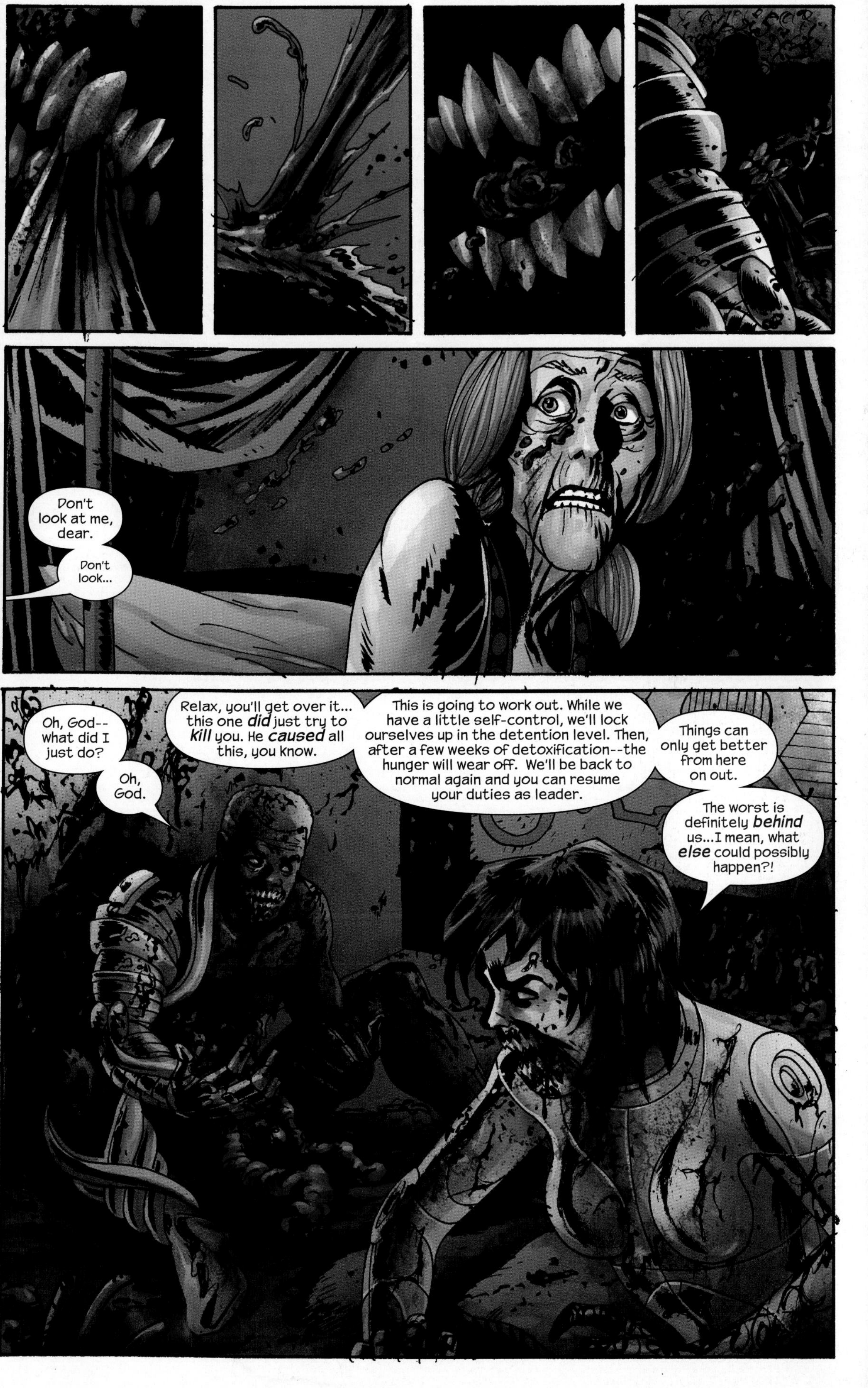
Don't look at me, dear.
Don't look...
Oh, God-- what did I just do?
Oh, God.
Relax, you'll get over it... this one did just try to kill you. He caused all this, you know.
This is going to work out. While we have a little self-control, we'll lock ourselves up in the detention level. Then, after a few weeks of detoxification--the hunger will wear off. We'll be back to normal again and you can resume your duties as leader.
Things can only get better from here on out.
The worst is definitely behind us...I mean, what else could possibly happen?!

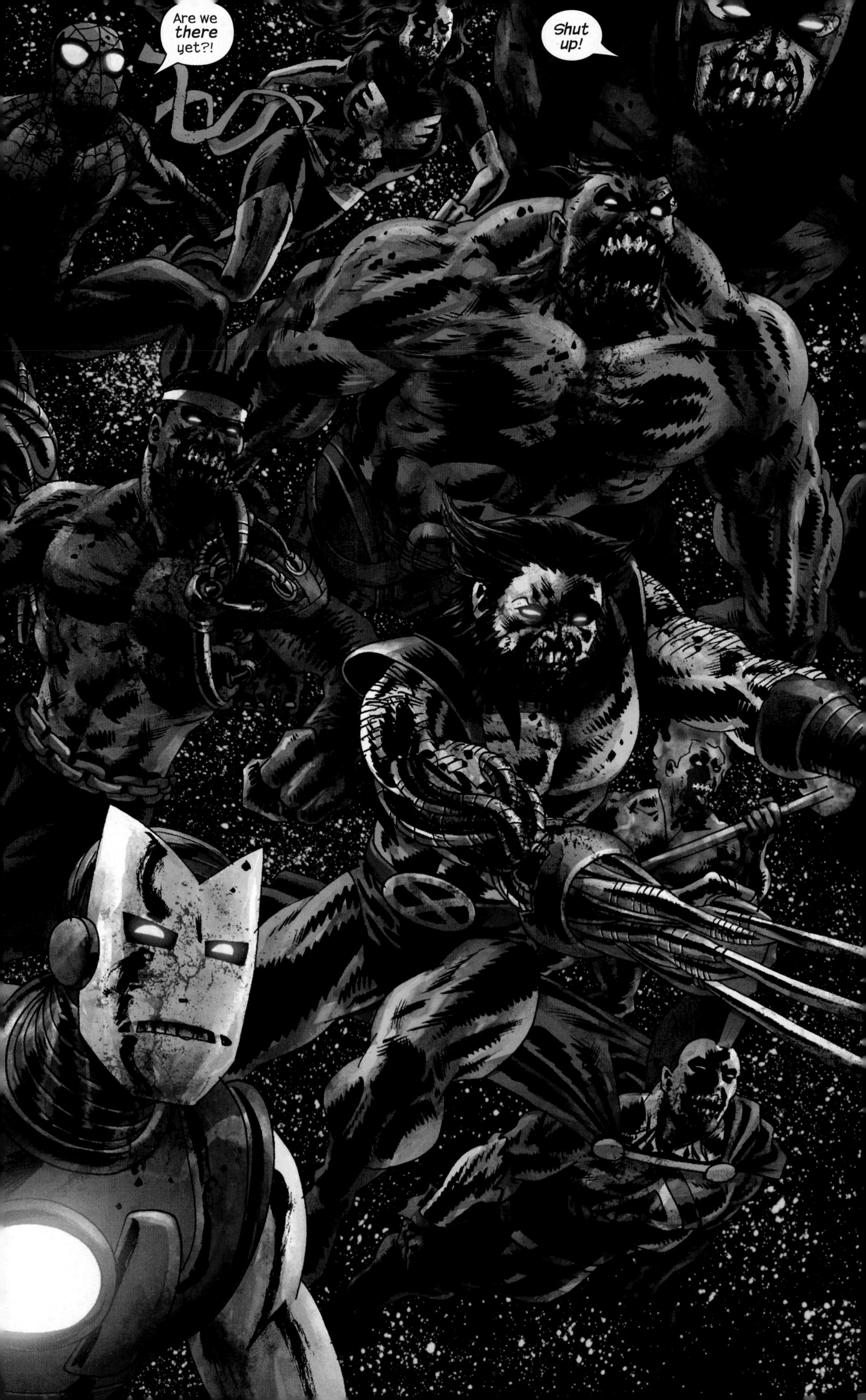
Are we there yet?!
Shut up!

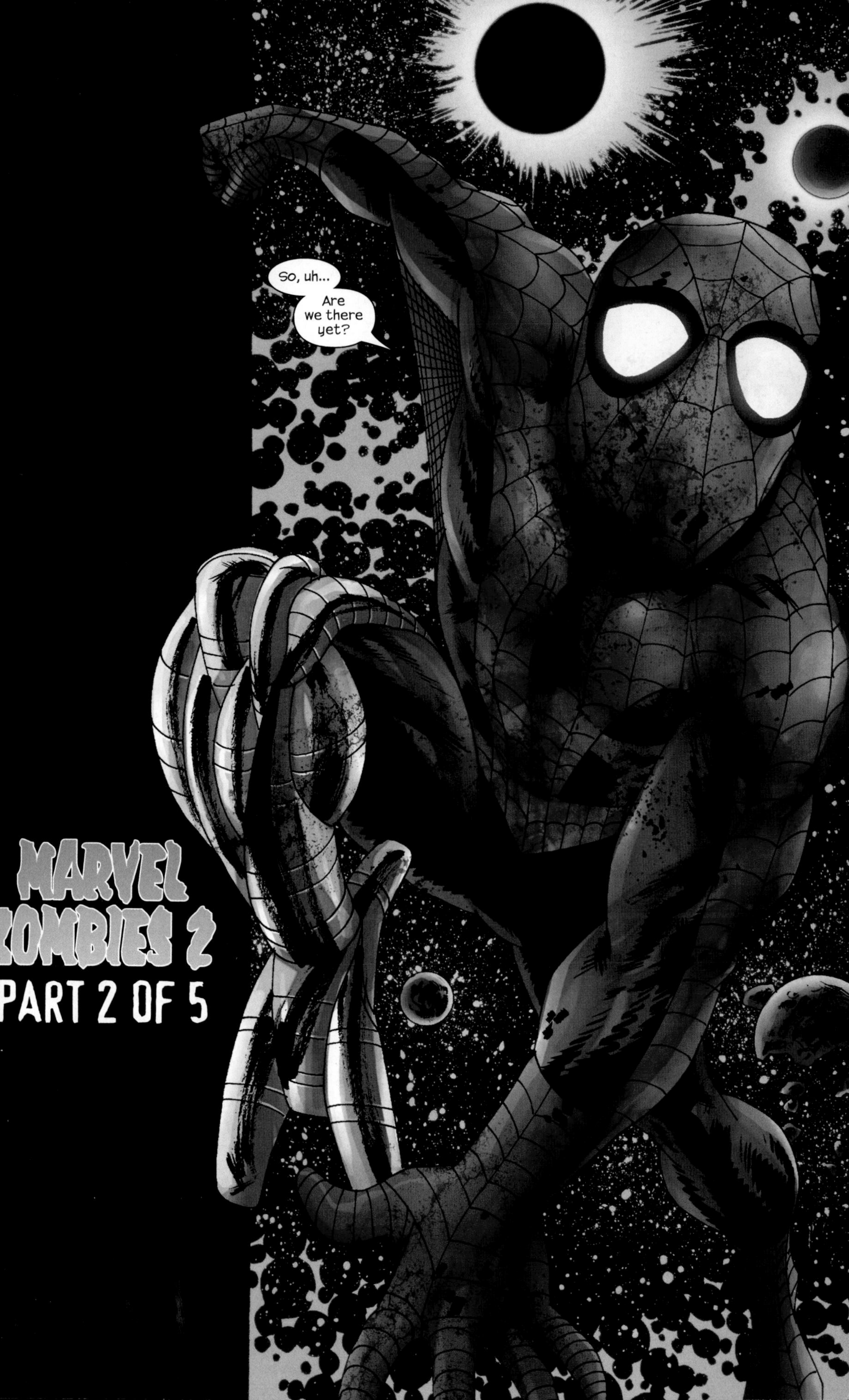
So, uh...
Are we there yet?
MARVEL
ZOMBIES 2
PART 2 OF 5

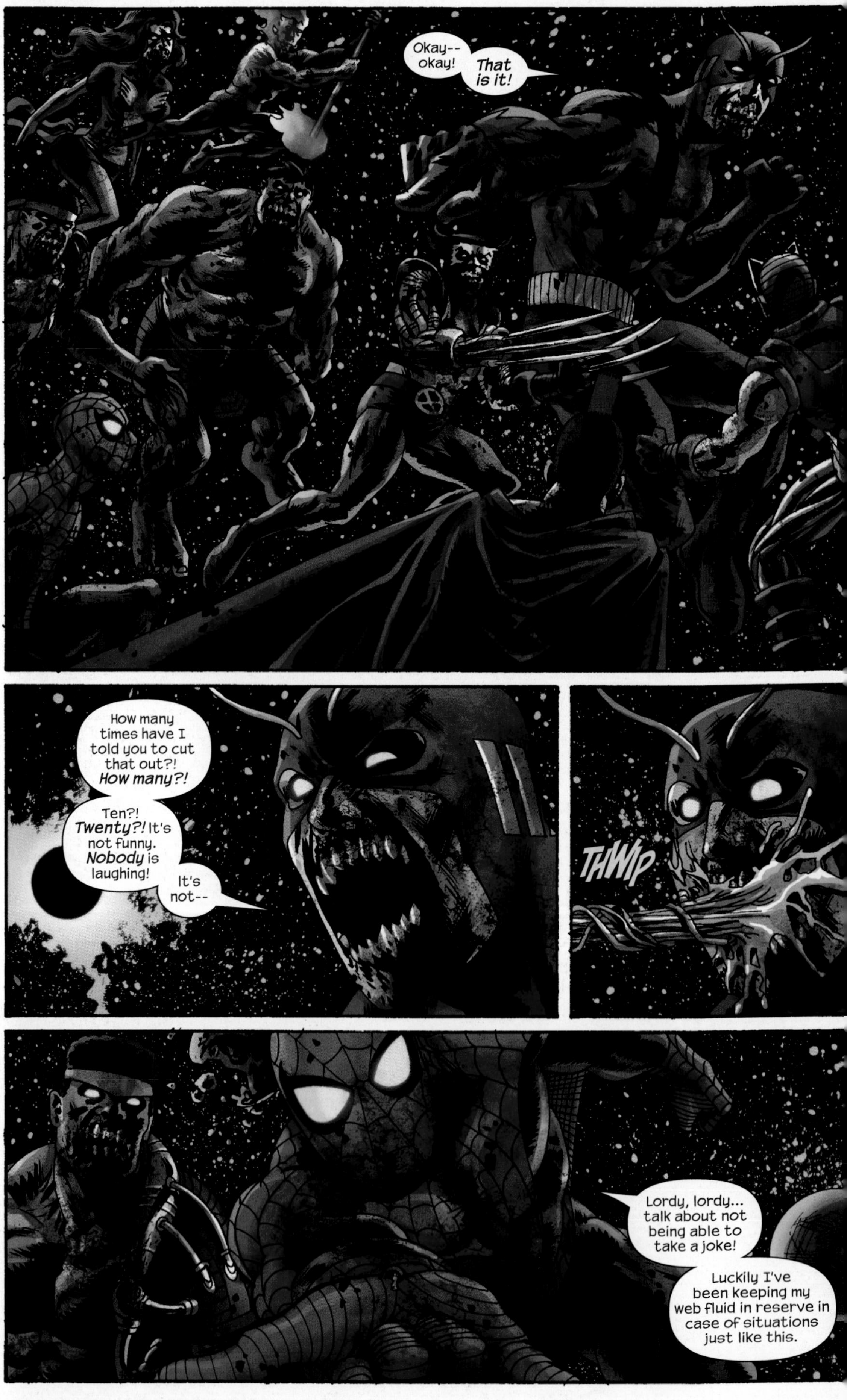

Okay-- okay! *That is it!*
How many times have I told you to cut that out?! *How many?!*
Ten?! *Twenty?!* It's not funny. *Nobody* is laughing!
It's not--
THWIP
Lordy, lordy... talk about not being able to take a joke!
Luckily I've been keeping my web fluid in reserve in case of situations just like this.

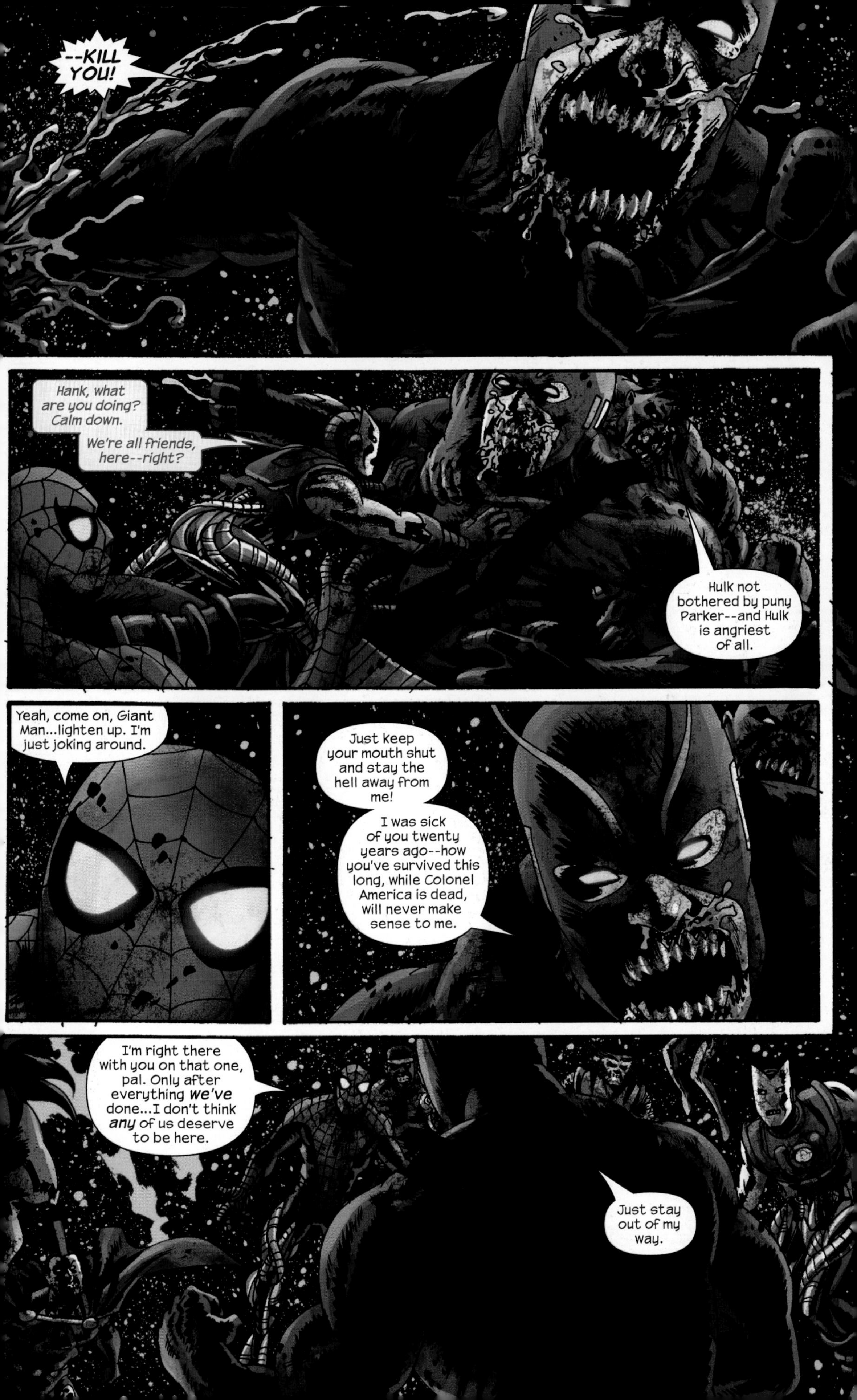
--KILL YOU!
Hank, what are you doing? Calm down.
We're all friends, here--right?
Hulk not bothered by puny Parker--and Hulk is angriest of all.
Yeah, come on, Giant Man...lighten up. I'm just joking around.
Just keep your mouth shut and stay the hell away from me!
I was sick of you twenty years ago--how you've survived this long, while Colonel America is dead, will never make sense to me.
I'm right there with you on that one, pal. Only after everything *we've* done...I don't think *any* of us deserve to be here.
Just stay out of my way.

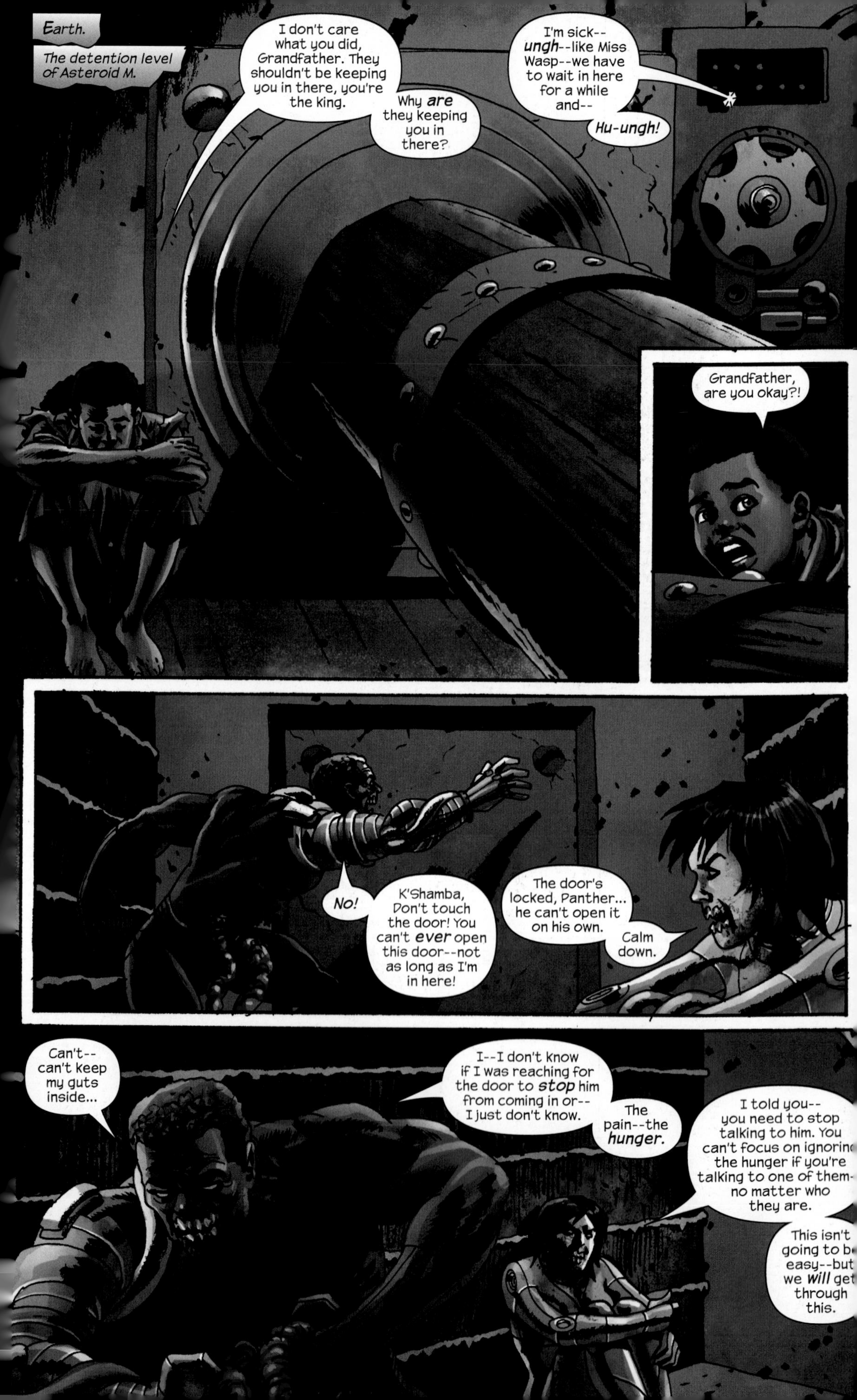
Earth.
The detention level of Asteroid M.
I don't care what you did, Grandfather. They shouldn't be keeping you in there, you're the king.
Why are they keeping you in there?
I'm sick-- ungh--like Miss Wasp--we have to wait in here for a while and--
Hu-ungh!
Grandfather, are you okay?!
No!
K'Shamba, Don't touch the door! You can't ever open this door--not as long as I'm in here!
The door's locked, Panther... he can't open it on his own.
Calm down.
Can't-- can't keep my guts inside...
I--I don't know if I was reaching for the door to stop him from coming in or-- I just don't know.
The pain--the hunger.
I told you-- you need to stop talking to him. You can't focus on ignorin the hunger if you're talking to one of them- no matter who they are.
This isn't going to b easy--but we will ge through this.

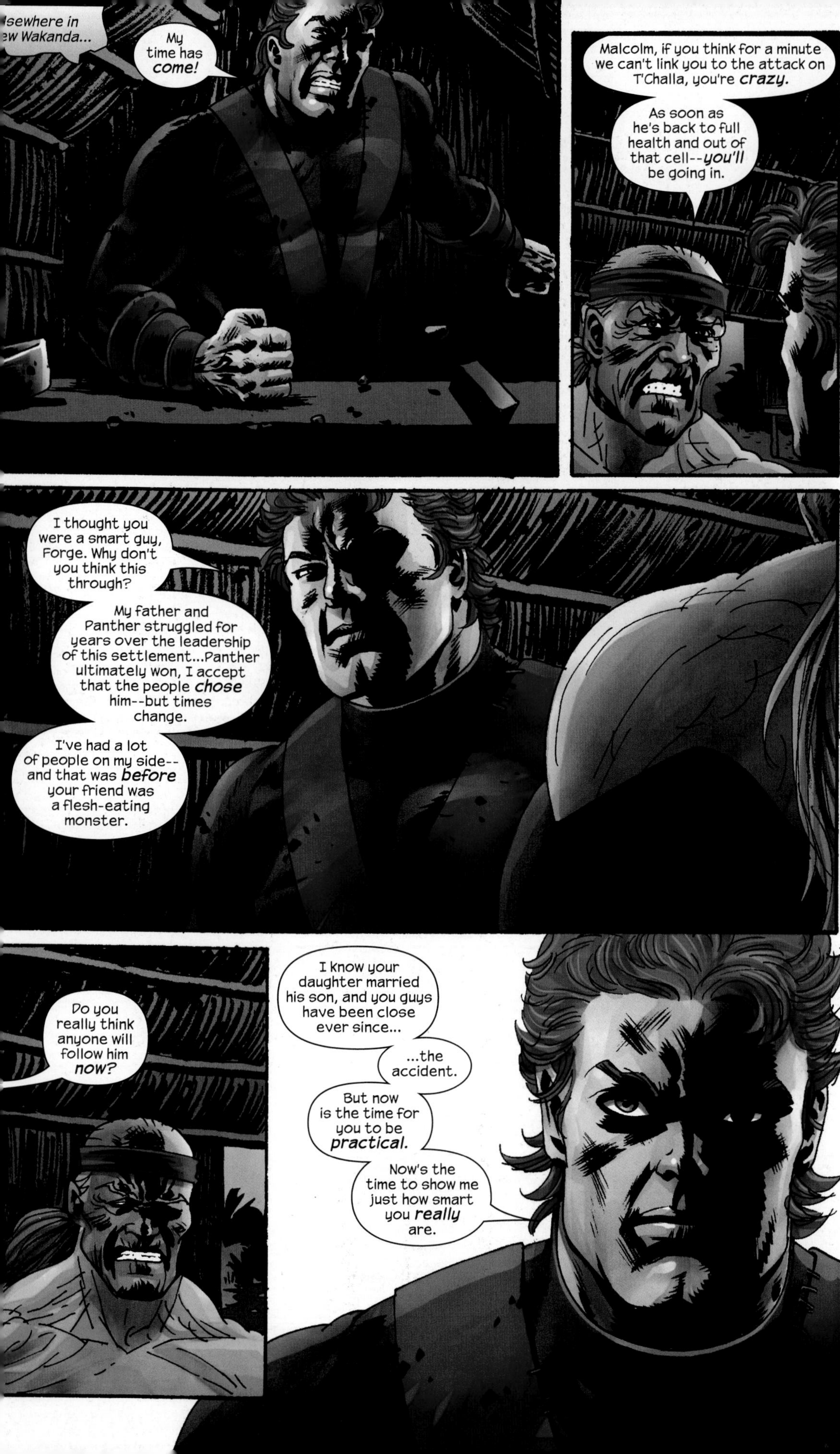

lsewhere in
ew Wakanda...
My time has come!
Malcolm, if you think for a minute we can't link you to the attack on T'Challa, you're crazy.
As soon as he's back to full health and out of that cell--you'll be going in.
I thought you were a smart guy, Forge. Why don't you think this through?
My father and Panther struggled for years over the leadership of this settlement...Panther ultimately won, I accept that the people chose him--but times change.
I've had a lot of people on my side--and that was before your friend was a flesh-eating monster.
Do you really think anyone will follow him now?
I know your daughter married his son, and you guys have been close ever since...
...the accident.
But now is the time for you to be practical.
Now's the time to show me just how smart you really are.

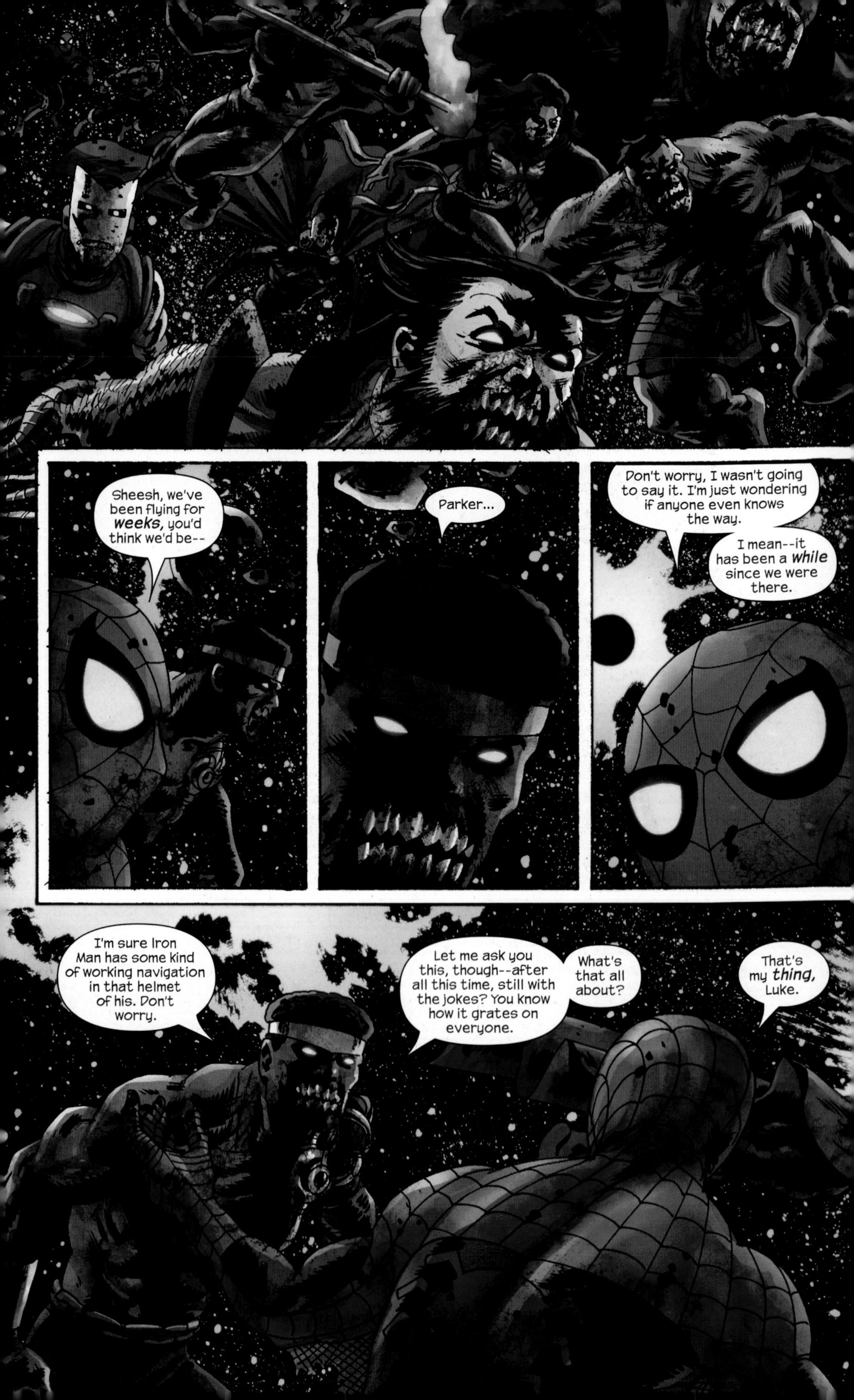
Sheesh, we've been flying for *weeks,* you'd think we'd be--
Parker...
Don't worry, I wasn't going to say it. I'm just wondering if anyone even knows the way.
I mean--it has been a *while* since we were there.
I'm sure Iron Man has some kind of working navigation in that helmet of his. Don't worry.
Let me ask you this, though--after all this time, still with the jokes? You know how it grates on everyone.
What's that all about?
That's my *thing,* Luke.

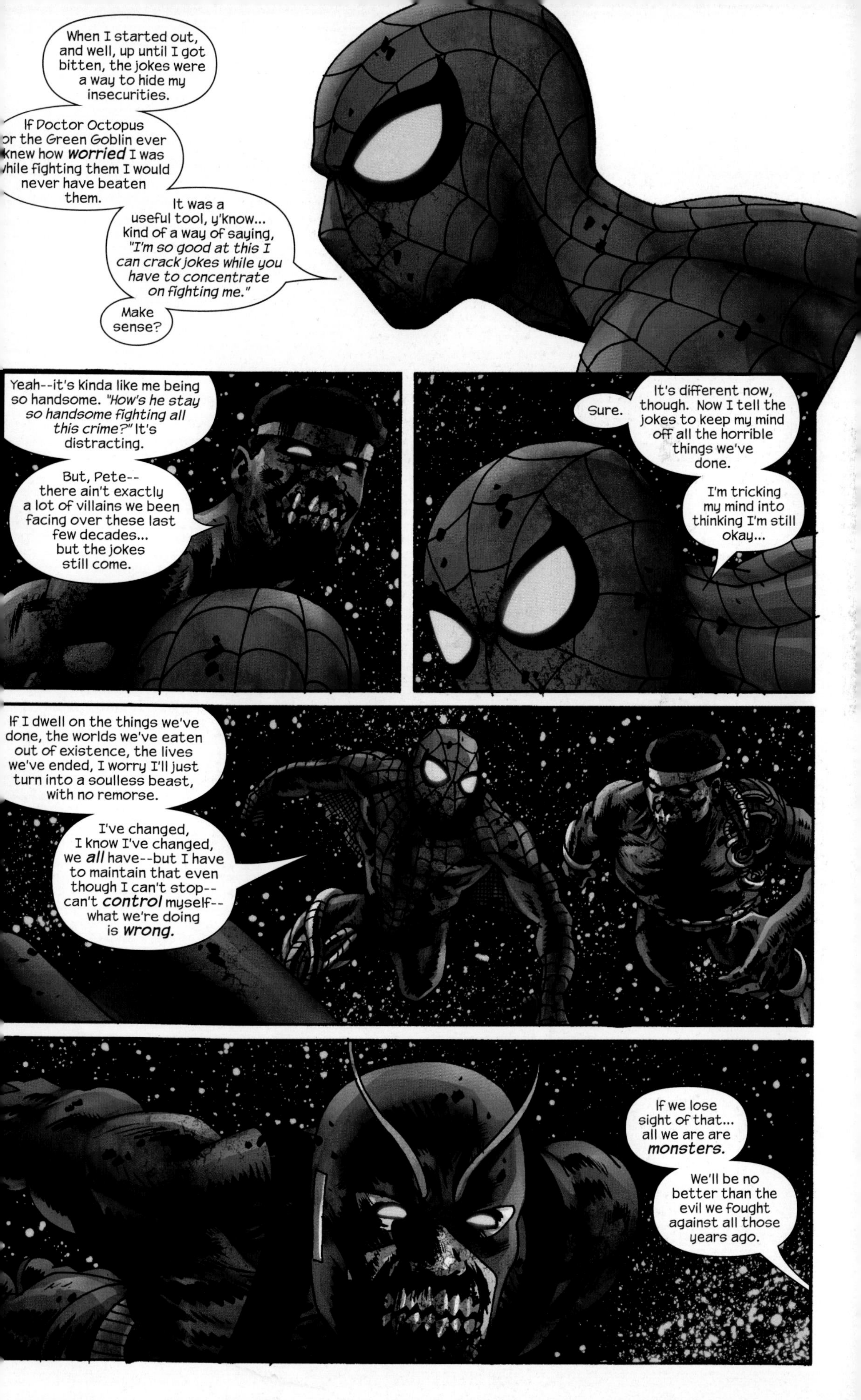
When I started out, and well, up until I got bitten, the jokes were a way to hide my insecurities.
If Doctor Octopus or the Green Goblin ever knew how *worried* I was while fighting them I would never have beaten them.
It was a useful tool, y'know... kind of a way of saying, *"I'm so good at this I can crack jokes while you have to concentrate on fighting me."*
Make sense?
Yeah--it's kinda like me being so handsome. *"How's he stay so handsome fighting all this crime?"* It's distracting.
But, Pete-- there ain't exactly a lot of villains we been facing over these last few decades... but the jokes still come.
Sure.
It's different now, though. Now I tell the jokes to keep my mind off all the horrible things we've done.
I'm tricking my mind into thinking I'm still okay...
If I dwell on the things we've done, the worlds we've eaten out of existence, the lives we've ended, I worry I'll just turn into a soulless beast, with no remorse.
I've changed, I know I've changed, we *all* have--but I have to maintain that even though I can't stop--can't **control** myself--what we're doing is **wrong.**
If we lose sight of that... all we are are ***monsters.***
We'll be no better than the evil we fought against all those years ago.

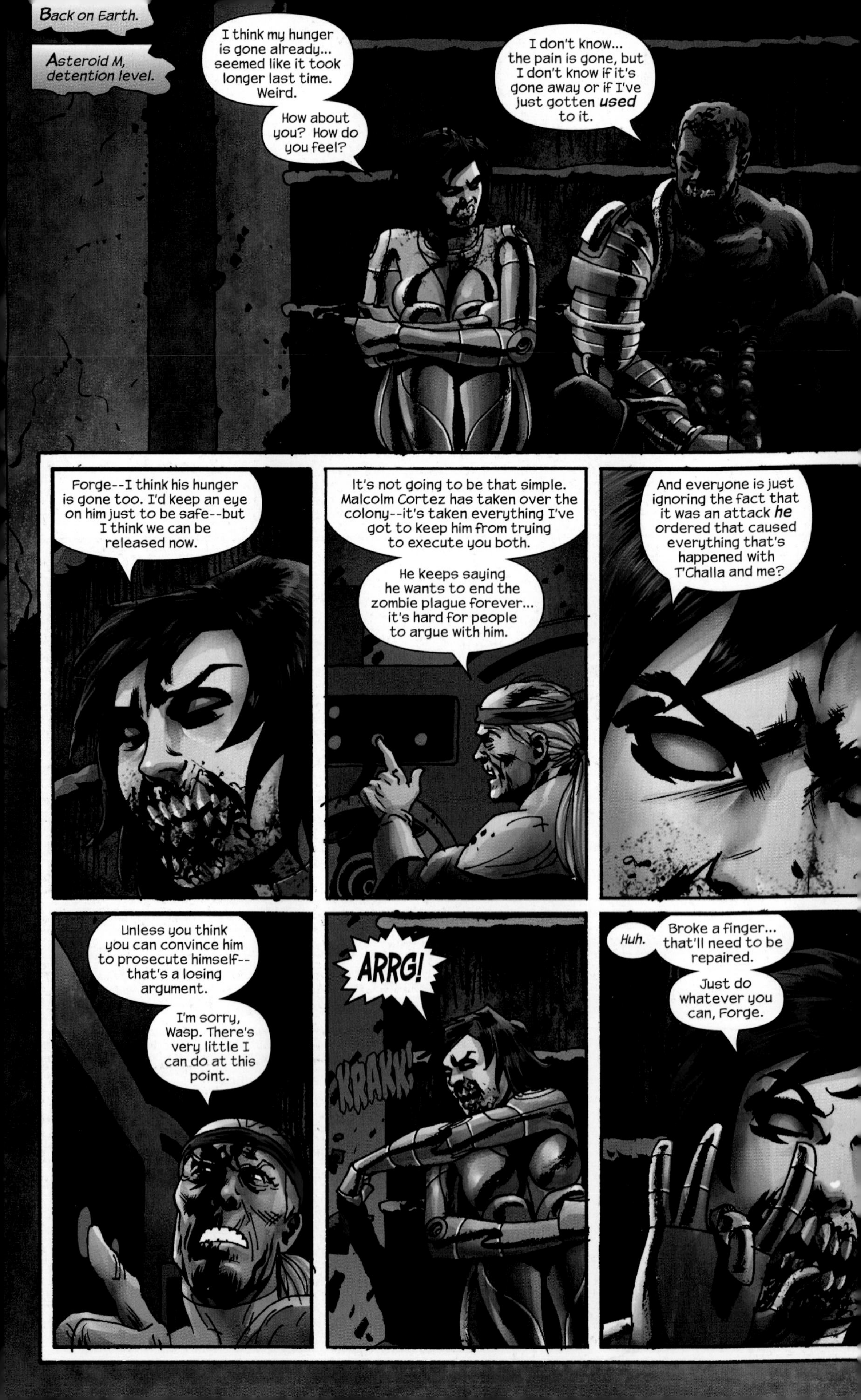
Back on Earth.
Asteroid M, detention level.
I think my hunger is gone already... seemed like it took longer last time. Weird.
How about you? How do you feel?
I don't know... the pain is gone, but I don't know if it's gone away or if I've just gotten *used* to it.
Forge--I think his hunger is gone too. I'd keep an eye on him just to be safe--but I think we can be released now.
It's not going to be that simple. Malcolm Cortez has taken over the colony--it's taken everything I've got to keep him from trying to execute you both.
He keeps saying he wants to end the zombie plague forever... it's hard for people to argue with him.
And everyone is just ignoring the fact that it was an attack *he* ordered that caused everything that's happened with T'Challa and me?
Unless you think you can convince him to prosecute himself--that's a losing argument.
I'm sorry, Wasp. There's very little I can do at this point.
ARRG!
KRAKK!
Huh.
Broke a finger... that'll need to be repaired.
Just do whatever you can, Forge.

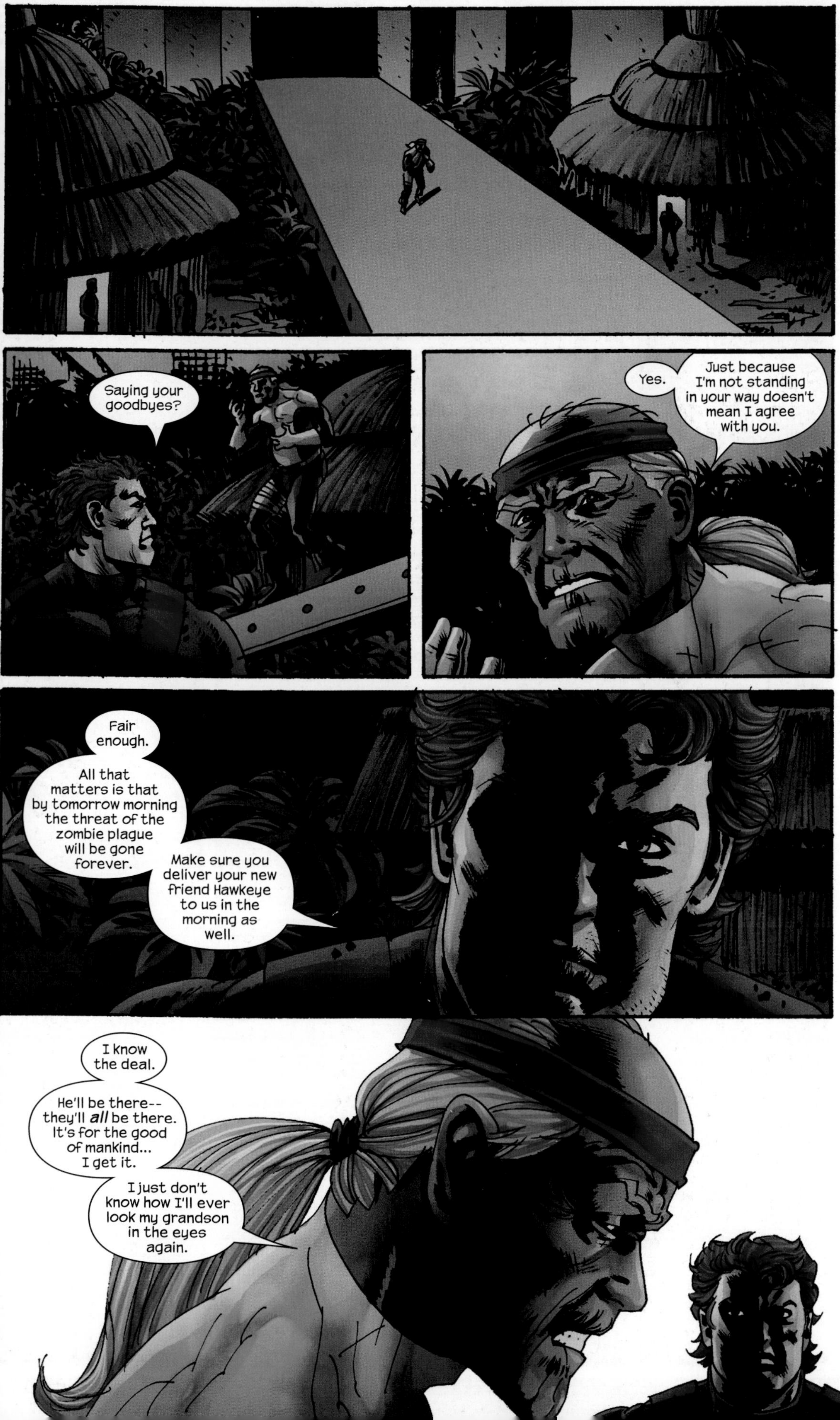
Saying your goodbyes?
Yes.
Just because I'm not standing in your way doesn't mean I agree with you.
Fair enough.
All that matters is that by tomorrow morning the threat of the zombie plague will be gone forever.
Make sure you deliver your new friend Hawkeye to us in the morning as well.
I know the deal.
He'll be there-- they'll *all* be there. It's for the good of mankind... I get it.
I just don't know how I'll ever look my grandson in the eyes again.

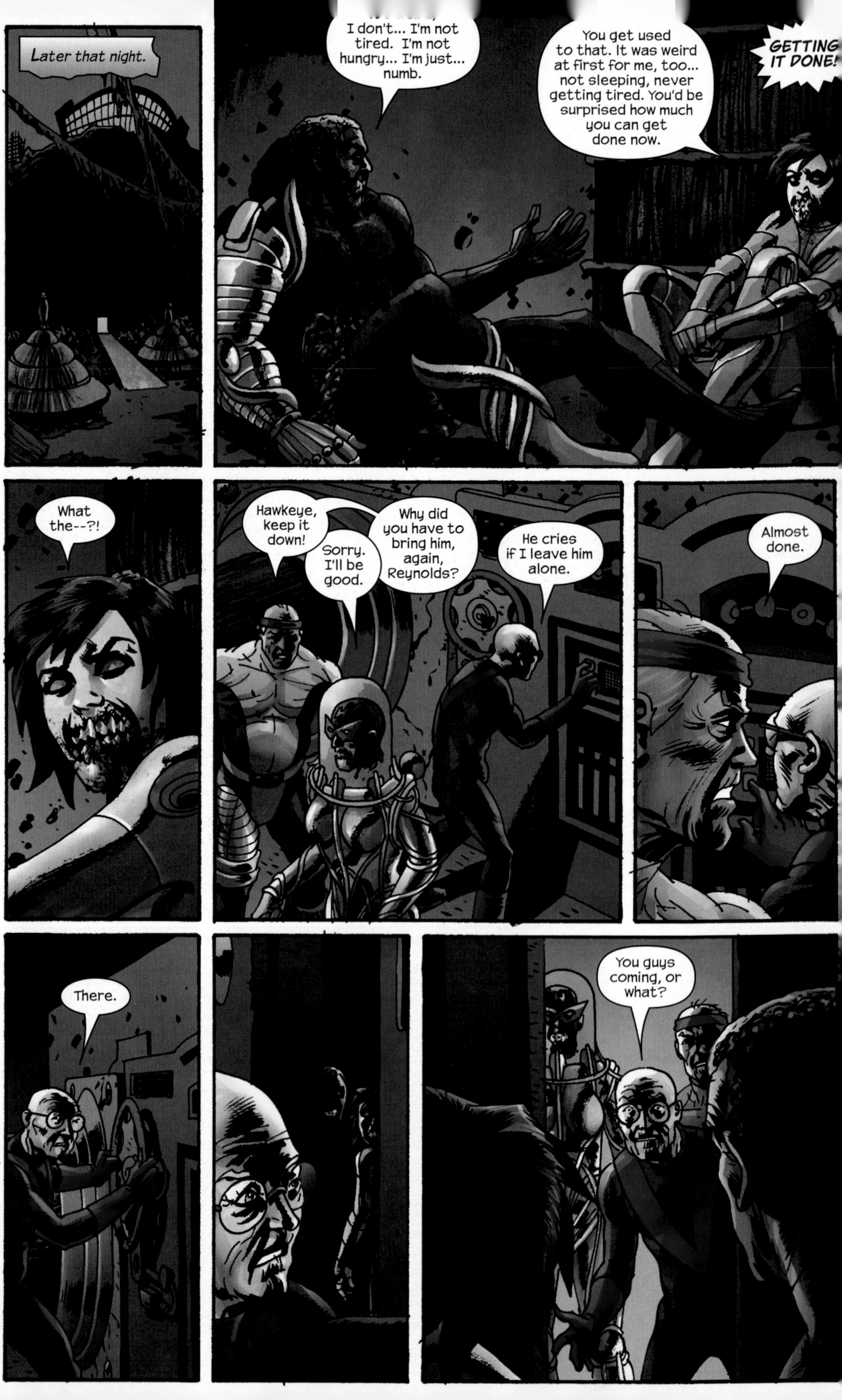

Later that night.
I don't... I'm not tired. I'm not hungry... I'm just... numb.
You get used to that. It was weird at first for me, too... not sleeping, never getting tired. You'd be surprised how much you can get done now.
GETTING IT DONE!
What the--?!
Hawkeye, keep it down!
Sorry. I'll be good.
Why did you have to bring him, again, Reynolds?
He cries if I leave him alone.
Almost done.
There.
You guys coming, or what?

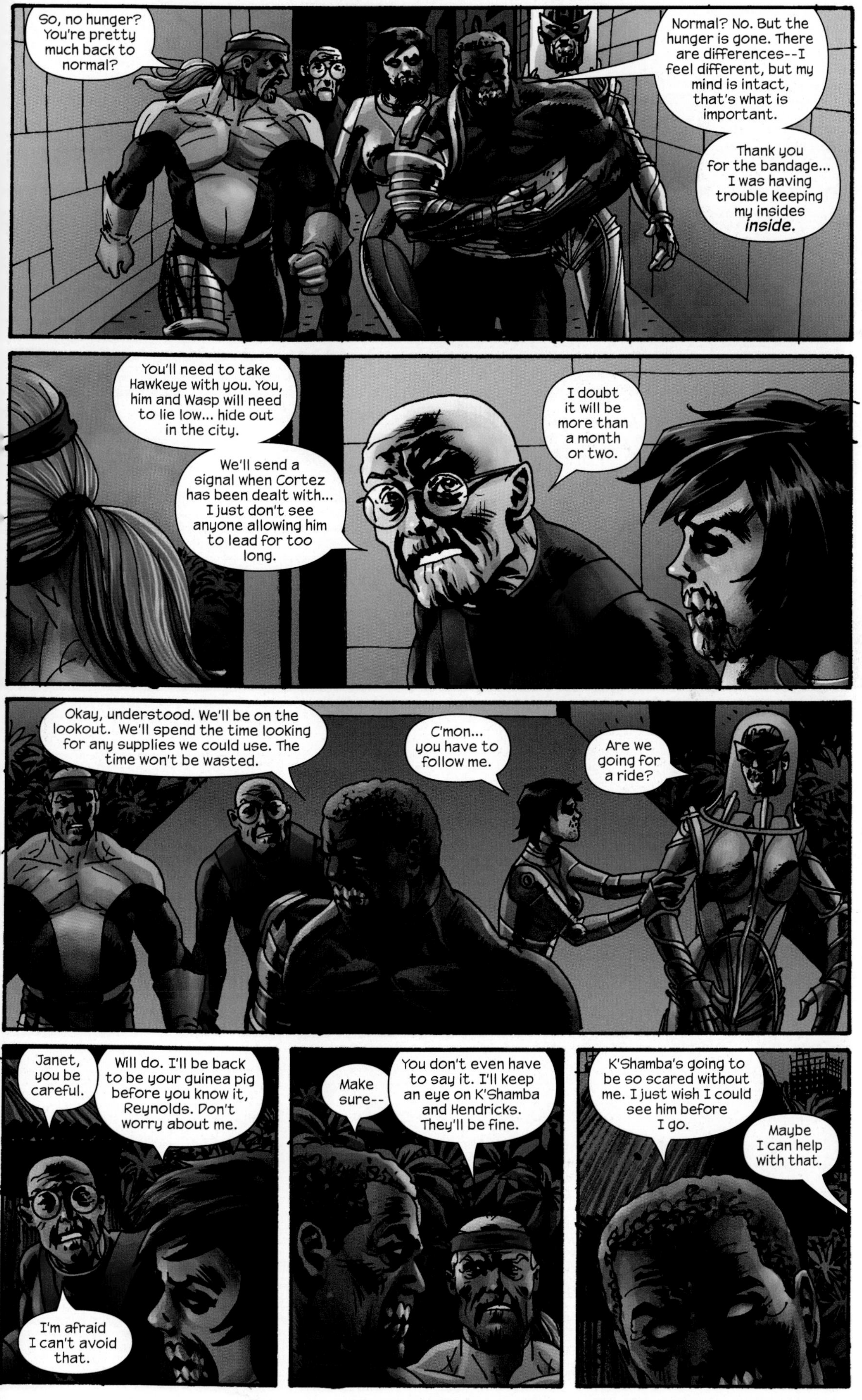

So, no hunger? You're pretty much back to normal?
Normal? No. But the hunger is gone. There are differences--I feel different, but my mind is intact, that's what is important.
Thank you for the bandage... I was having trouble keeping my insides *inside.*
You'll need to take Hawkeye with you. You, him and Wasp will need to lie low... hide out in the city.
We'll send a signal when Cortez has been dealt with... I just don't see anyone allowing him to lead for too long.
I doubt it will be more than a month or two.
Okay, understood. We'll be on the lookout. We'll spend the time looking for any supplies we could use. The time won't be wasted.
C'mon... you have to follow me.
Are we going for a ride?
Janet, you be careful.
Will do. I'll be back to be your guinea pig before you know it, Reynolds. Don't worry about me.
I'm afraid I can't avoid that.
Make sure--
You don't even have to say it. I'll keep an eye on K'Shamba and Hendricks. They'll be fine.
K'Shamba's going to be so scared without me. I just wish I could see him before I go.
Maybe I can help with that.

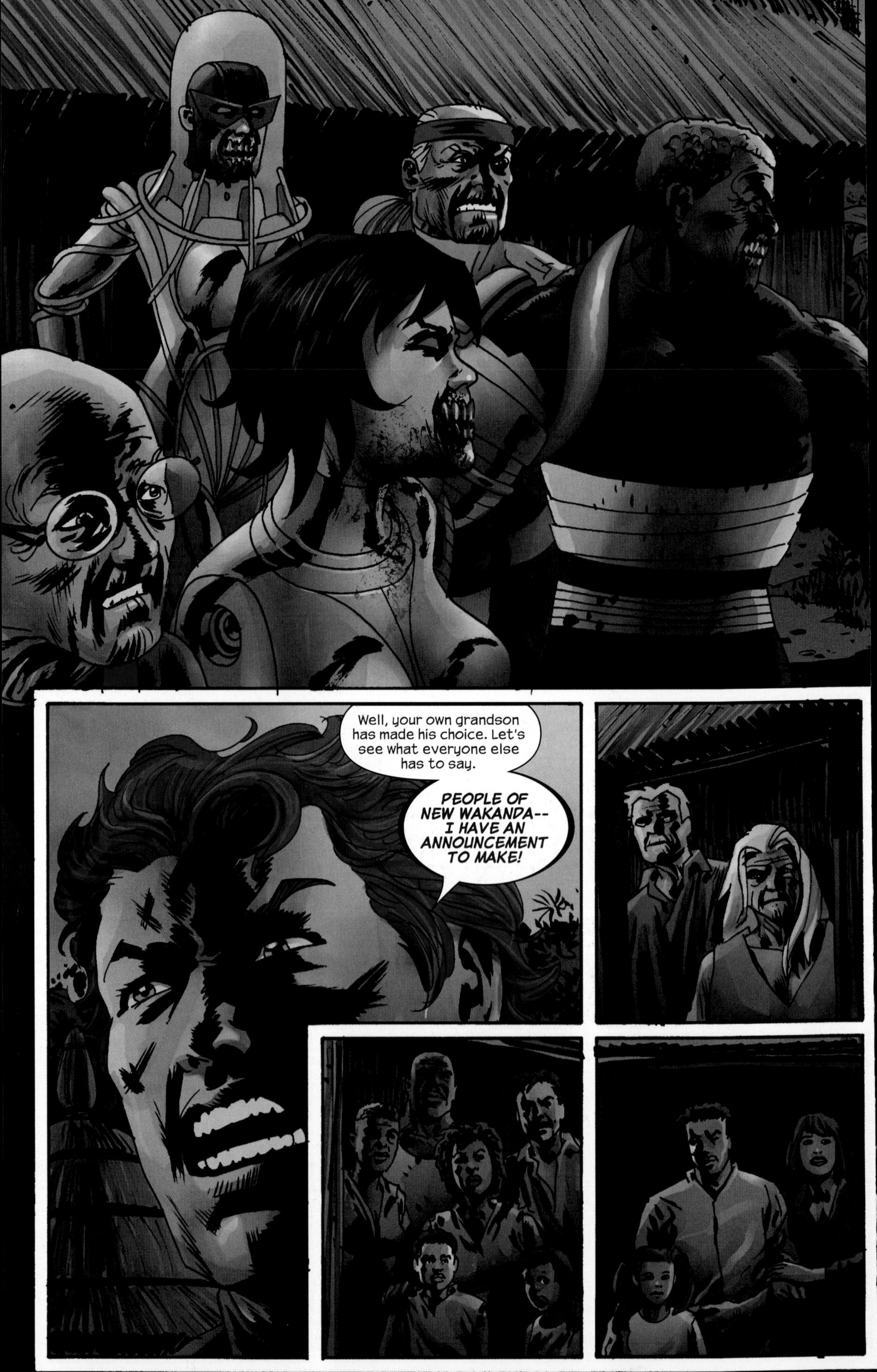
Well, your own grandson has made his choice. Let's see what everyone else has to say.
PEOPLE OF NEW WAKANDA-- I HAVE AN ANNOUNCEMENT TO MAKE!

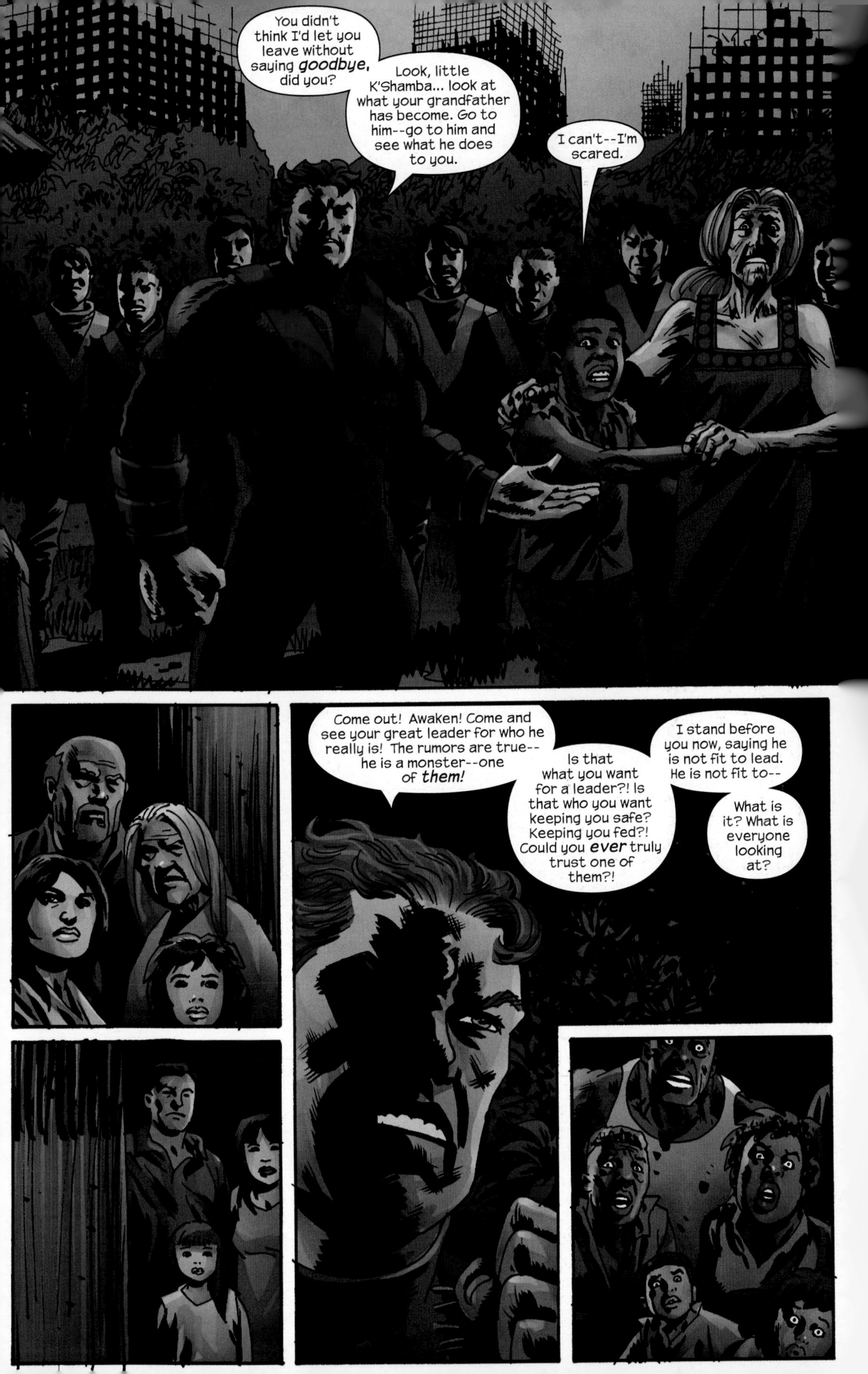
You didn't think I'd let you leave without saying *goodbye*, did you?
Look, little K'Shamba... look at what your grandfather has become. Go to him--go to him and see what he does to you.
I can't--I'm scared.
Come out! Awaken! Come and see your great leader for who he really is! The rumors are true--he is a monster--one of *them!*
Is that what you want for a leader?! Is that who you want keeping you safe? Keeping you fed?! Could you *ever* truly trust one of them?!
I stand before you now, saying he is not fit to lead. He is not fit to--
What is it? What is everyone looking at?

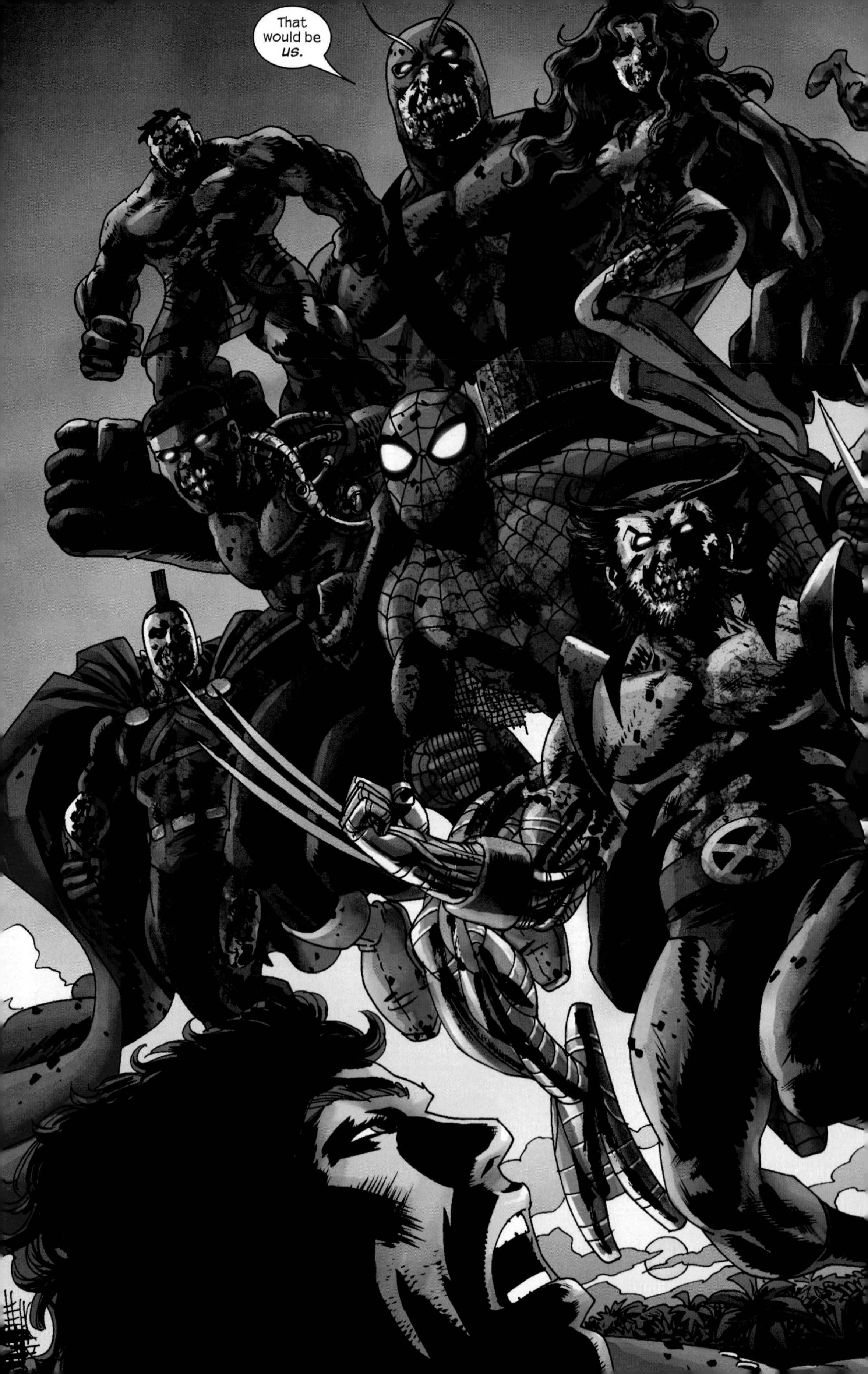
That would be *us.*

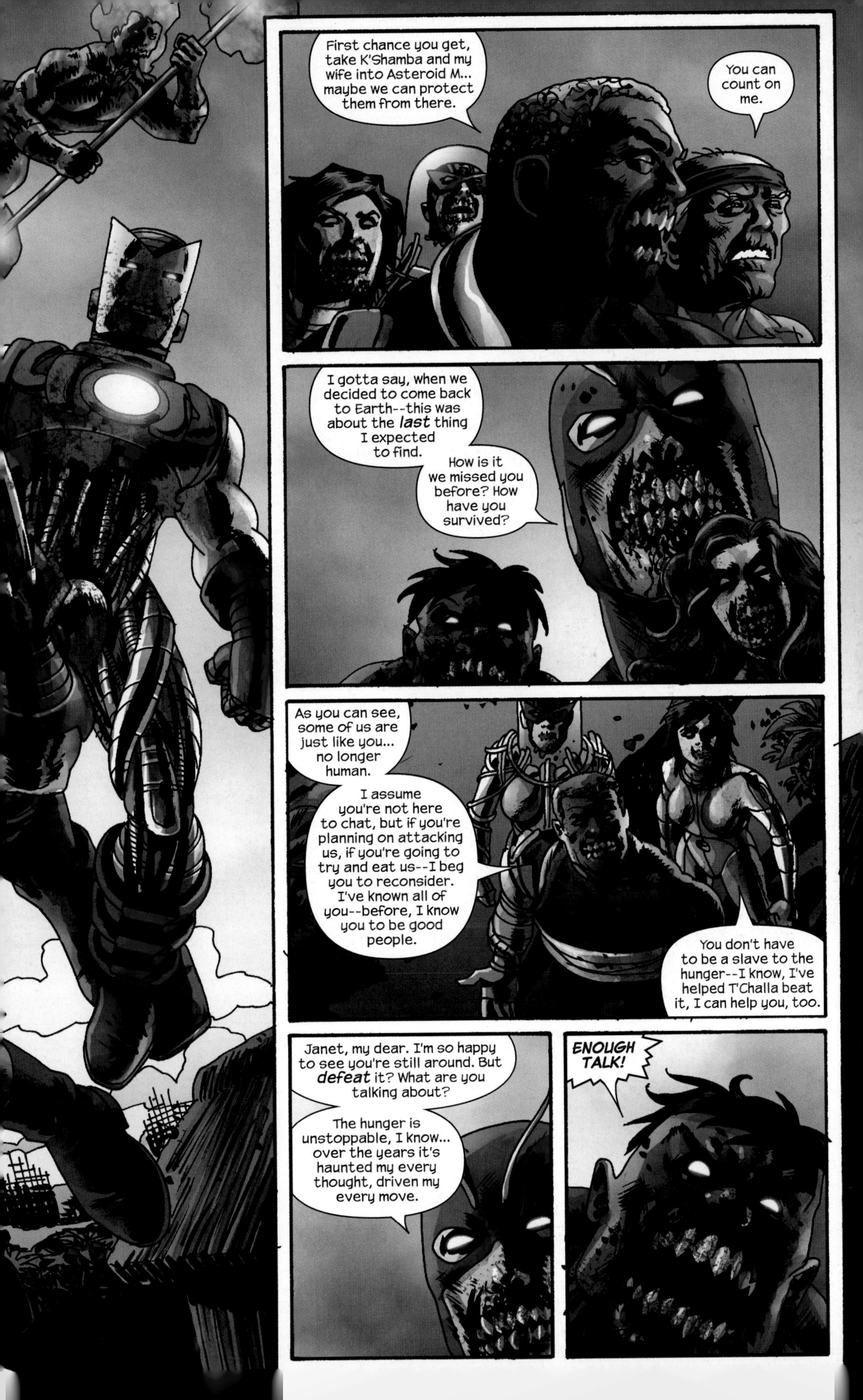
First chance you get, take K'Shamba and my wife into Asteroid M... maybe we can protect them from there.
You can count on me.
I gotta say, when we decided to come back to Earth--this was about the *last* thing I expected to find.
How is it we missed you before? How have you survived?
As you can see, some of us are just like you... no longer human.
I assume you're not here to chat, but if you're planning on attacking us, if you're going to try and eat us--I beg you to reconsider. I've known all of you--before, I know you to be good people.
You don't have to be a slave to the hunger--I know, I've helped T'Challa beat it, I can help you, too.
Janet, my dear. I'm so happy to see you're still around. But **defeat** it? What are you talking about?
The hunger is unstoppable, I know... over the years it's haunted my every thought, driven my every move.
ENOUGH TALK!

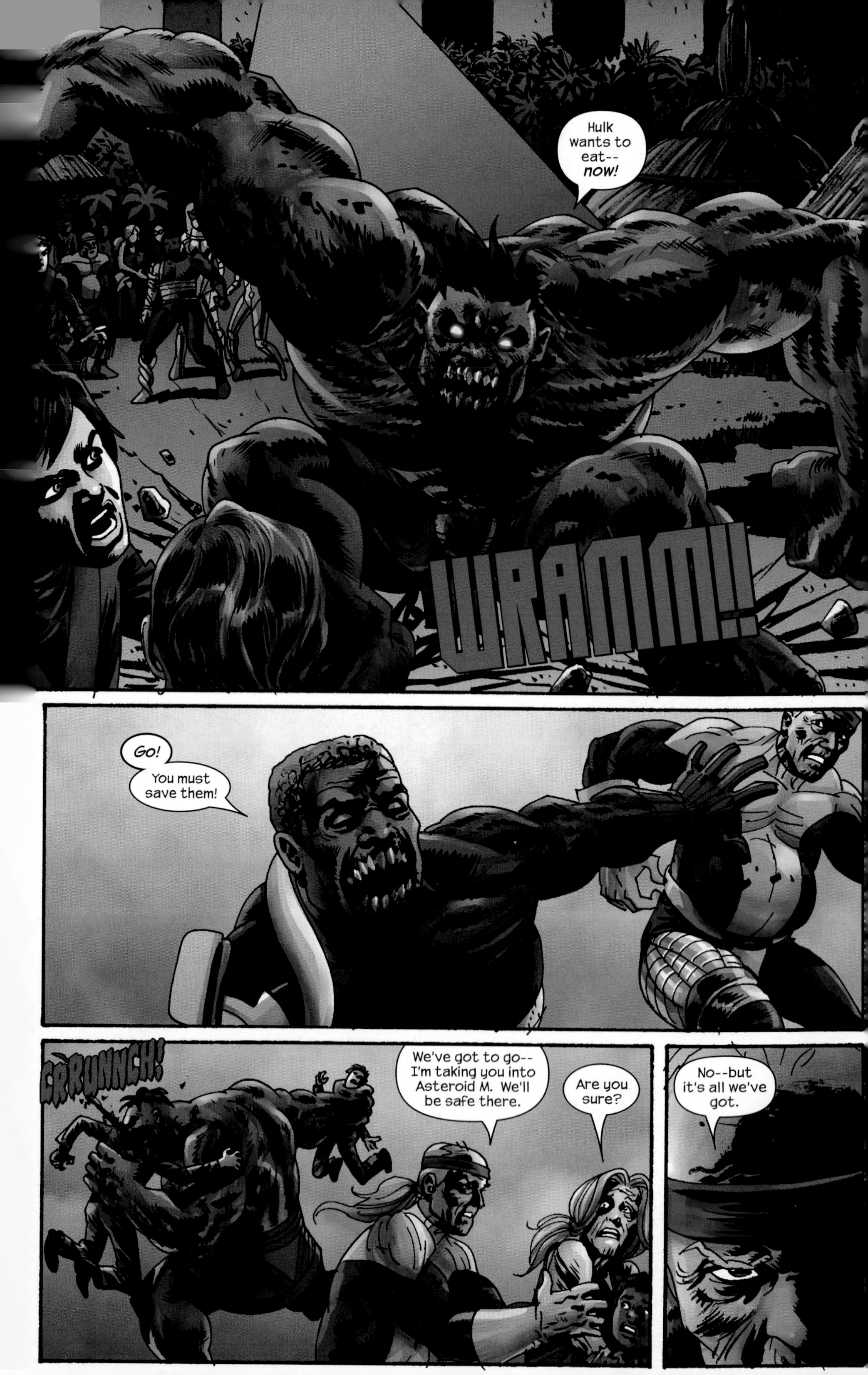
Hulk wants to eat-- now!
WRAMM!!
Go!
You must save them!
CRUNNCH!
We've got to go-- I'm taking you into Asteroid M. We'll be safe there.
Are you sure?
No--but it's all we've got.

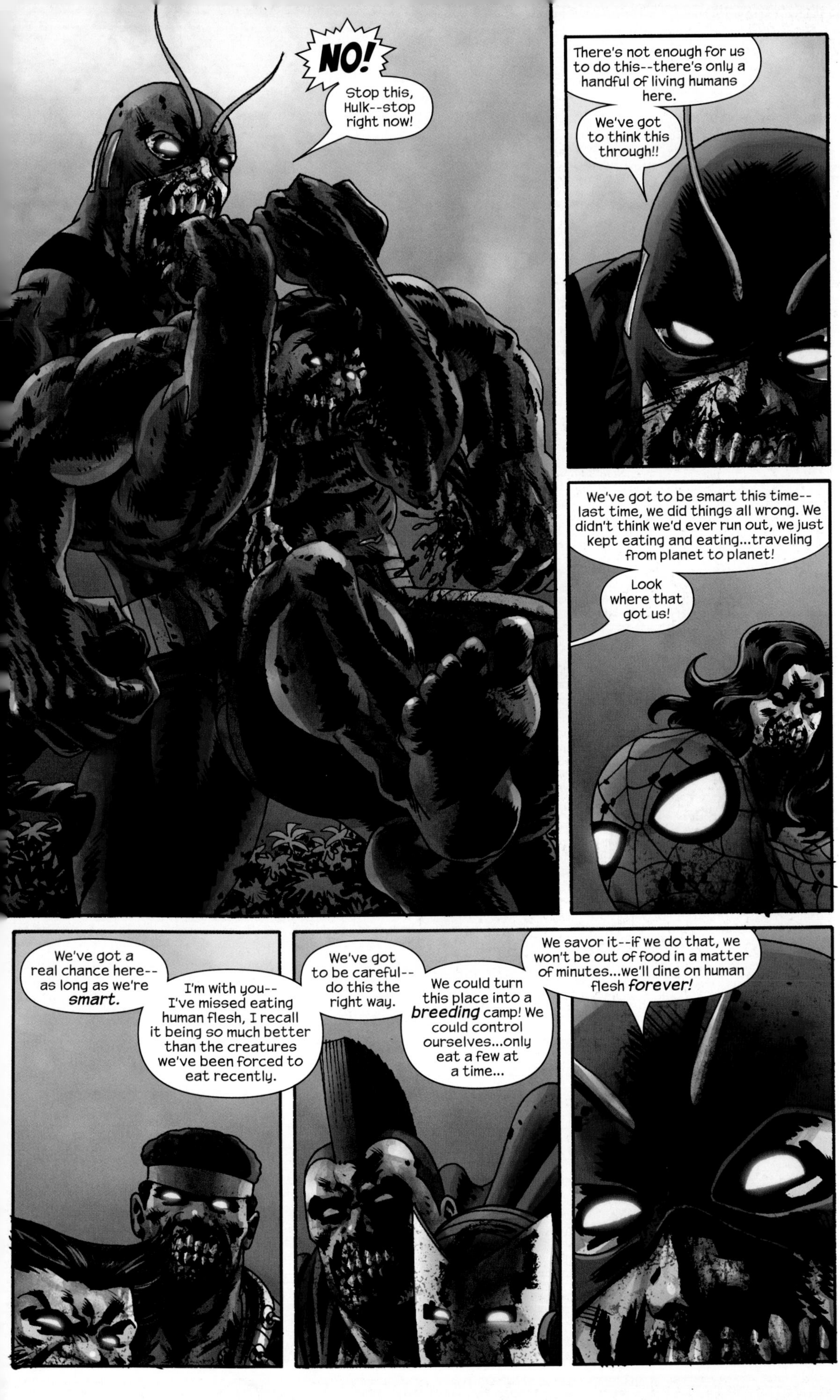
NO!
Stop this, Hulk--stop right now!
There's not enough for us to do this--there's only a handful of living humans here.
We've got to think this through!!
We've got to be smart this time--last time, we did things all wrong. We didn't think we'd ever run out, we just kept eating and eating...traveling from planet to planet!
Look where that got us!
We've got a real chance here--as long as we're *smart.*
I'm with you--I've missed eating human flesh, I recall it being so much better than the creatures we've been forced to eat recently.
We've got to be careful--do this the right way.
We could turn this place into a *breeding* camp! We could control ourselves...only eat a few at a time...
We savor it--if we do that, we won't be out of food in a matter of minutes...we'll dine on human flesh *forever!*

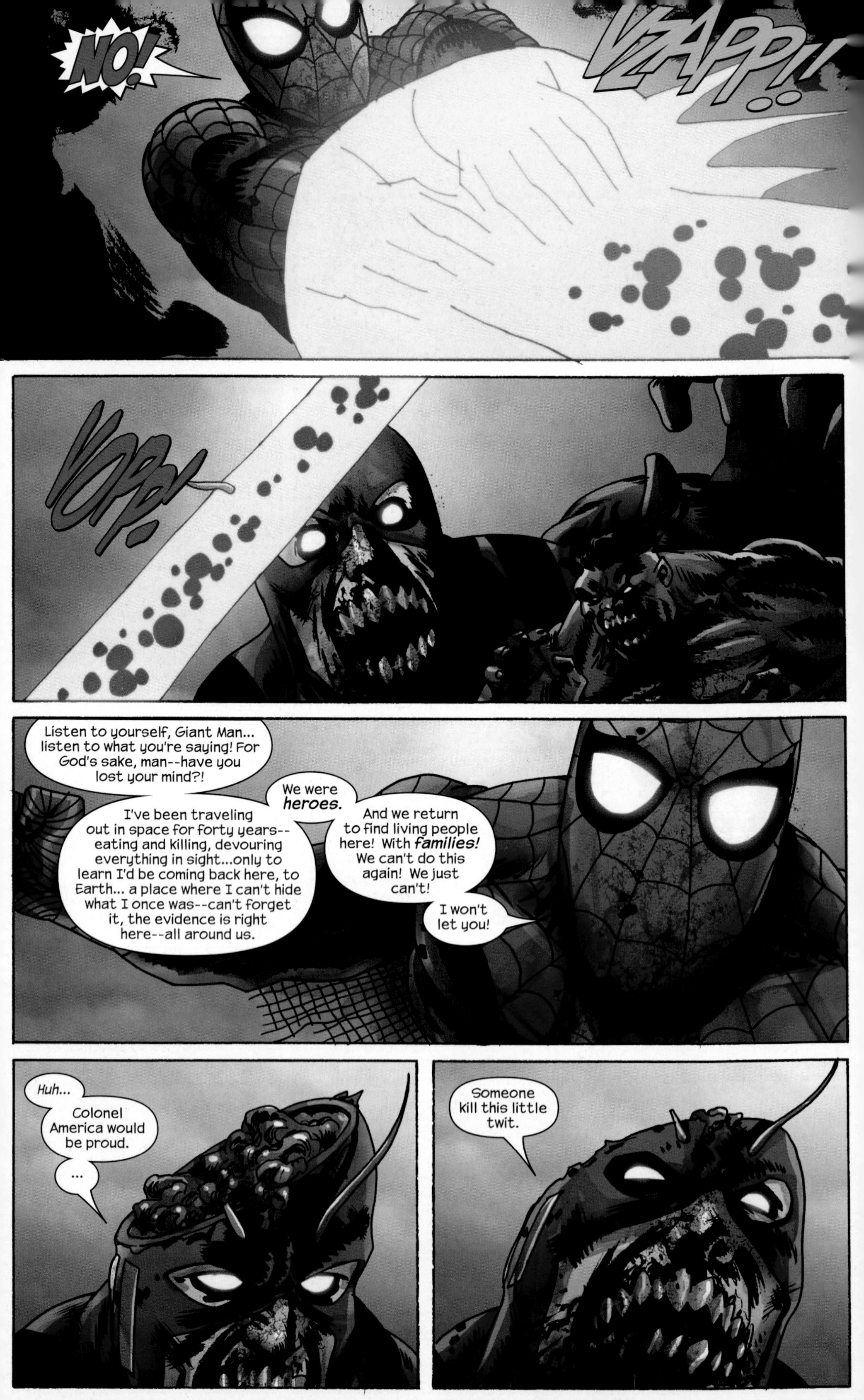
NO!
VZAPP!!
VOPP!
Listen to yourself, Giant Man... listen to what you're saying! For God's sake, man--have you lost your mind?!
I've been traveling out in space for forty years--eating and killing, devouring everything in sight...only to learn I'd be coming back here, to Earth... a place where I can't hide what I once was--can't forget it, the evidence is right here--all around us.
We were heroes.
And we return to find living people here! With families! We can't do this again! We just can't!
I won't let you!
Huh...
Colonel America would be proud.
...
Someone kill this little twit.

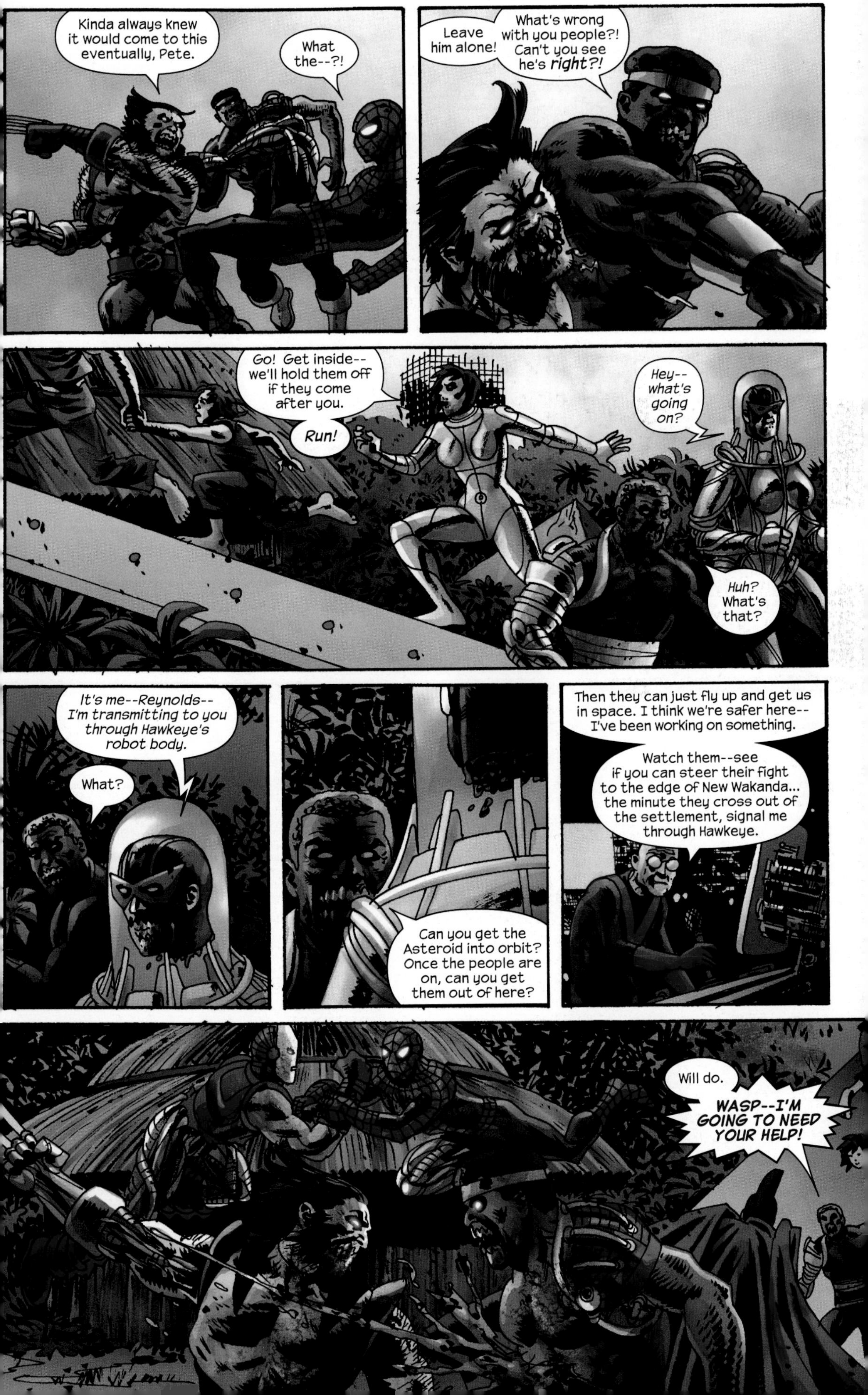

Kinda always knew it would come to this eventually, Pete.
What the--?!
Leave him alone!
What's wrong with you people?! Can't you see he's right?!
Go! Get inside-- we'll hold them off if they come after you.
Run!
Hey-- what's going on?
Huh? What's that?
It's me--Reynolds-- I'm transmitting to you through Hawkeye's robot body.
What?
Can you get the Asteroid into orbit? Once the people are on, can you get them out of here?
Then they can just fly up and get us in space. I think we're safer here-- I've been working on something.
Watch them--see if you can steer their fight to the edge of New Wakanda... the minute they cross out of the settlement, signal me through Hawkeye.
Will do.
WASP--I'M GOING TO NEED YOUR HELP!

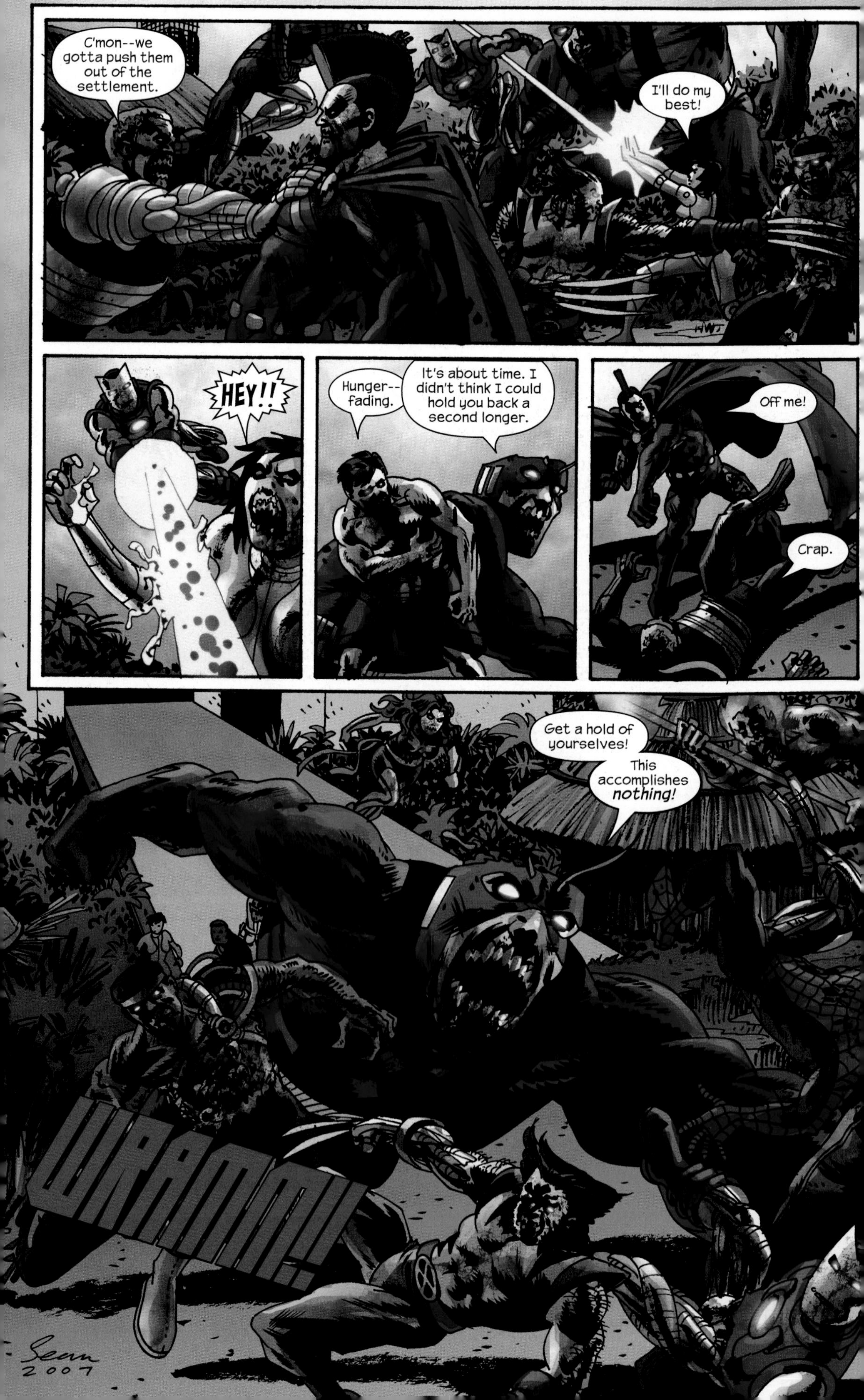
C'mon--we gotta push them out of the settlement.
I'll do my best!
HEY!!
Hunger--fading.
It's about time. I didn't think I could hold you back a second longer.
Off me!
Crap.
Get a hold of yourselves!
This accomplishes *nothing*!
WHAMM!
Sean 2007

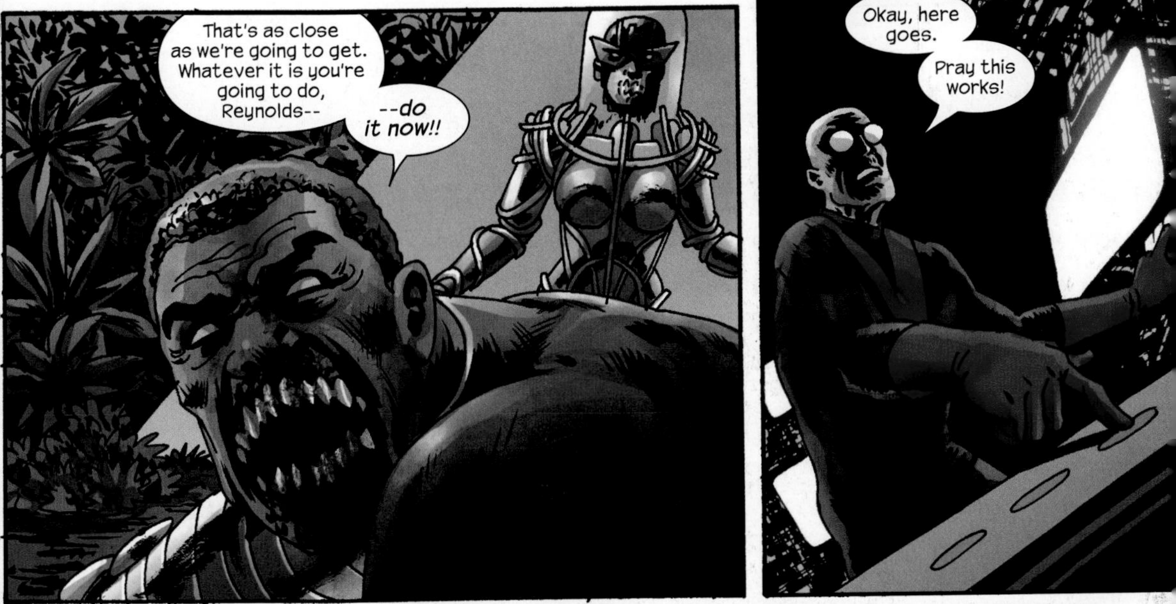
That's as close as we're going to get. Whatever it is you're going to do, Reynolds--
--do it now!!
Okay, here goes.
Pray this works!

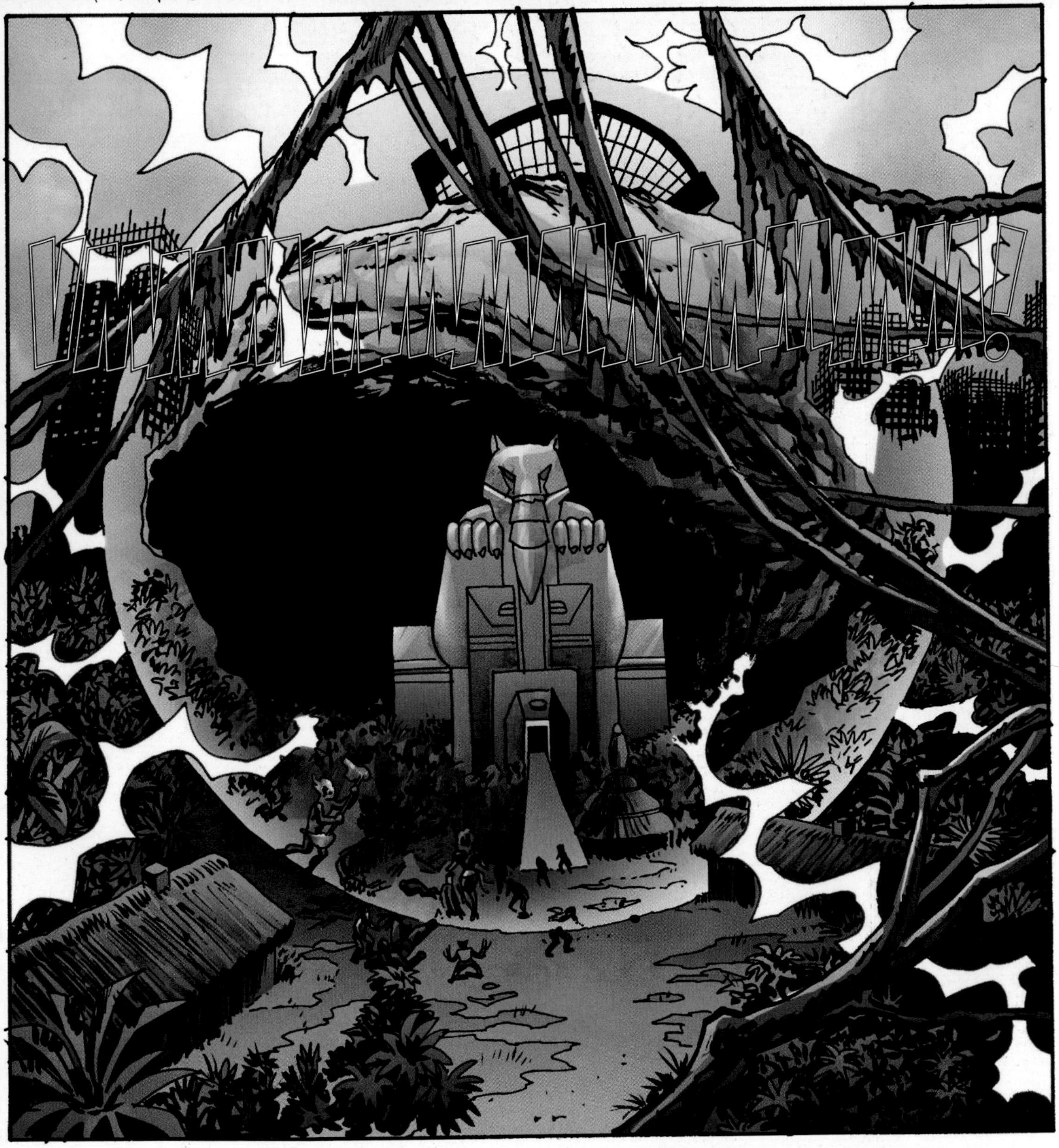

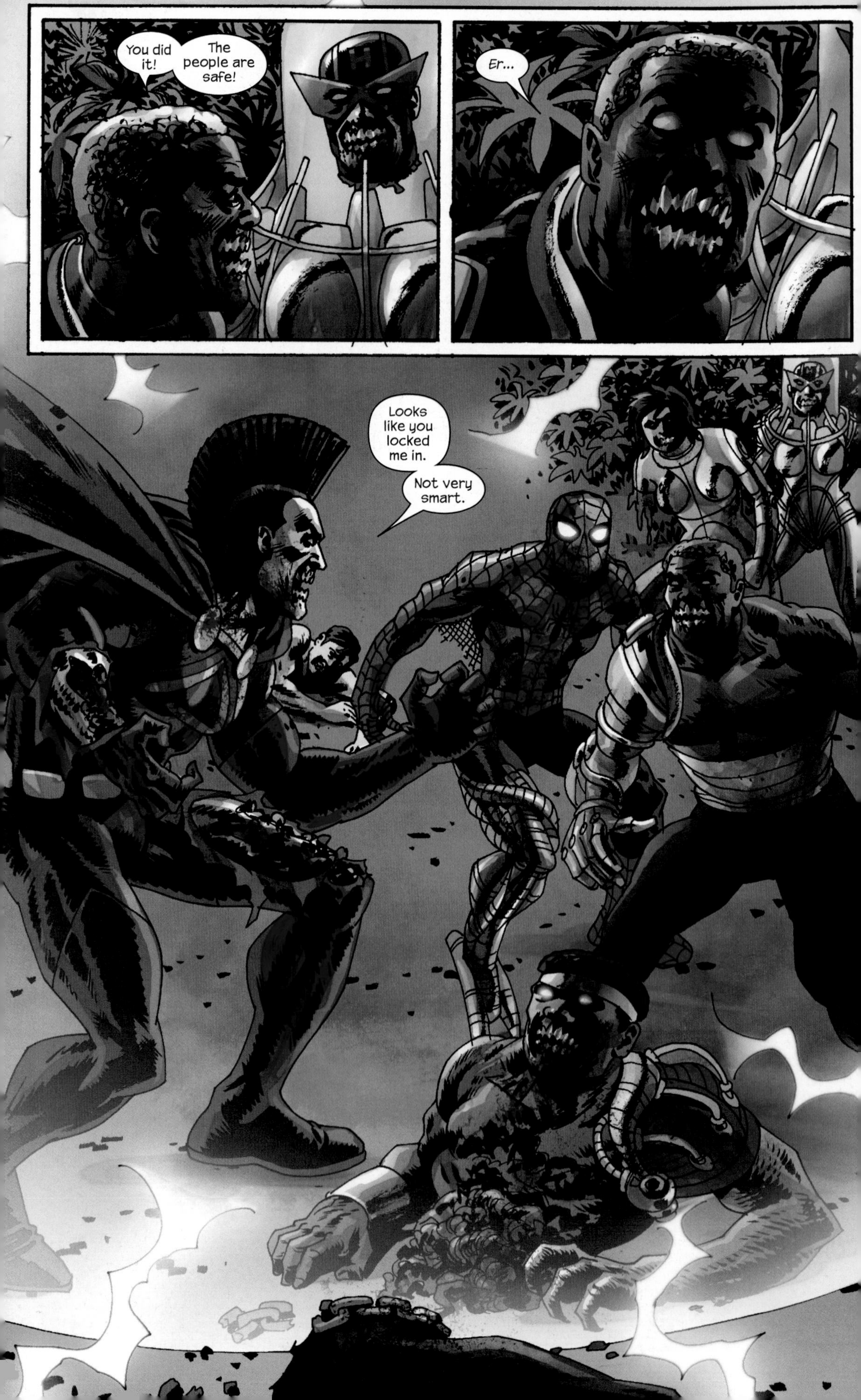
You did it!
The people are safe!
Er...
Looks like you locked me in.
Not very smart.

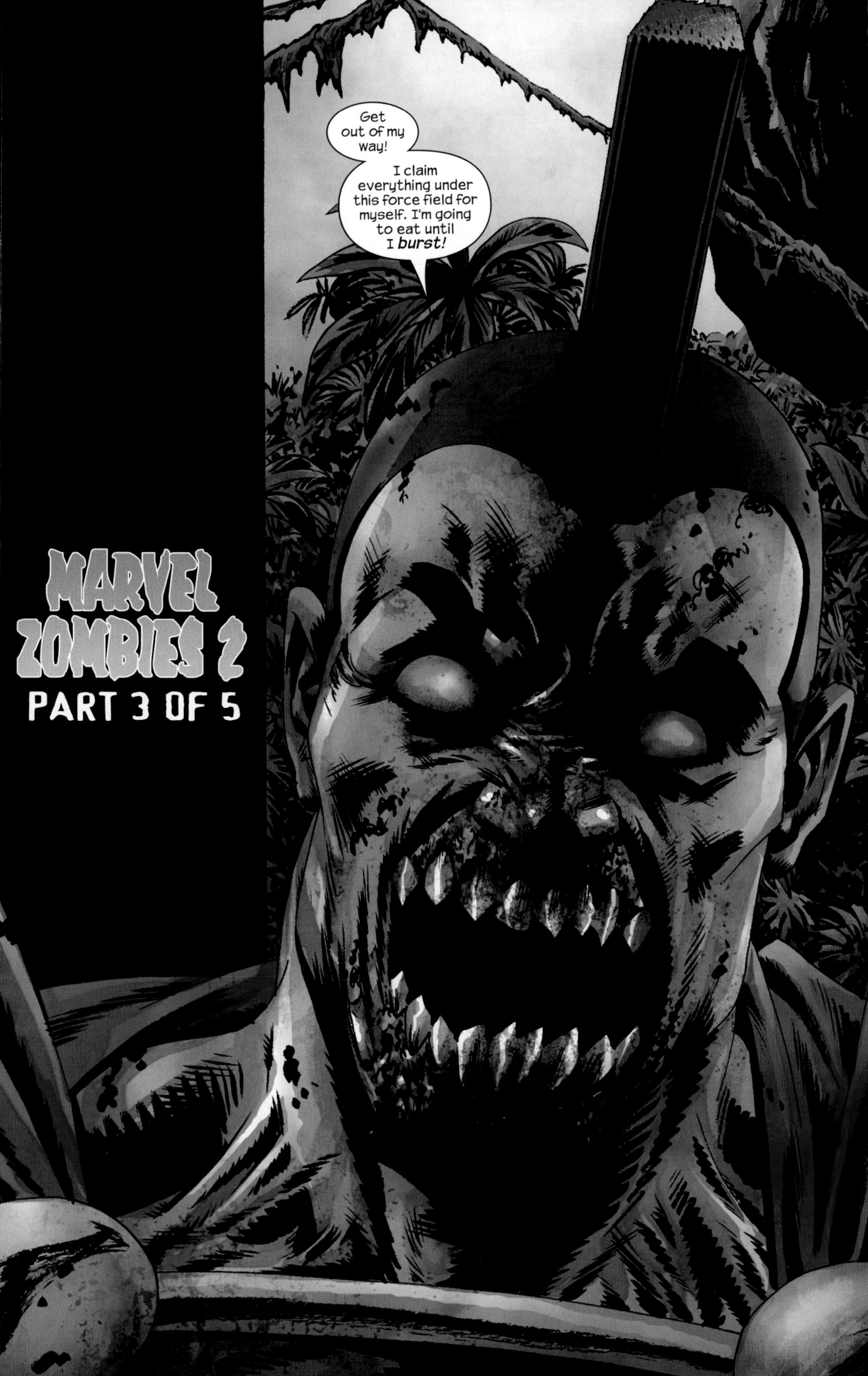
Get out of my way!
I claim everything under this force field for myself. I'm going to eat until I *burst!*
MARVEL ZOMBIES 2
PART 3 OF 5

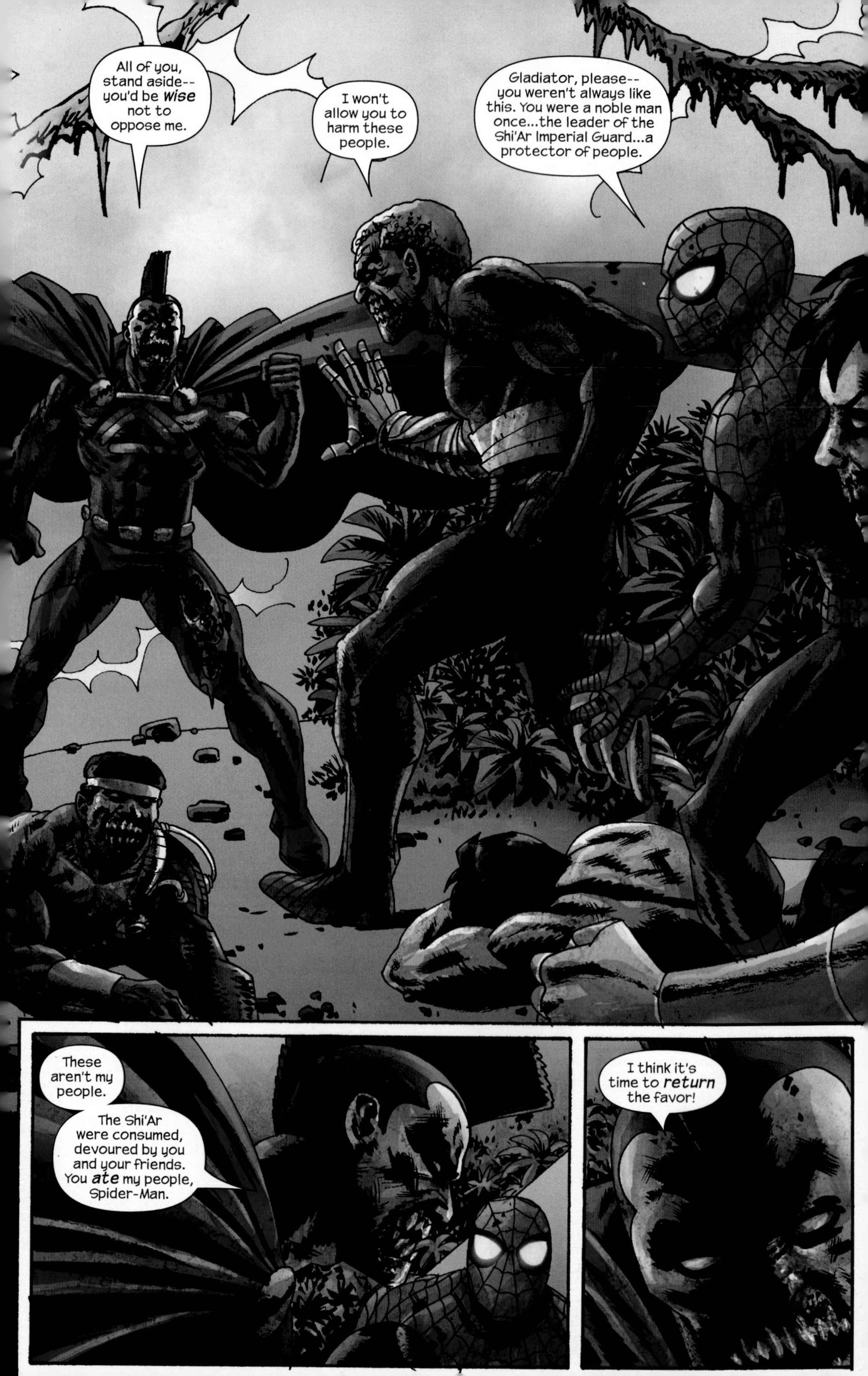
All of you, stand aside--you'd be *wise* not to oppose me.
I won't allow you to harm these people.
Gladiator, please--you weren't always like this. You were a noble man once...the leader of the Shi'Ar Imperial Guard...a protector of people.
These aren't my people.
The Shi'Ar were consumed, devoured by you and your friends. You *ate* my people, Spider-Man.
I think it's time to *return* the favor!

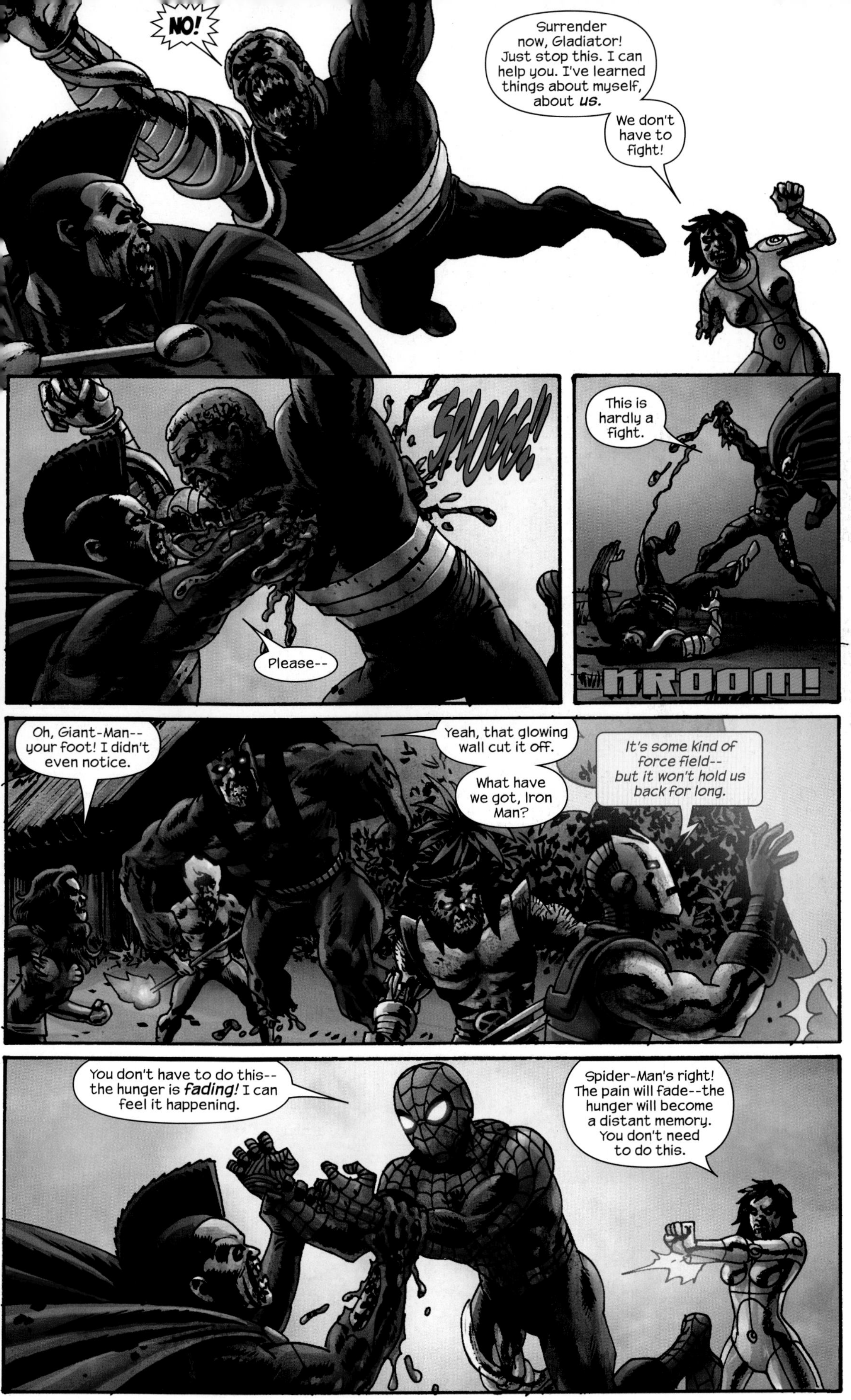
NO!
Surrender now, Gladiator! Just stop this. I can help you. I've learned things about myself, about *us.*
We don't have to fight!
SPLOOGE!!
Please--
This is hardly a fight.
KROOM!
Oh, Giant-Man-- your foot! I didn't even notice.
Yeah, that glowing wall cut it off.
What have we got, Iron Man?
It's some kind of force field-- but it won't hold us back for long.
You don't have to do this-- the hunger is *fading!* I can feel it happening.
Spider-Man's right! The pain will fade--the hunger will become a distant memory. You don't need to do this.

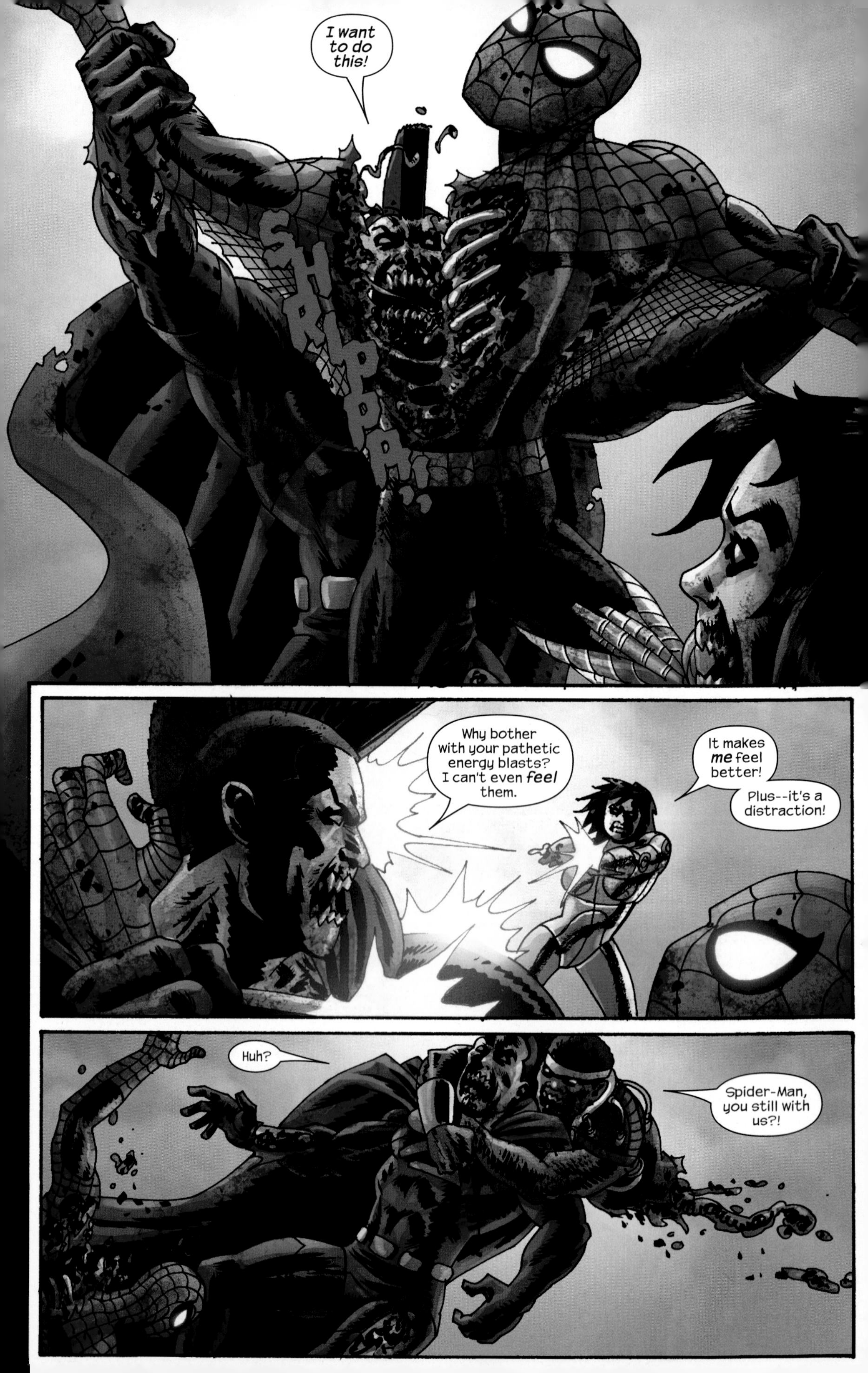
I want to do this!
SHRLPPP!!
Why bother with your pathetic energy blasts? I can't even *feel* them.
It makes *me* feel better!
Plus--it's a distraction!
Huh?
Spider-Man, you still with us?!

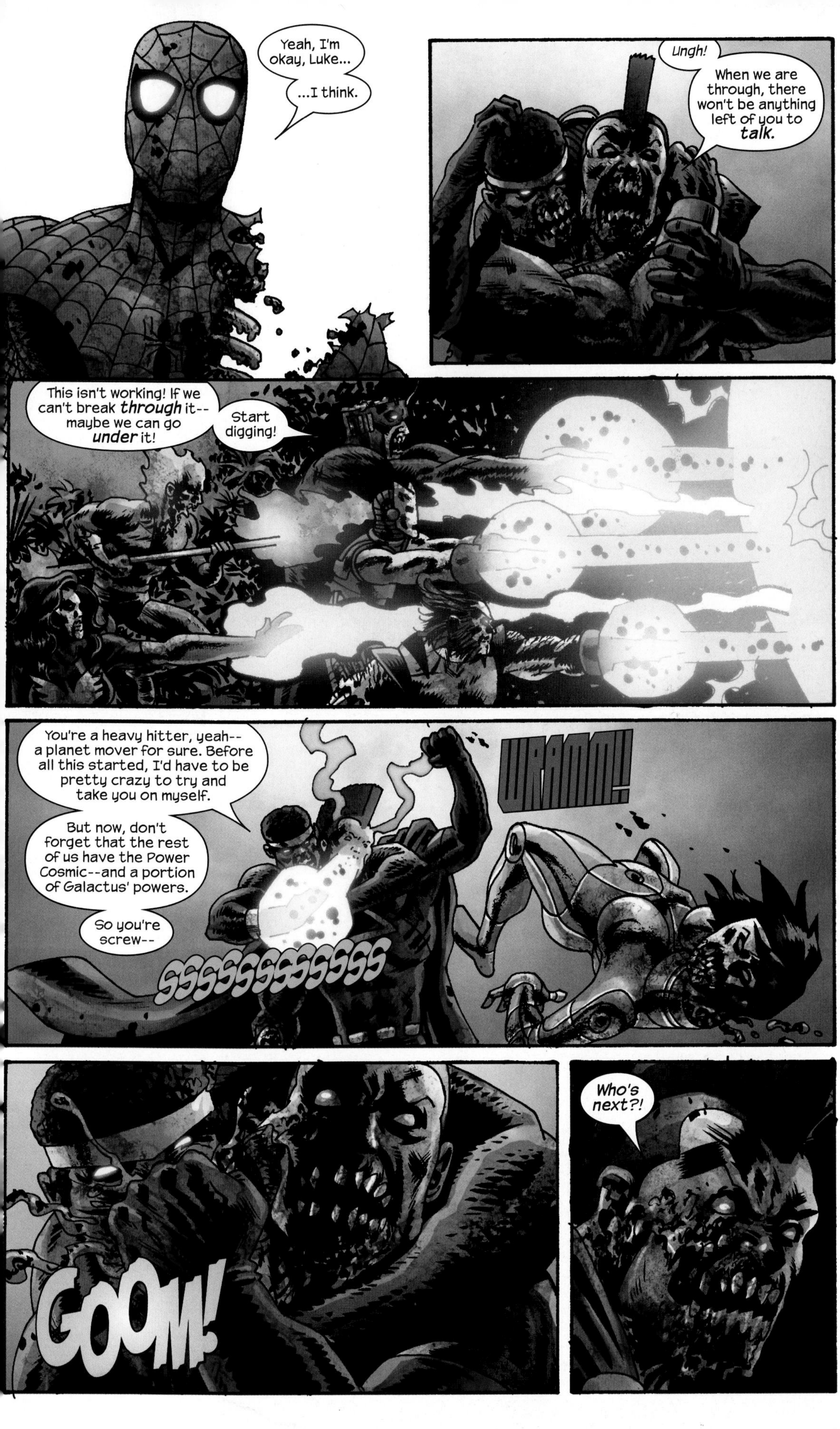
Yeah, I'm okay, Luke...
...I think.
Ungh!
When we are through, there won't be anything left of you to talk.
This isn't working! If we can't break through it-- maybe we can go under it!
Start digging!
You're a heavy hitter, yeah-- a planet mover for sure. Before all this started, I'd have to be pretty crazy to try and take you on myself.
But now, don't forget that the rest of us have the Power Cosmic--and a portion of Galactus' powers.
So you're screw--
WRAMM!!
SSSSSSSSSSSS
GOOM!
Who's next?!

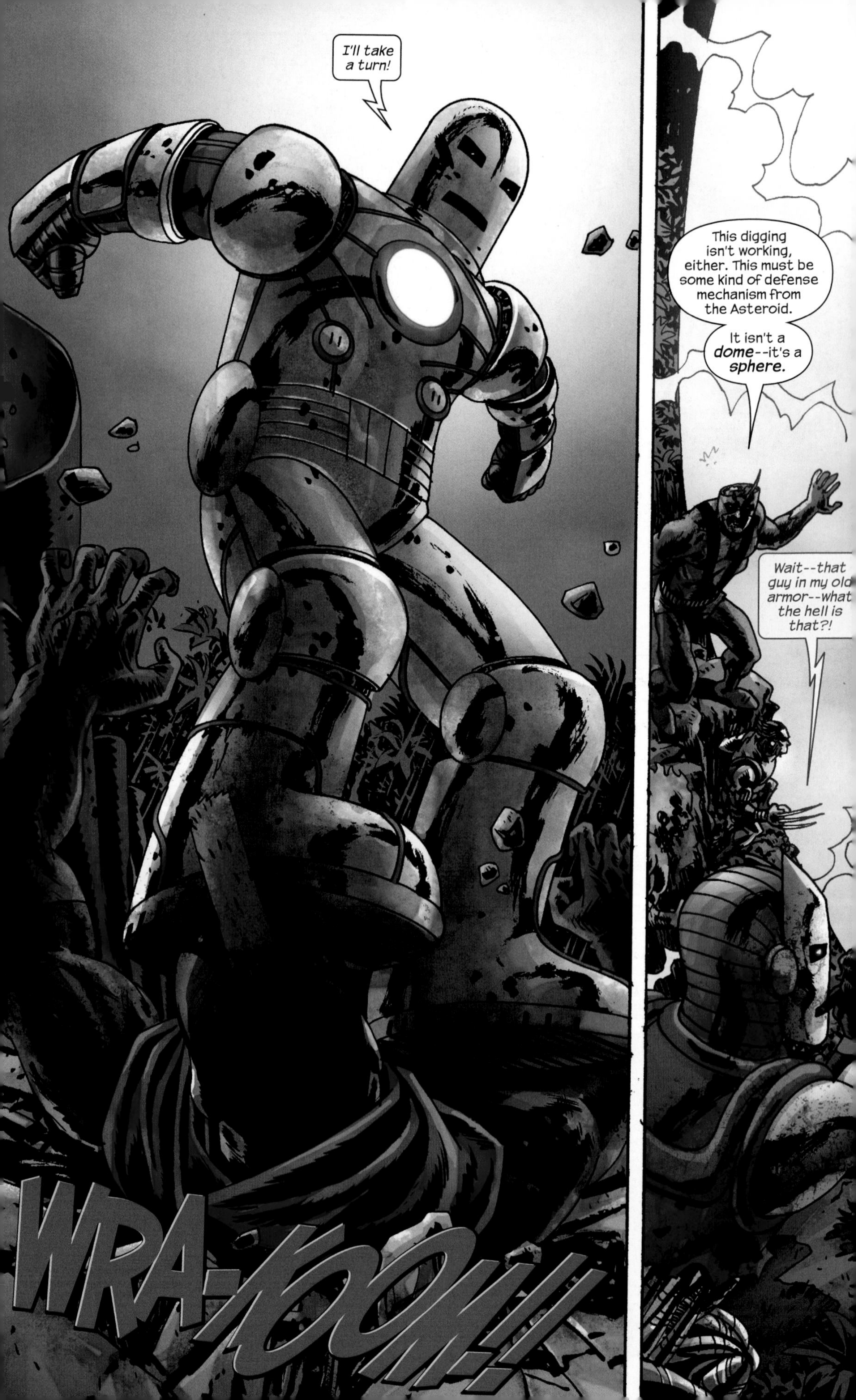
I'll take a turn!
This digging isn't working, either. This must be some kind of defense mechanism from the Asteroid.
It isn't a dome--it's a sphere.
Wait--that guy in my old armor--what the hell is that?!
WRA-KOOM!!

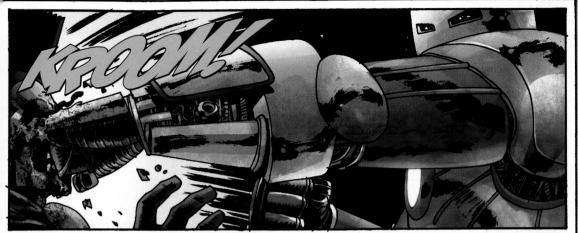

KROOM!

Wow.

Heh. Now we get to find out who's inside.

VZAPP!

Quickly-- while he's stunned-- hold him in place!

I'll do what I can-- just make this quick!

Can't-- move!

Can't-- think!

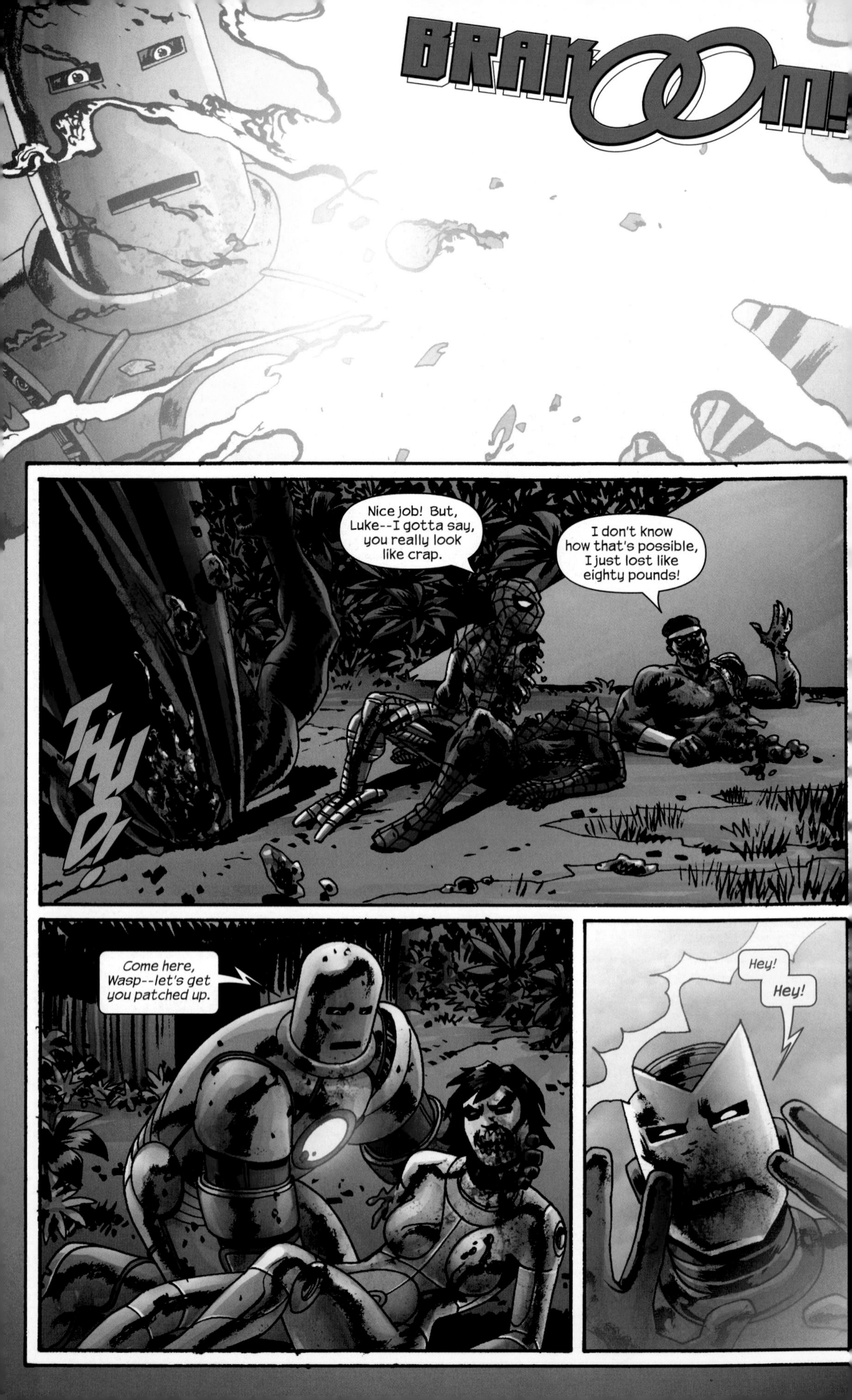
BRAKOOOM!
Nice job! But, Luke--I gotta say, you really look like crap.
I don't know how that's possible, I just lost like eighty pounds!
THUD!
Come here, Wasp--let's get you patched up.
Hey!
Hey!

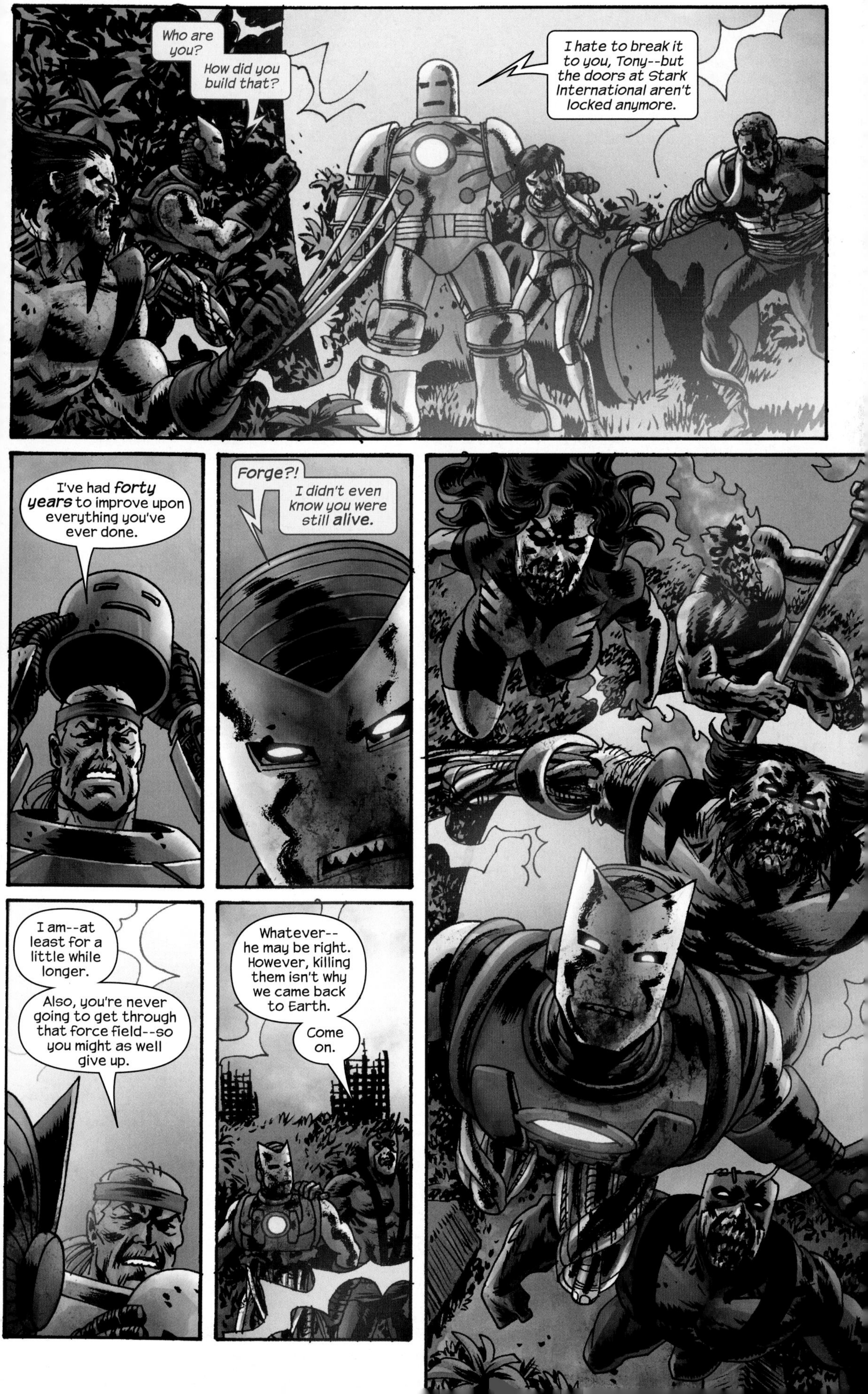
Who are you?
How did you build that?
I hate to break it to you, Tony--but the doors at Stark International aren't locked anymore.
I've had **forty years** to improve upon everything you've ever done.
Forge?!
I didn't even know you were still **alive.**
I am--at least for a little while longer.
Also, you're never going to get through that force field--so you might as well give up.
Whatever--he may be right. However, killing them isn't why we came back to Earth.
Come on.

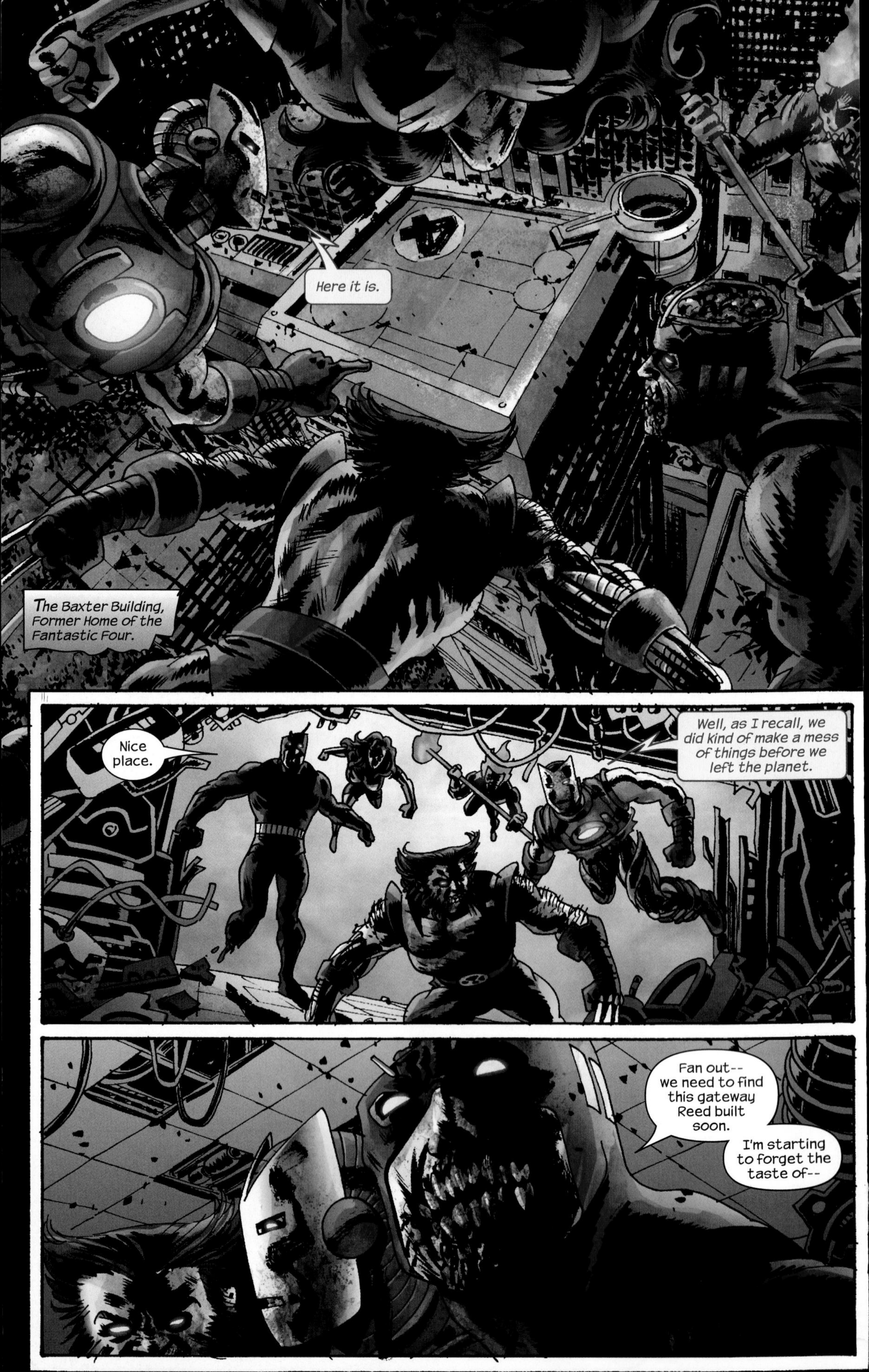
Here it is.
The Baxter Building, Former Home of the Fantastic Four.
Nice place.
Well, as I recall, we did kind of make a mess of things before we left the planet.
Fan out-- we need to find this gateway Reed built soon.
I'm starting to forget the taste of--

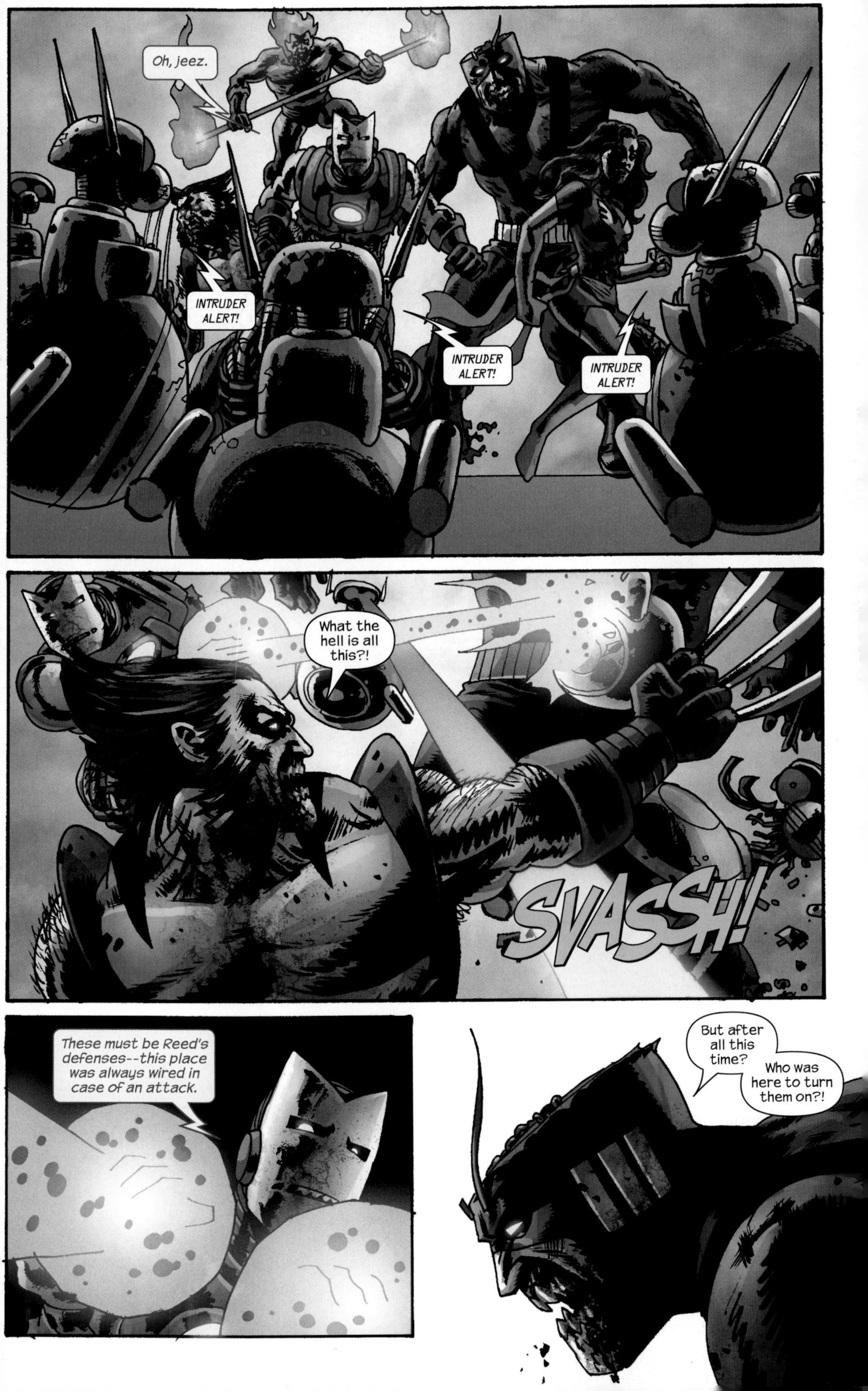
Oh, jeez.
INTRUDER ALERT!
INTRUDER ALERT!
INTRUDER ALERT!
What the hell is all this?!
SVASSH!
These must be Reed's defenses--this place was always wired in case of an attack.
But after all this time?
Who was here to turn them on?!

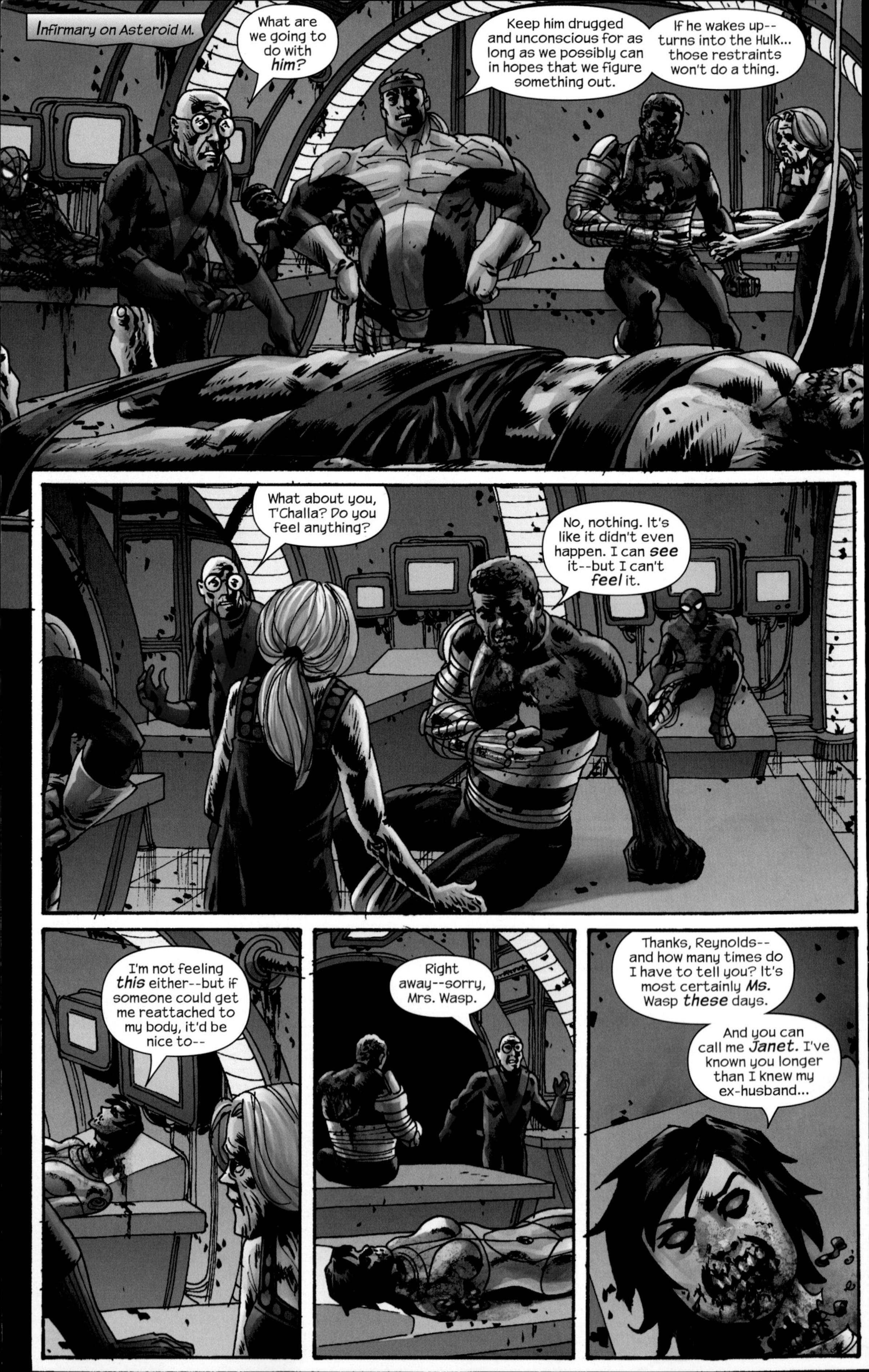
Infirmary on Asteroid M.
What are we going to do with *him*?
Keep him drugged and unconscious for as long as we possibly can in hopes that we figure something out.
If he wakes up--turns into the Hulk... those restraints won't do a thing.
What about you, T'Challa? Do you feel anything?
No, nothing. It's like it didn't even happen. I can *see* it--but I can't *feel* it.
I'm not feeling *this* either--but if someone could get me reattached to my body, it'd be nice to--
Right away--sorry, Mrs. Wasp.
Thanks, Reynolds--and how many times do I have to tell you? It's most certainly *Ms.* Wasp *these* days.
And you can call me *Janet*. I've known you longer than I knew my ex-husband...

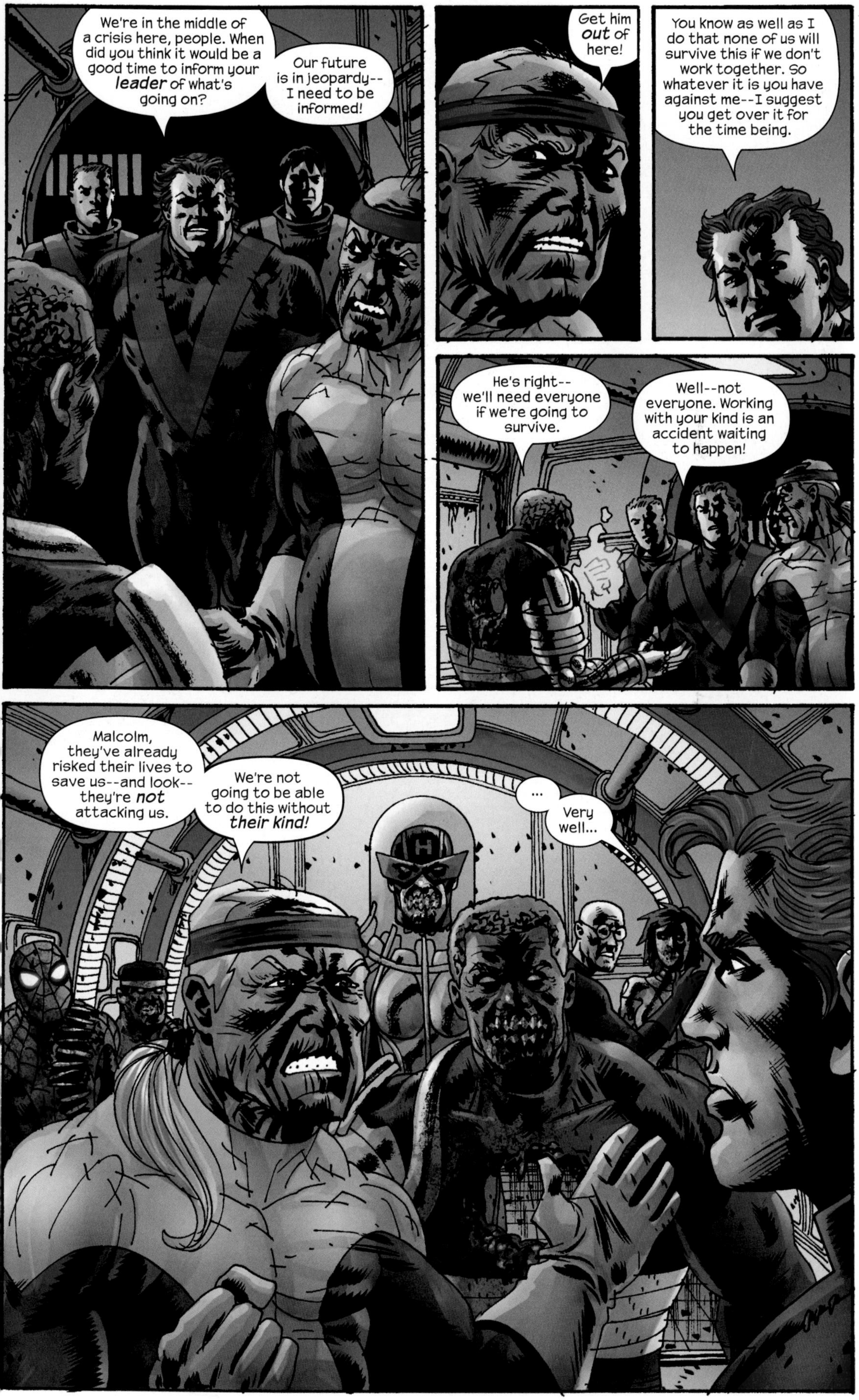

We're in the middle of a crisis here, people. When did you think it would be a good time to inform your *leader* of what's going on?
Our future is in jeopardy-- I need to be informed!
Get him *out* of here!
You know as well as I do that none of us will survive this if we don't work together. So whatever it is you have against me--I suggest you get over it for the time being.
He's right-- we'll need everyone if we're going to survive.
Well--not everyone. Working with your kind is an accident waiting to happen!
Malcolm, they've already risked their lives to save us--and look-- they're *not* attacking us.
We're not going to be able to do this without *their kind!*
...
Very well...

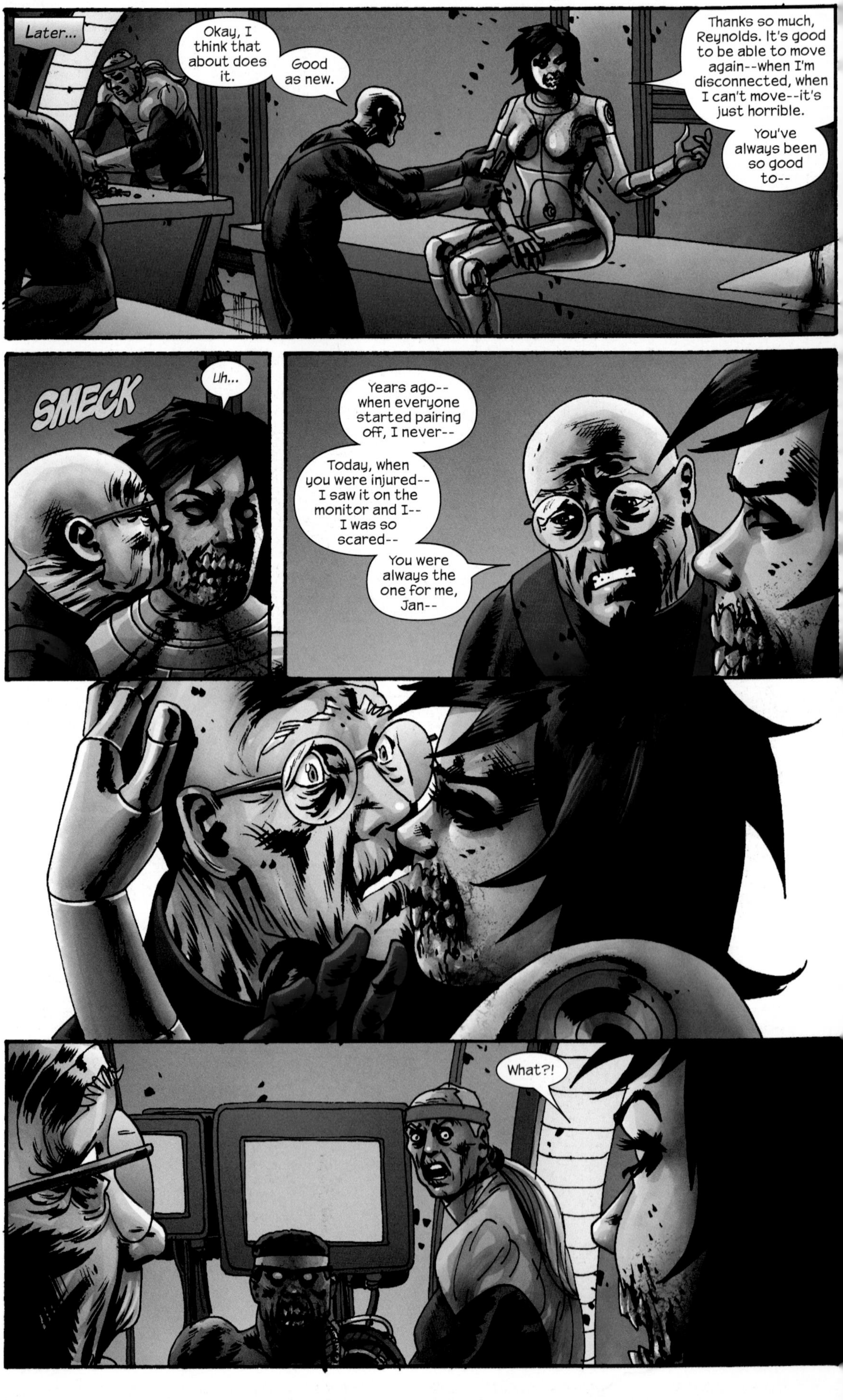
Later...
Okay, I think that about does it.
Good as new.
Thanks so much, Reynolds. It's good to be able to move again--when I'm disconnected, when I can't move--it's just horrible.
You've always been so good to--
SMECK
Uh...
Years ago--when everyone started pairing off, I never--
Today, when you were injured--I saw it on the monitor and I--I was so scared--
You were always the one for me, Jan--
What?!

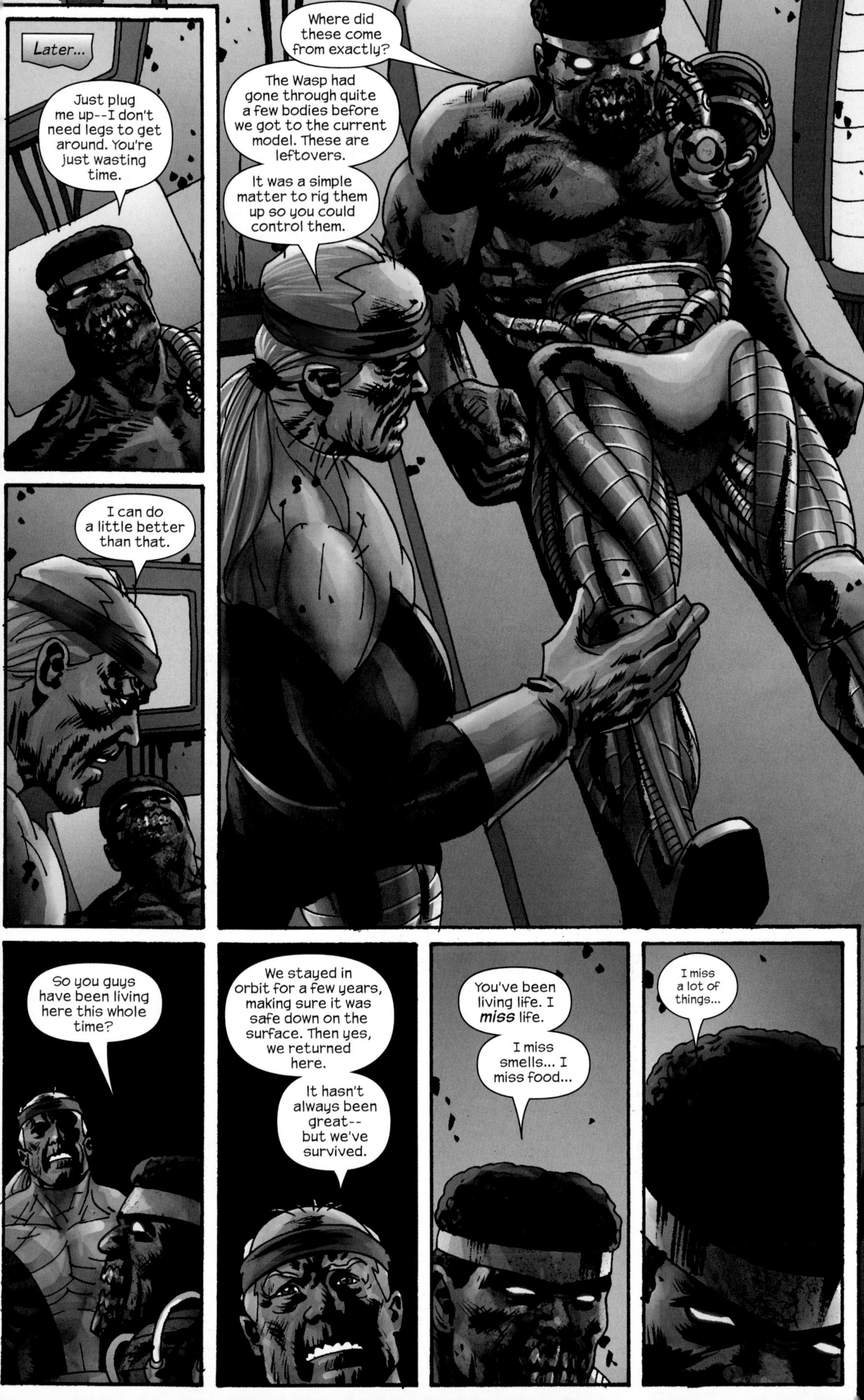
Later...
Just plug me up--I don't need legs to get around. You're just wasting time.
Where did these come from exactly?
The Wasp had gone through quite a few bodies before we got to the current model. These are leftovers.
It was a simple matter to rig them up so you could control them.
I can do a little better than that.
So you guys have been living here this whole time?
We stayed in orbit for a few years, making sure it was safe down on the surface. Then yes, we returned here.
It hasn't always been great--but we've survived.
You've been living life. I *miss* life.
I miss smells... I miss food...
I miss a lot of things...

I'm sorry, he-- he wanted to see you.

Please, come. Don't be afraid, K'Shamba. You have nothing to fear from me.

I'm not afraid. I'm--

Are-- are you *dead*?

Do I sound dead to you?

No...but you *look* dead.

What have I told you in your studies? Looks can be deceiving... never judge anything by looks alone.

I am still your grandfather.

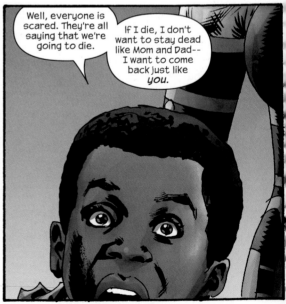

Well, everyone is scared. They're all saying that we're going to die.

If I die, I don't want to stay dead like Mom and Dad-- I want to come back just like *you*.

What can the two of you tell us about your group? Any information would be useful.

Why are they here? Why have they come back?

The same reason we went everywhere else in the galaxy: for more *food...*

They're looking for a place that has it.

Then why *here*? They had to know that even if there were survivors here--it wouldn't be *enough*.

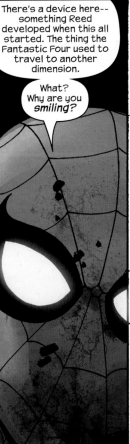

There's a device here-- something Reed developed when this all started. The thing the Fantastic Four used to travel to another dimension.

What? Why are you *smiling*?

Follow me. There's something I'd like to show you.

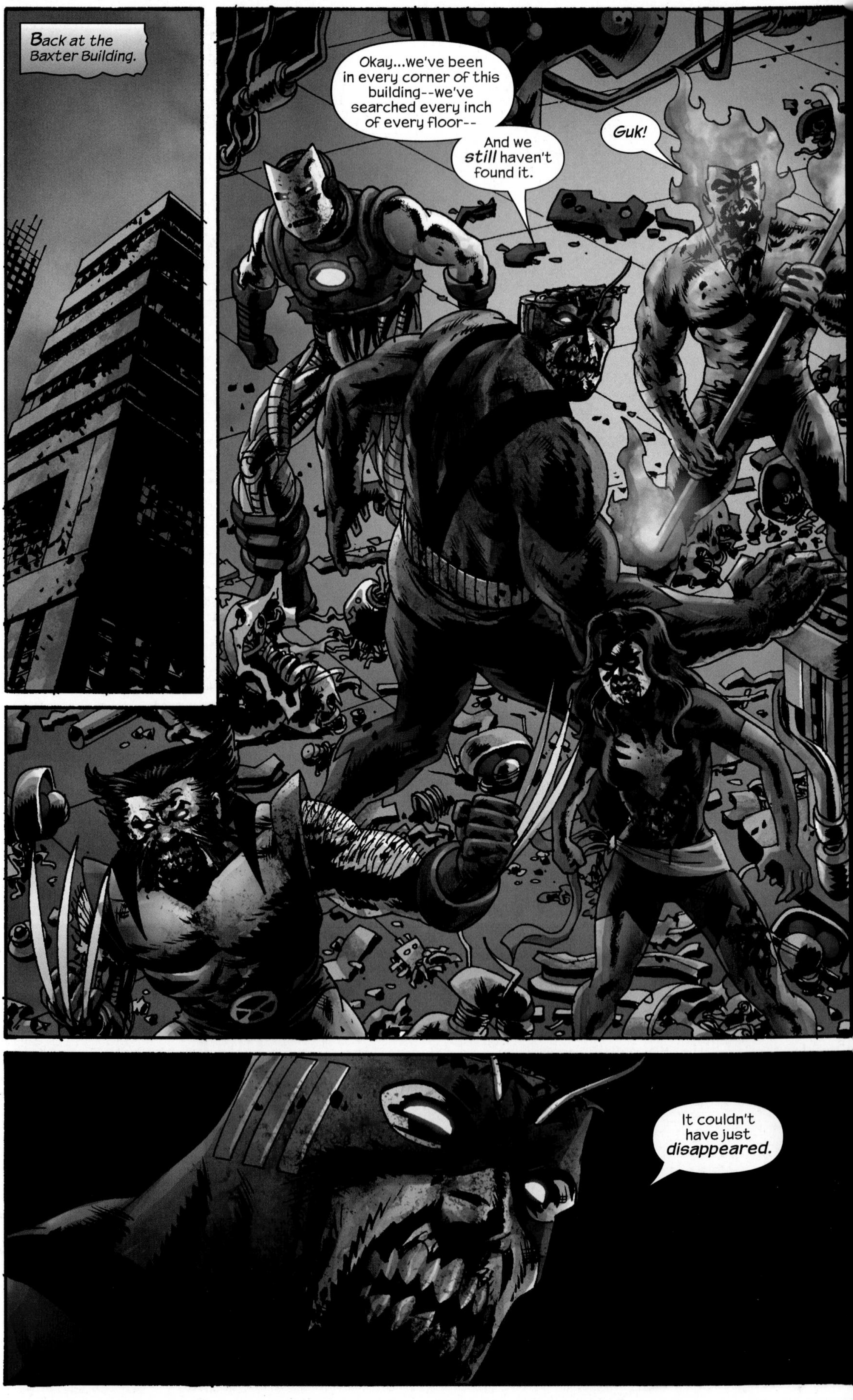
Back at the Baxter Building.
Okay...we've been in every corner of this building--we've searched every inch of every floor--
And we still haven't found it.
Guk!
It couldn't have just disappeared.

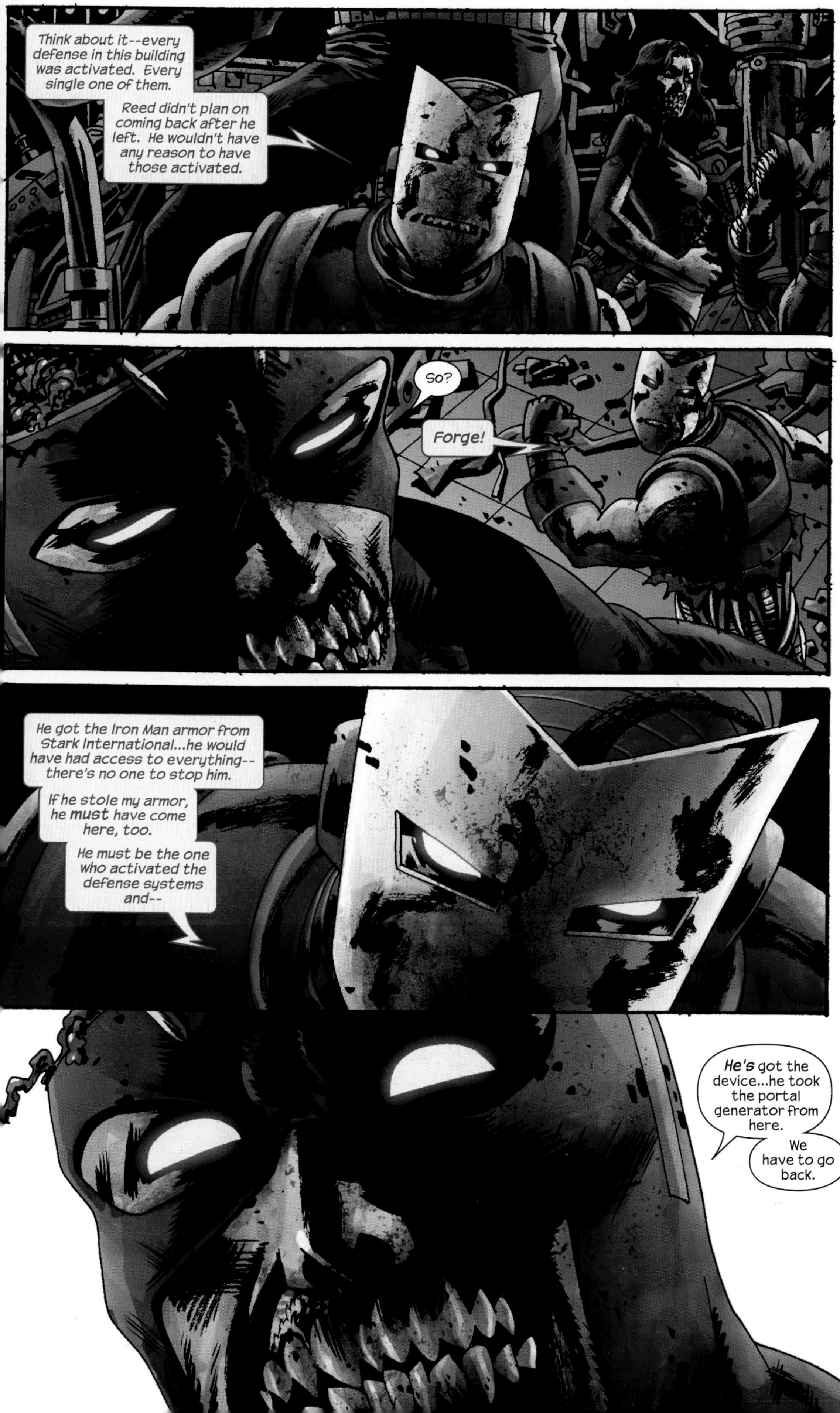
Think about it--every defense in this building was activated. Every single one of them.
Reed didn't plan on coming back after he left. He wouldn't have any reason to have those activated.
So?
Forge!
He got the Iron Man armor from Stark International...he would have had access to everything--there's no one to stop him.
If he stole my armor, he **must** have come here, too.
He must be the one who activated the defense systems and--
He's got the device...he took the portal generator from here.
We have to go back.

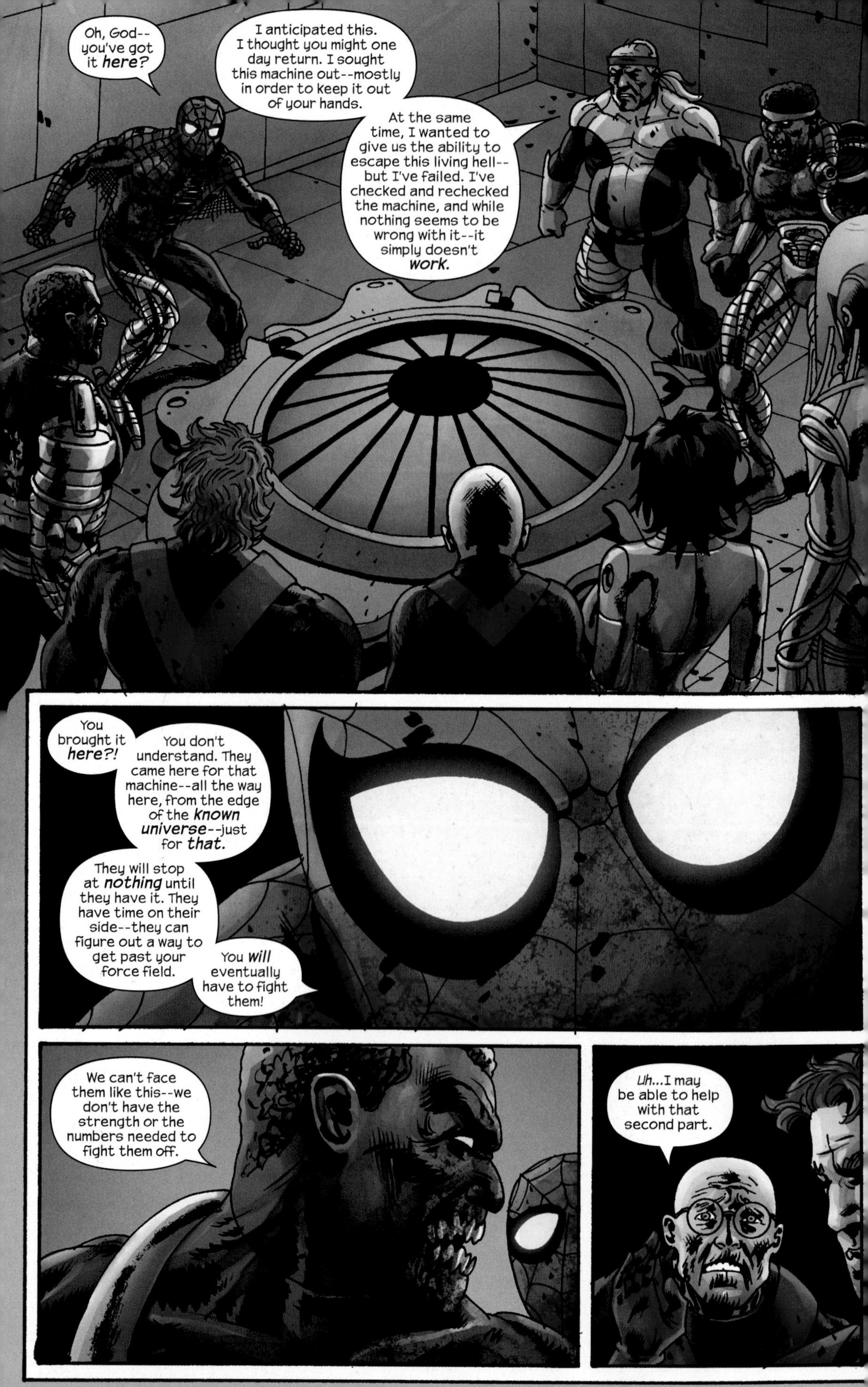
Oh, God-- you've got it *here?*
I anticipated this. I thought you might one day return. I sought this machine out--mostly in order to keep it out of your hands.
At the same time, I wanted to give us the ability to escape this living hell-- but I've failed. I've checked and rechecked the machine, and while nothing seems to be wrong with it--it simply doesn't *work.*
You brought it *here?!*
You don't understand. They came here for that machine--all the way here, from the edge of the *known universe*--just for *that.*
They will stop at *nothing* until they have it. They have time on their side--they can figure out a way to get past your force field.
You *will* eventually have to fight them!
We can't face them like this--we don't have the strength or the numbers needed to fight them off.
Uh...I may be able to help with that second part.

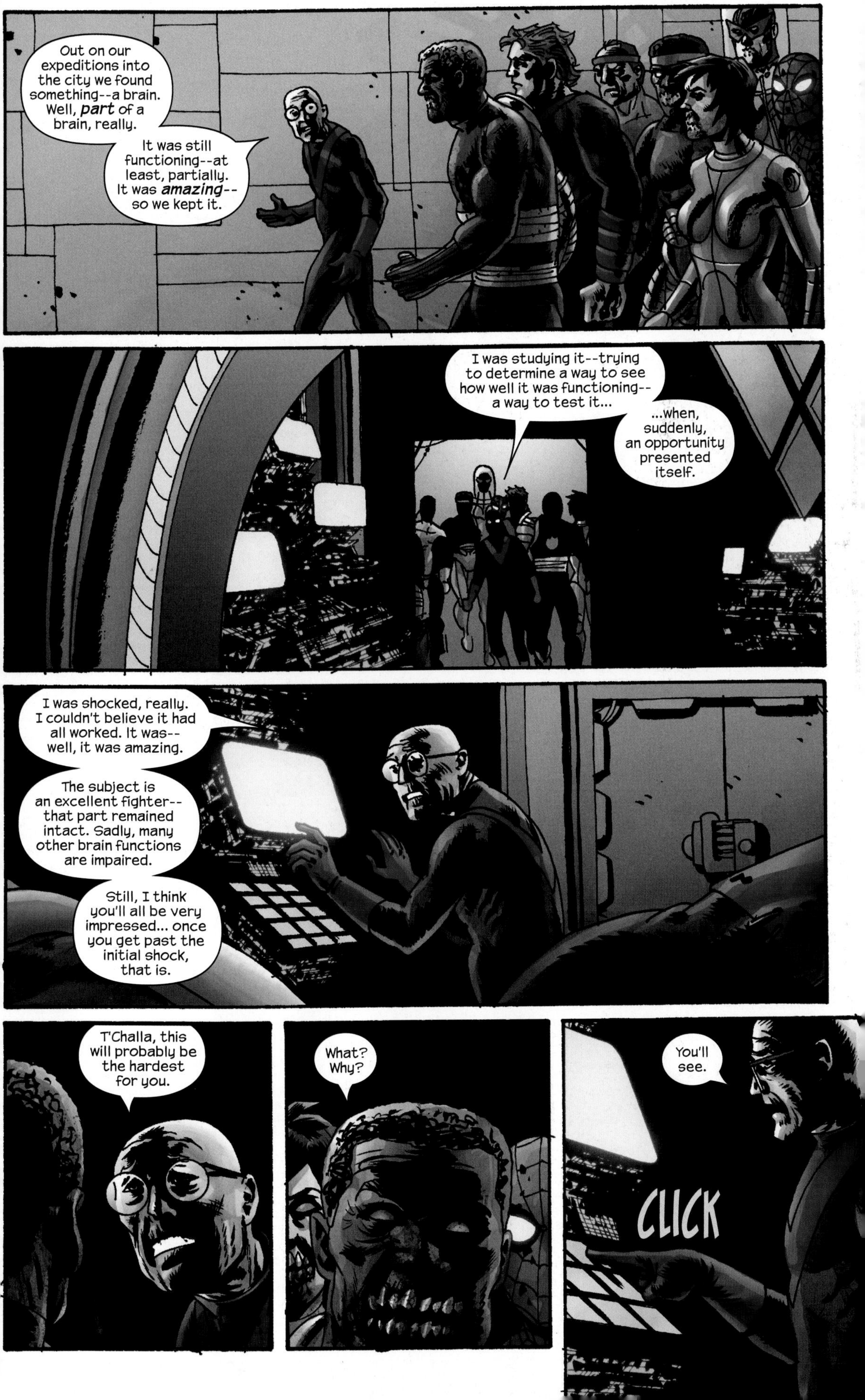
Out on our expeditions into the city we found something--a brain. Well, *part* of a brain, really.
It was still functioning--at least, partially. It was *amazing*--so we kept it.
I was studying it--trying to determine a way to see how well it was functioning--a way to test it...
...when, suddenly, an opportunity presented itself.
I was shocked, really. I couldn't believe it had all worked. It was--well, it was amazing.
The subject is an excellent fighter--that part remained intact. Sadly, many other brain functions are impaired.
Still, I think you'll all be very impressed... once you get past the initial shock, that is.
T'Challa, this will probably be the hardest for you.
What? Why?
You'll see.
CLICK

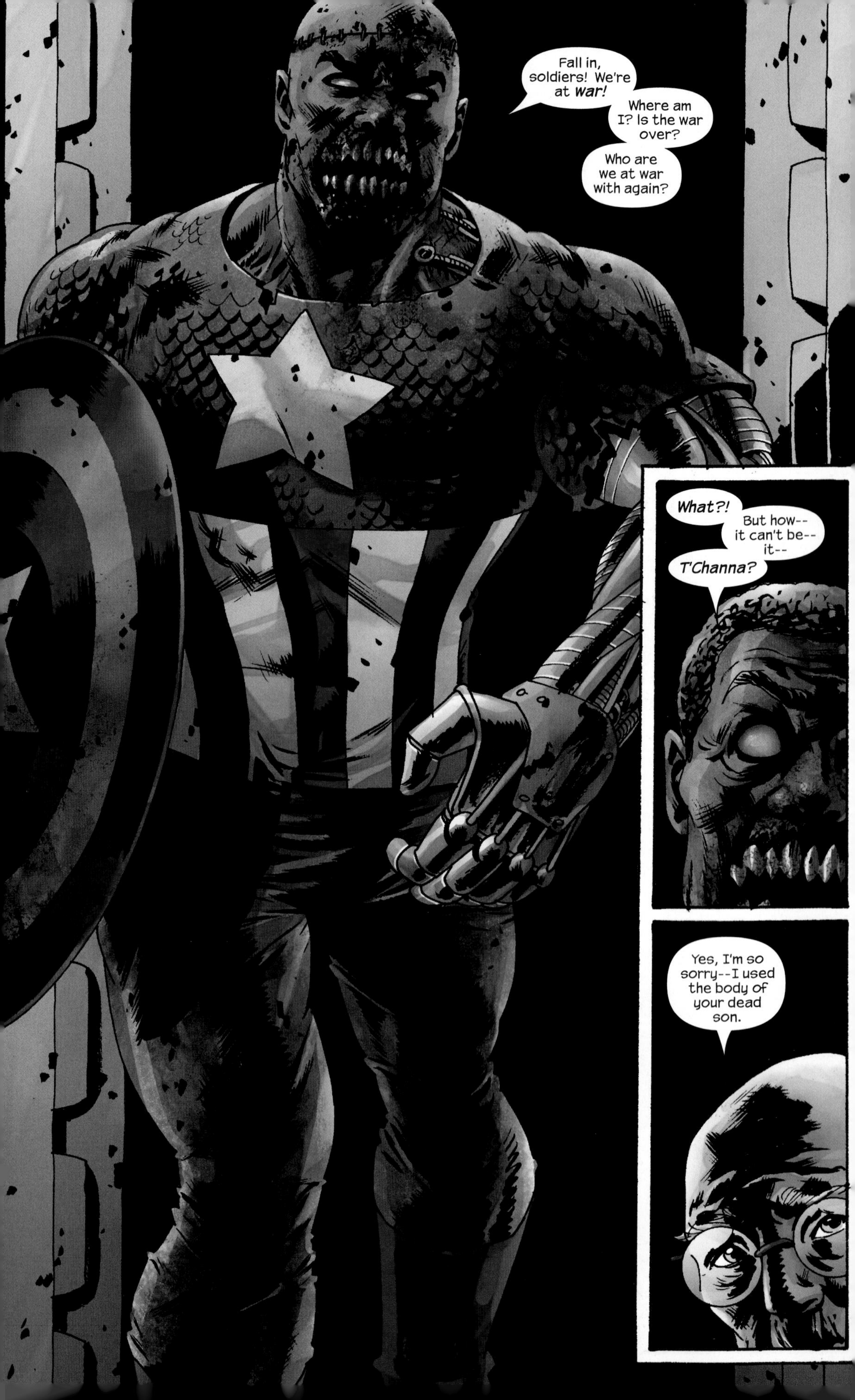
Fall in, soldiers! We're at *war!*
Where am I? Is the war over?
Who are we at war with again?
What?!
But how-- it can't be-- it--
T'Channa?
Yes, I'm so sorry--I used the body of your dead son.

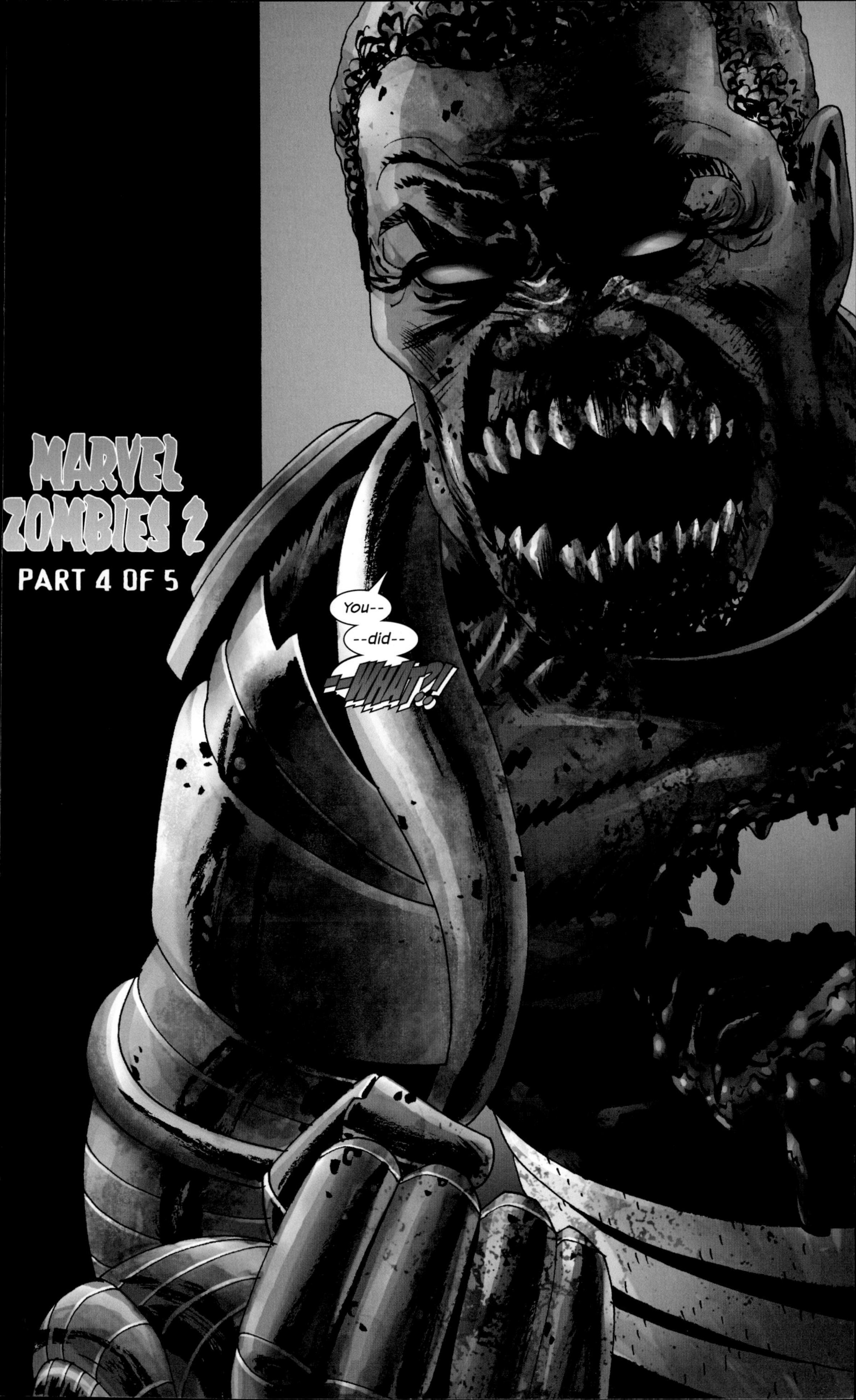
MARVEL ZOMBIES 2
PART 4 OF 5
You--
--did--
--WHAT?!

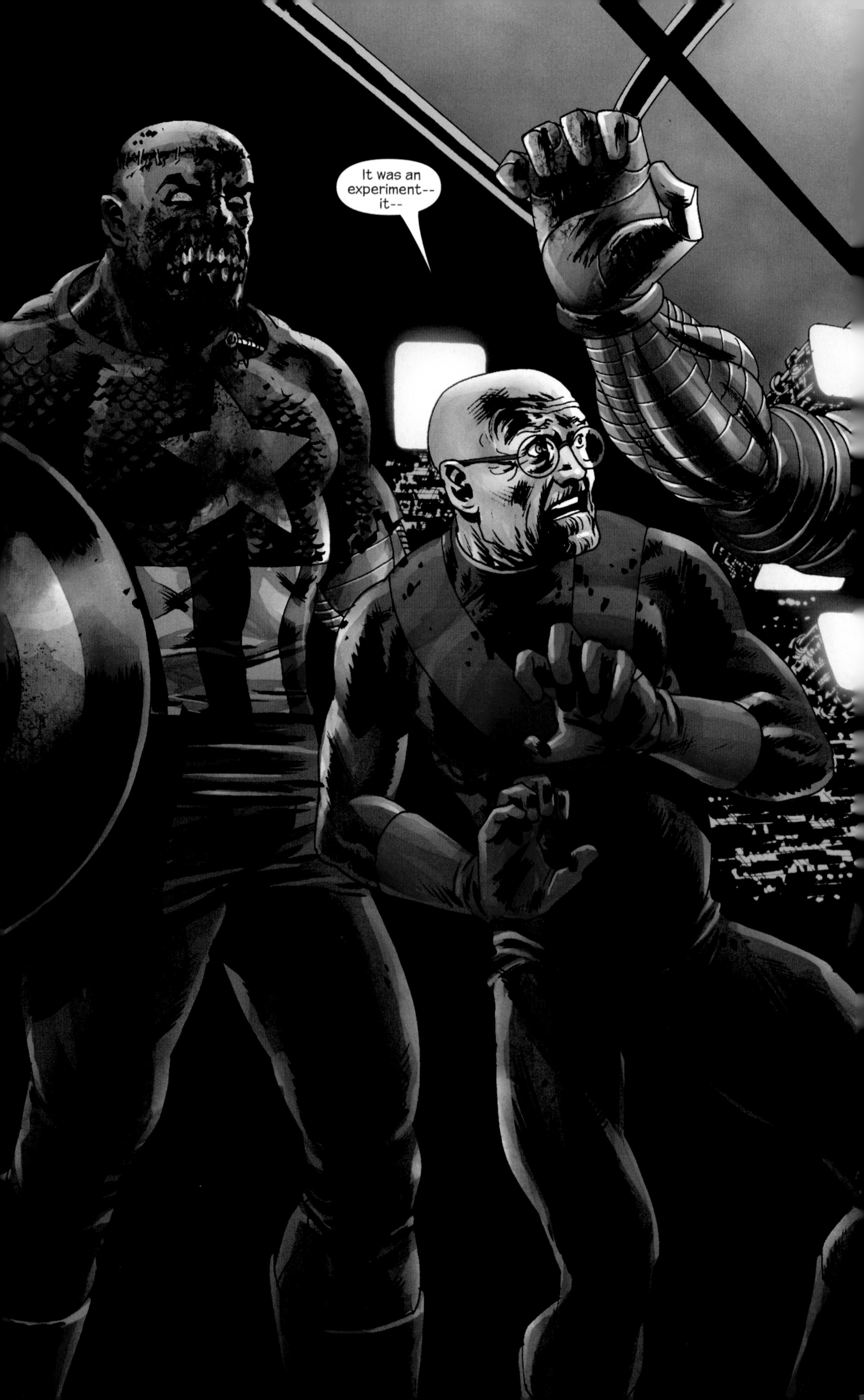
It was an experiment-- it--

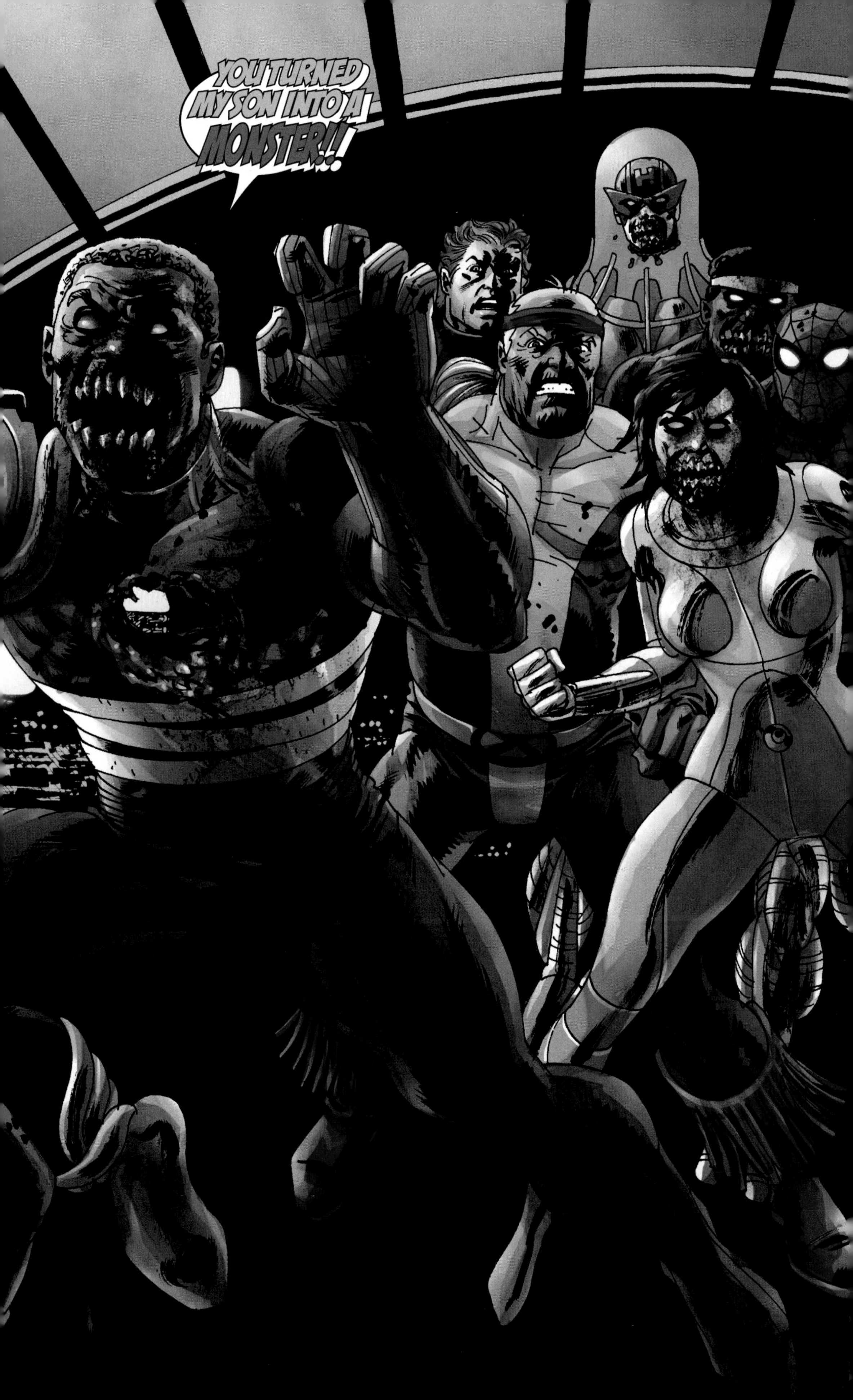
YOU TURNED MY SON INTO A MONSTER!!

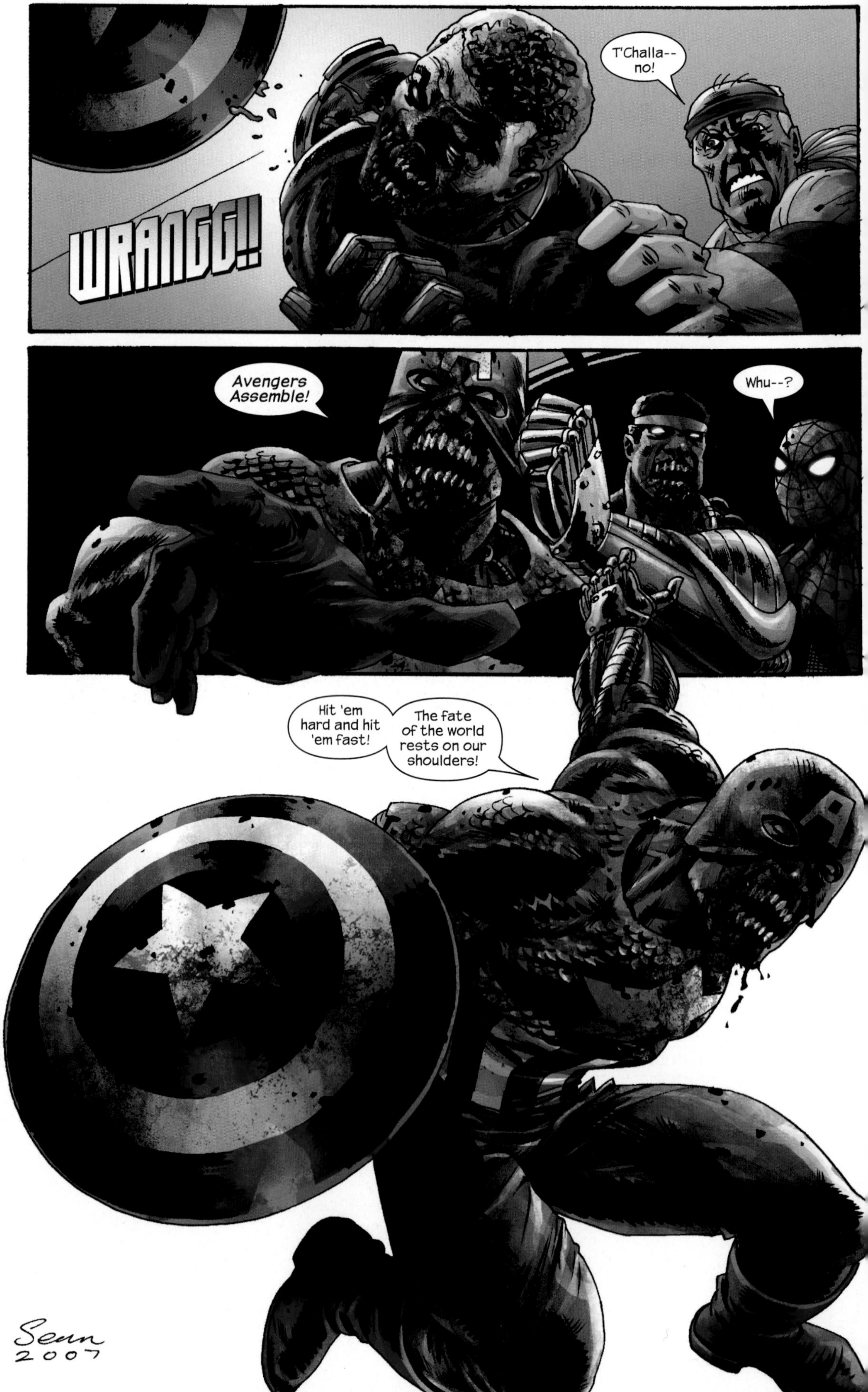
T'Challa--
no!
WRANGG!!
Avengers
Assemble!
Whu--?
Hit 'em
hard and hit
'em fast!
The fate
of the world
rests on our
shoulders!
Sean
2007

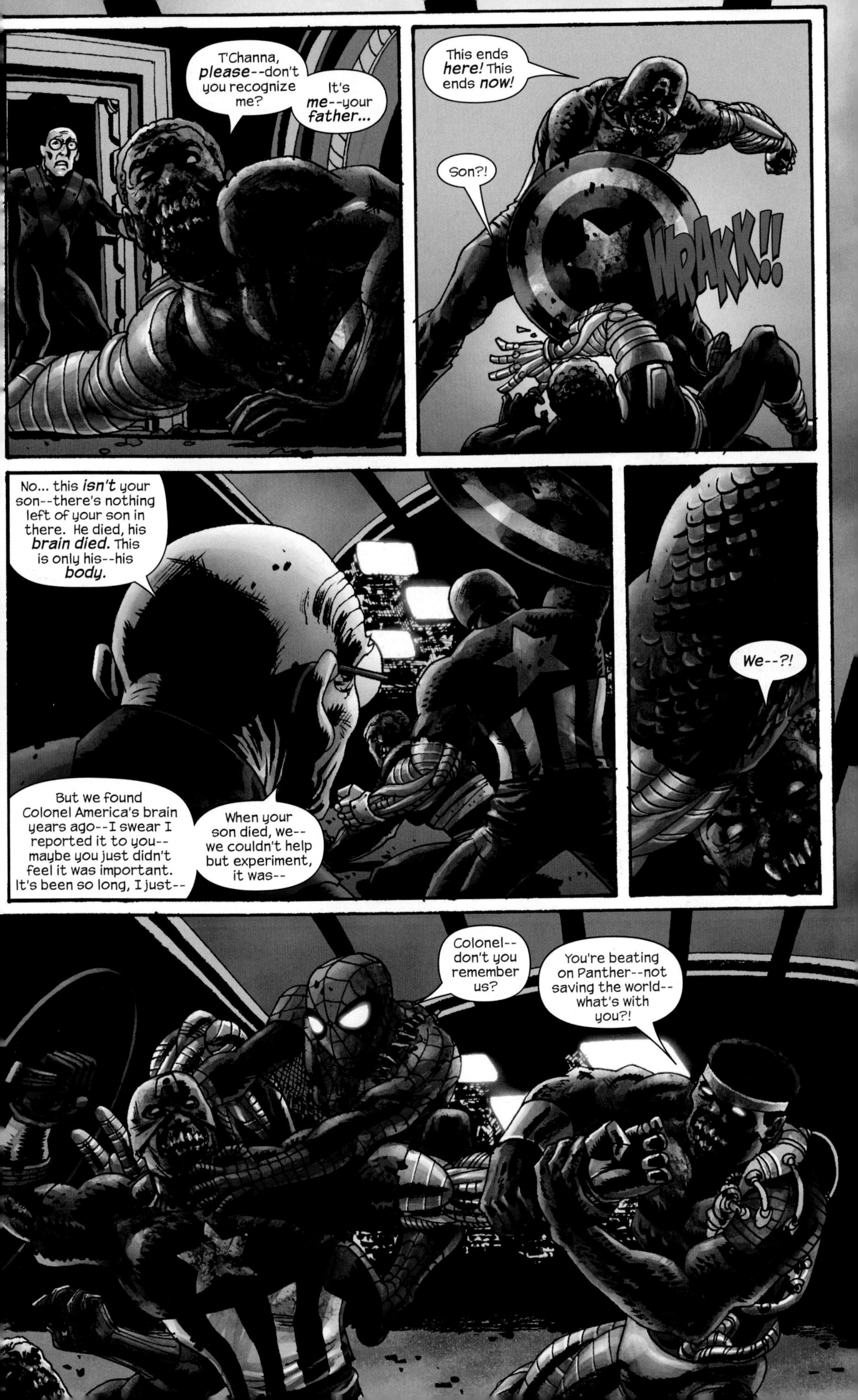
T'Channa, please--don't you recognize me?
It's me--your father...
This ends here! This ends now!
Son?!
WRAKK!!
No... this isn't your son--there's nothing left of your son in there. He died, his brain died. This is only his--his body.
But we found Colonel America's brain years ago--I swear I reported it to you--maybe you just didn't feel it was important. It's been so long, I just--
When your son died, we--we couldn't help but experiment, it was--
We--?!
Colonel--don't you remember us?
You're beating on Panther--not saving the world--what's with you?!

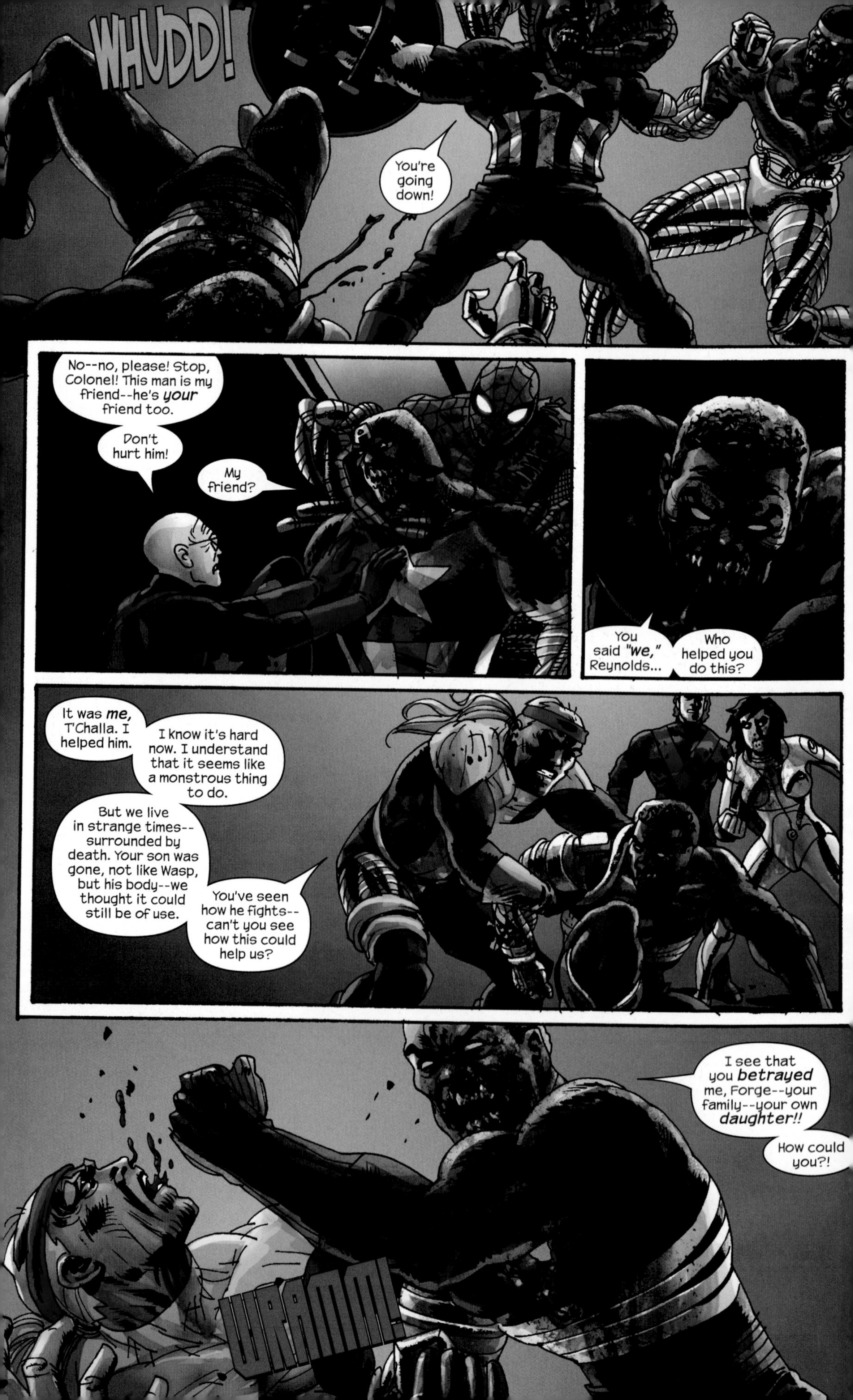
WHUDD!
You're going down!
No--no, please! Stop, Colonel! This man is my friend--he's your friend too.
Don't hurt him!
My friend?
You said "we," Reynolds...
Who helped you do this?
It was me, T'Challa. I helped him.
I know it's hard now. I understand that it seems like a monstrous thing to do.
But we live in strange times--surrounded by death. Your son was gone, not like Wasp, but his body--we thought it could still be of use.
You've seen how he fights--can't you see how this could help us?
I see that you betrayed me, Forge--your family--your own daughter!!
How could you?!
WRAMM!

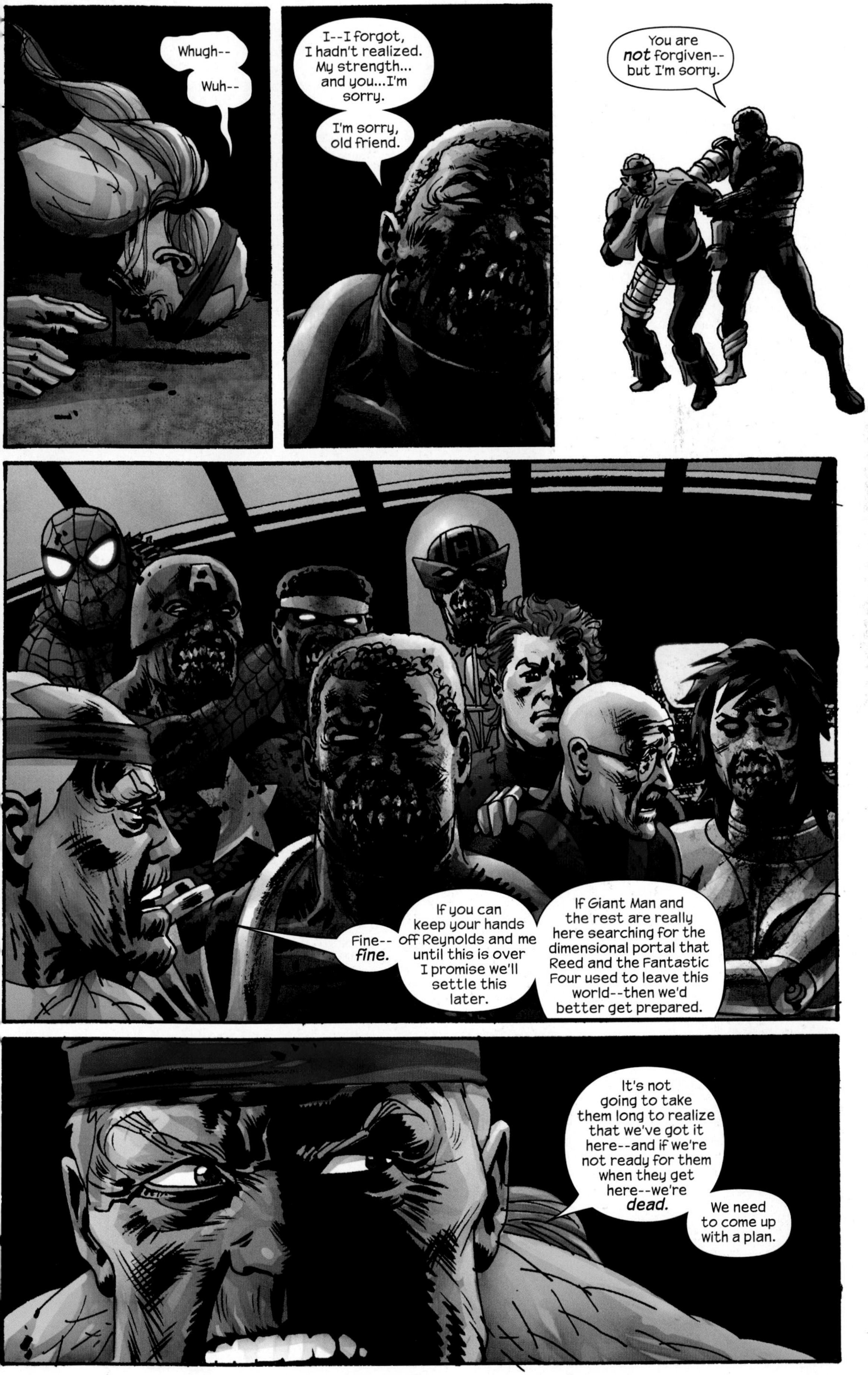
Whugh--
Wuh--
I--I forgot, I hadn't realized. My strength... and you...I'm sorry.
I'm sorry, old friend.
You are *not* forgiven-- but I'm sorry.
Fine-- *fine.*
If you can keep your hands off Reynolds and me until this is over I promise we'll settle this later.
If Giant Man and the rest are really here searching for the dimensional portal that Reed and the Fantastic Four used to leave this world--then we'd better get prepared.
It's not going to take them long to realize that we've got it here--and if we're not ready for them when they get here--we're *dead.*
We need to come up with a plan.

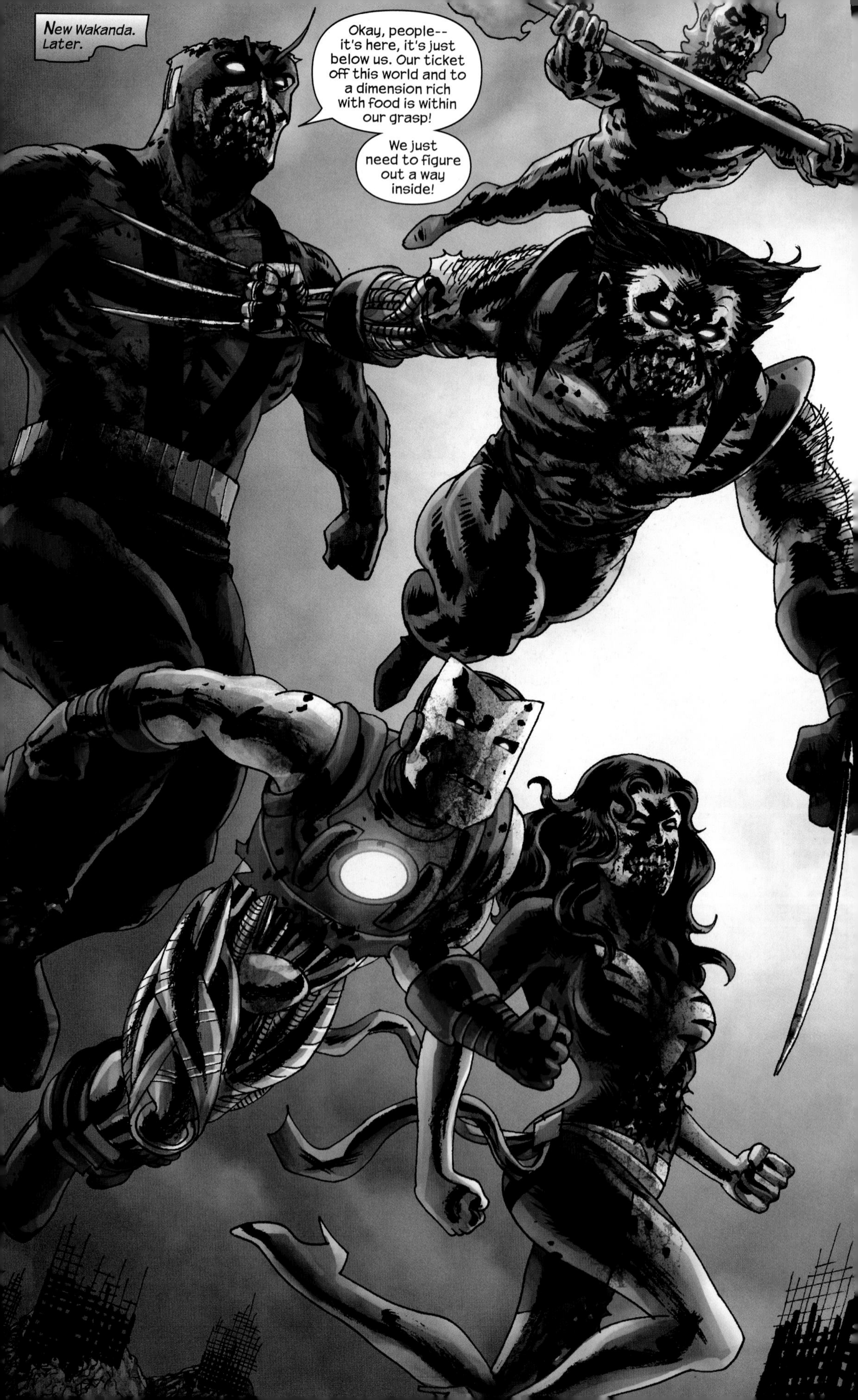
New Wakanda. Later.
Okay, people-- it's here, it's just below us. Our ticket off this world and to a dimension rich with food is within our grasp!
We just need to figure out a way inside!

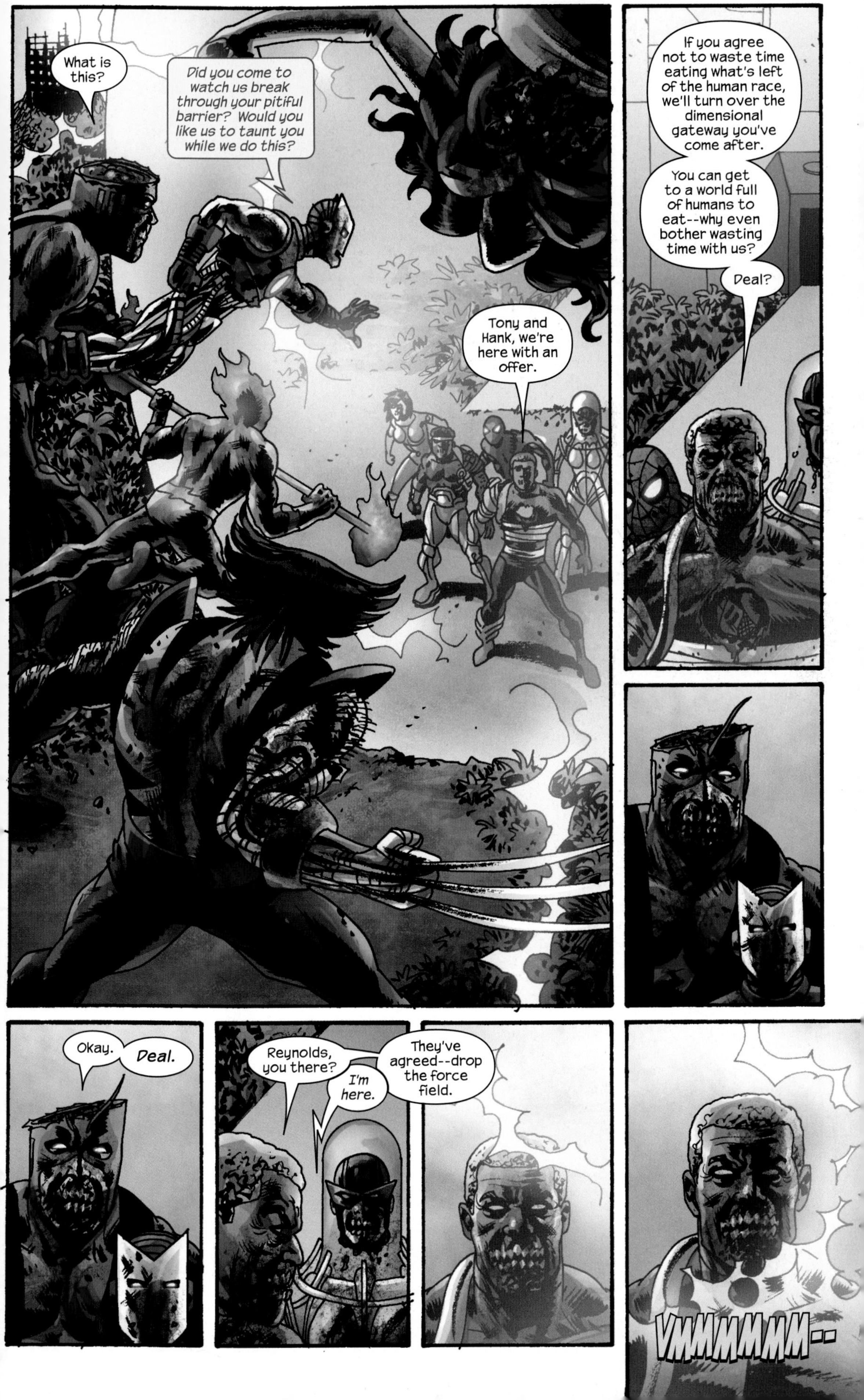

What is this?
Did you come to watch us break through your pitiful barrier? Would you like us to taunt you while we do this?
Tony and Hank, we're here with an offer.
If you agree not to waste time eating what's left of the human race, we'll turn over the dimensional gateway you've come after.
You can get to a world full of humans to eat--why even bother wasting time with us?
Deal?
Okay.
Deal.
Reynolds, you there?
I'm here.
They've agreed--drop the force field.
VMMMMMM--

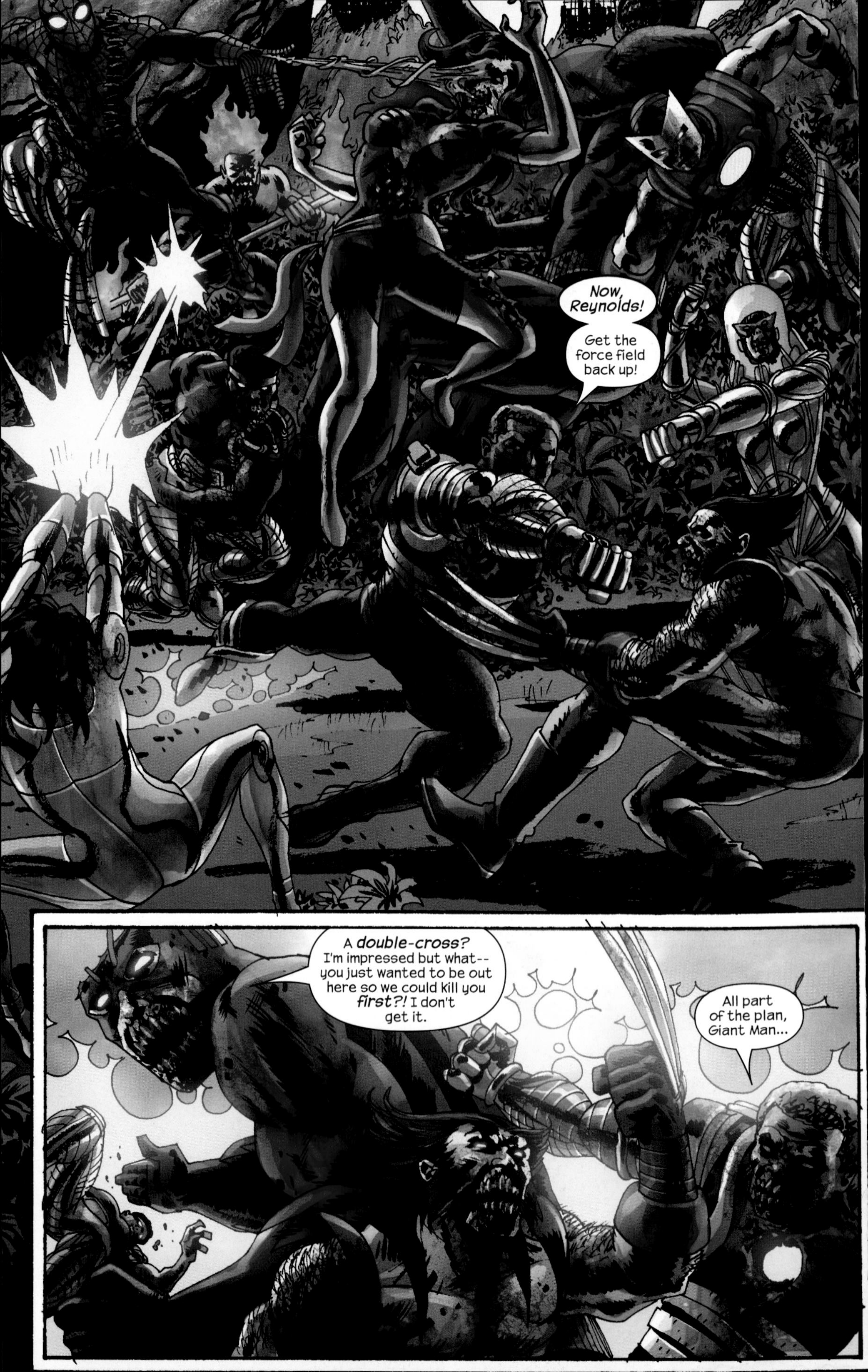
Now, Reynolds!
Get the force field back up!
A double-cross? I'm impressed but what-- you just wanted to be out here so we could kill you first?! I don't get it.
All part of the plan, Giant Man...

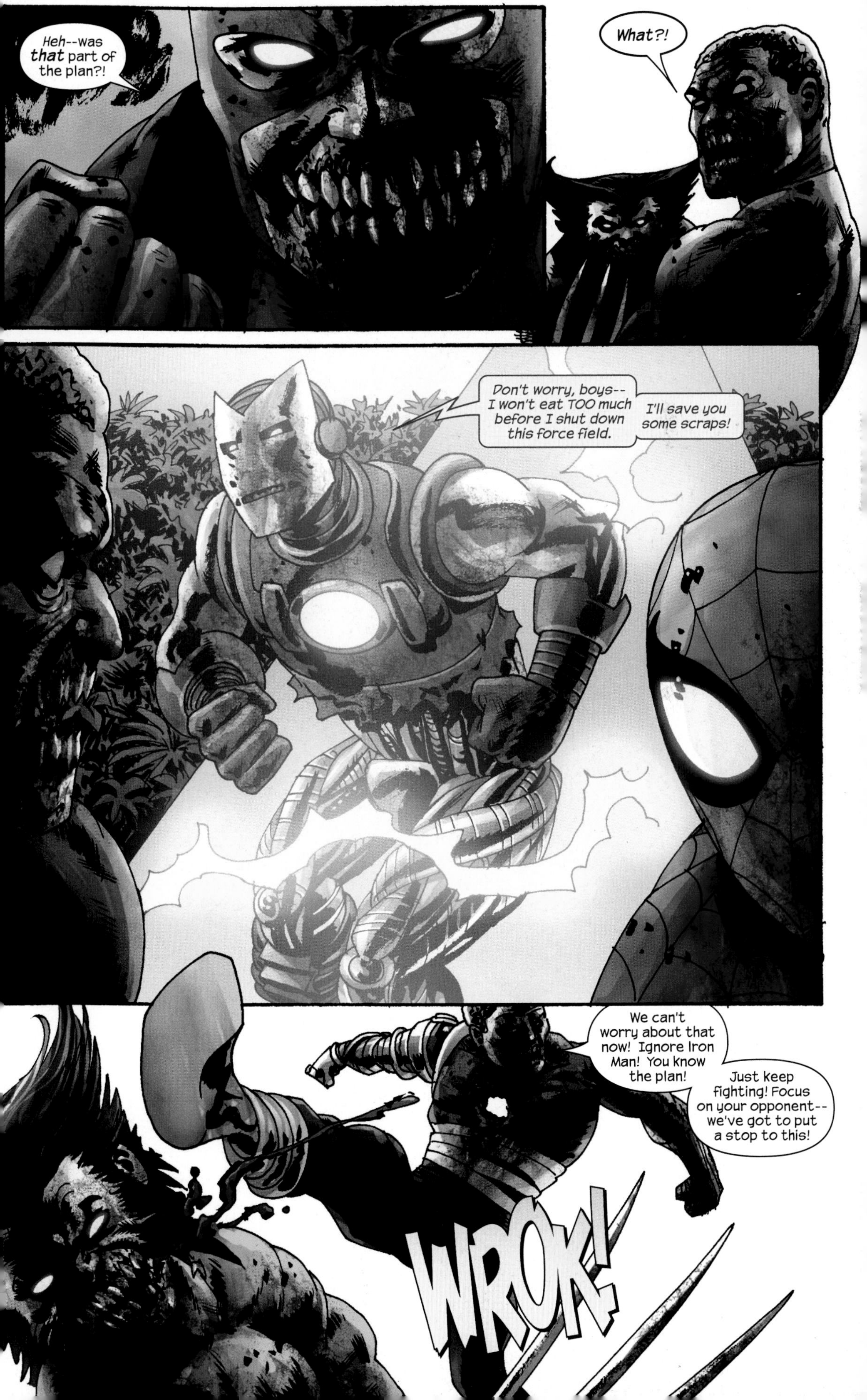
Heh--was *that* part of the plan?!
What?!
Don't worry, boys-- I won't eat TOO much before I shut down this force field.
I'll save you some scraps!
We can't worry about that now! Ignore Iron Man! You know the plan!
Just keep fighting! Focus on your opponent-- we've got to put a stop to this!
WROK!

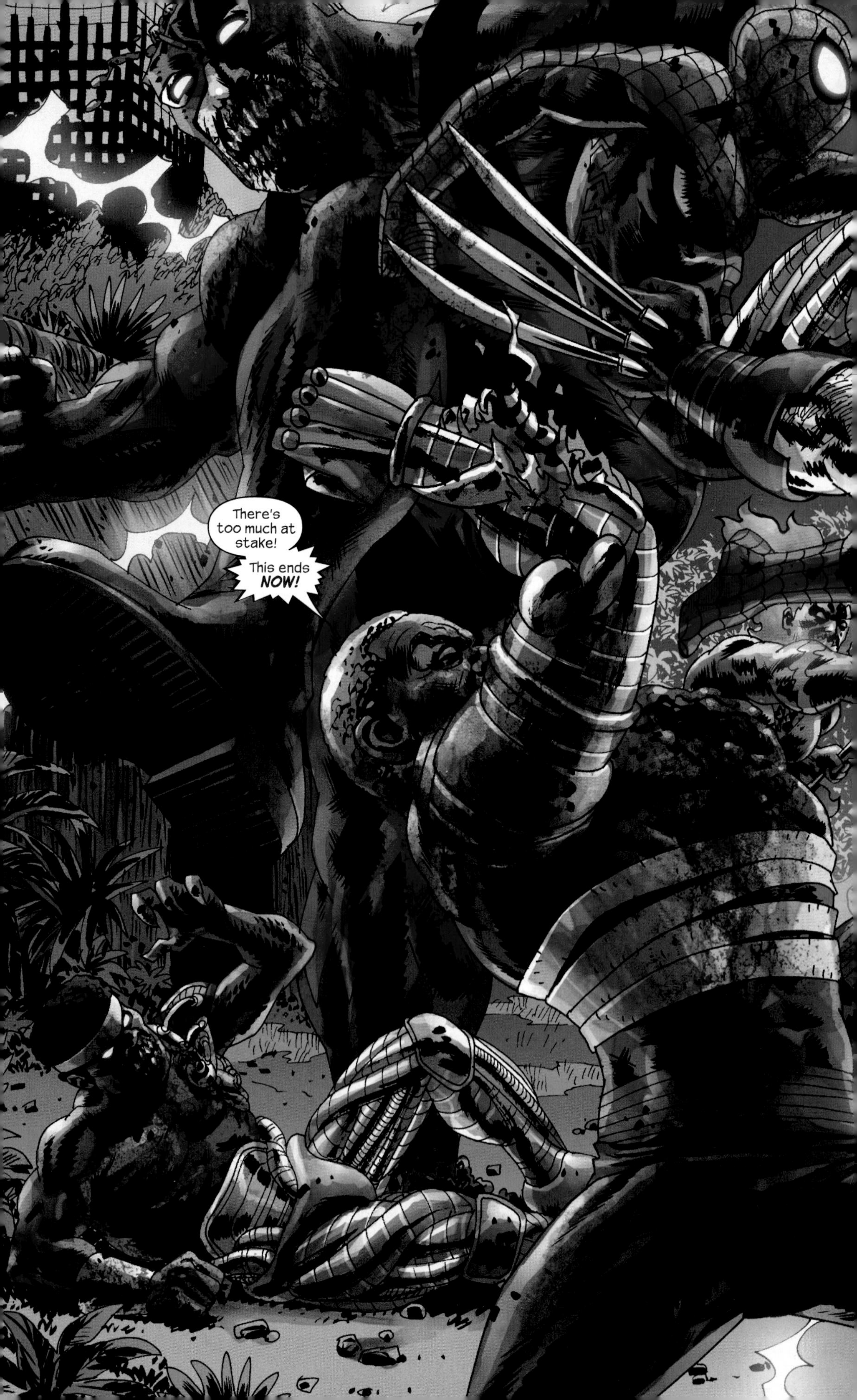
There's too much at stake!
This ends NOW!

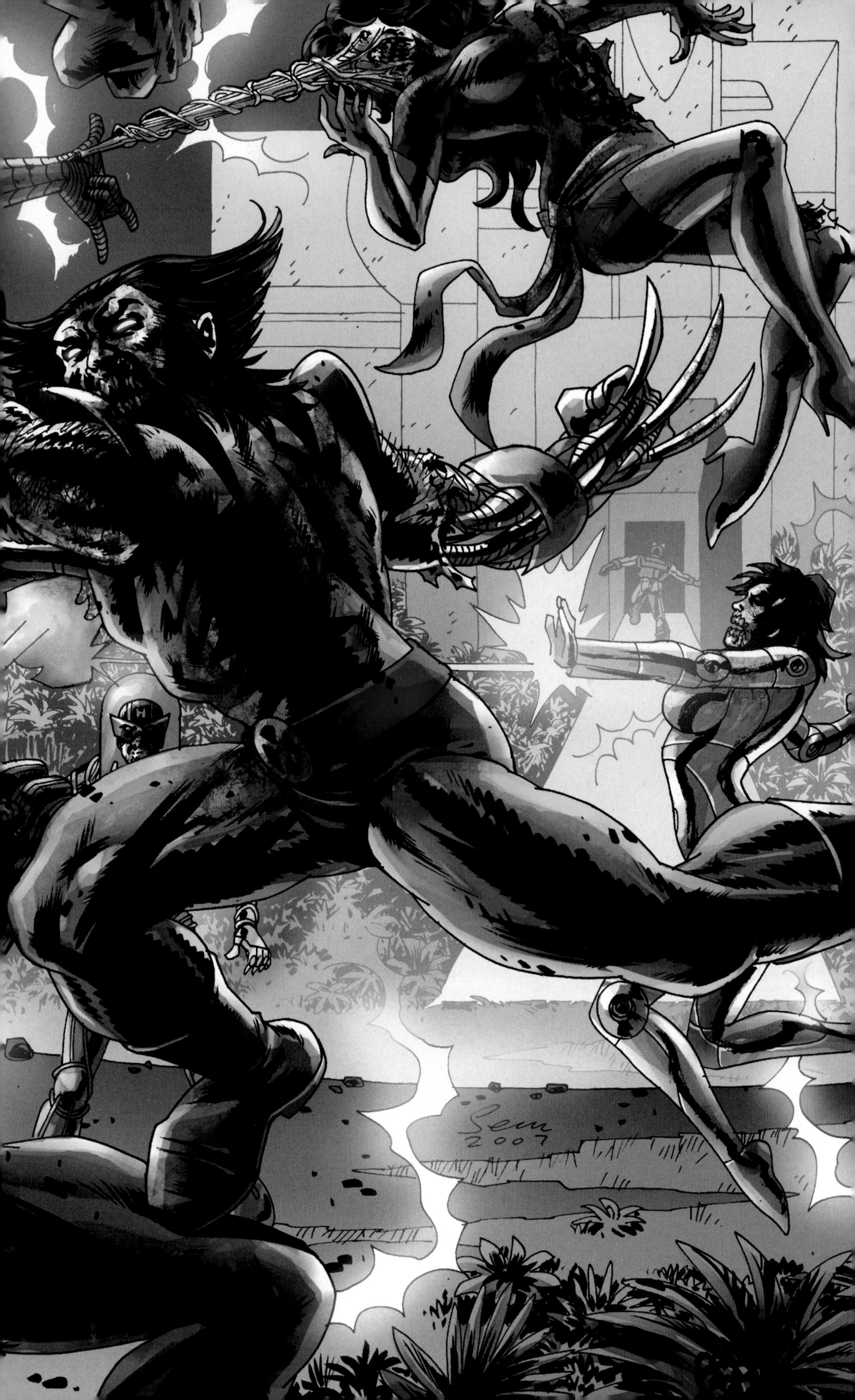

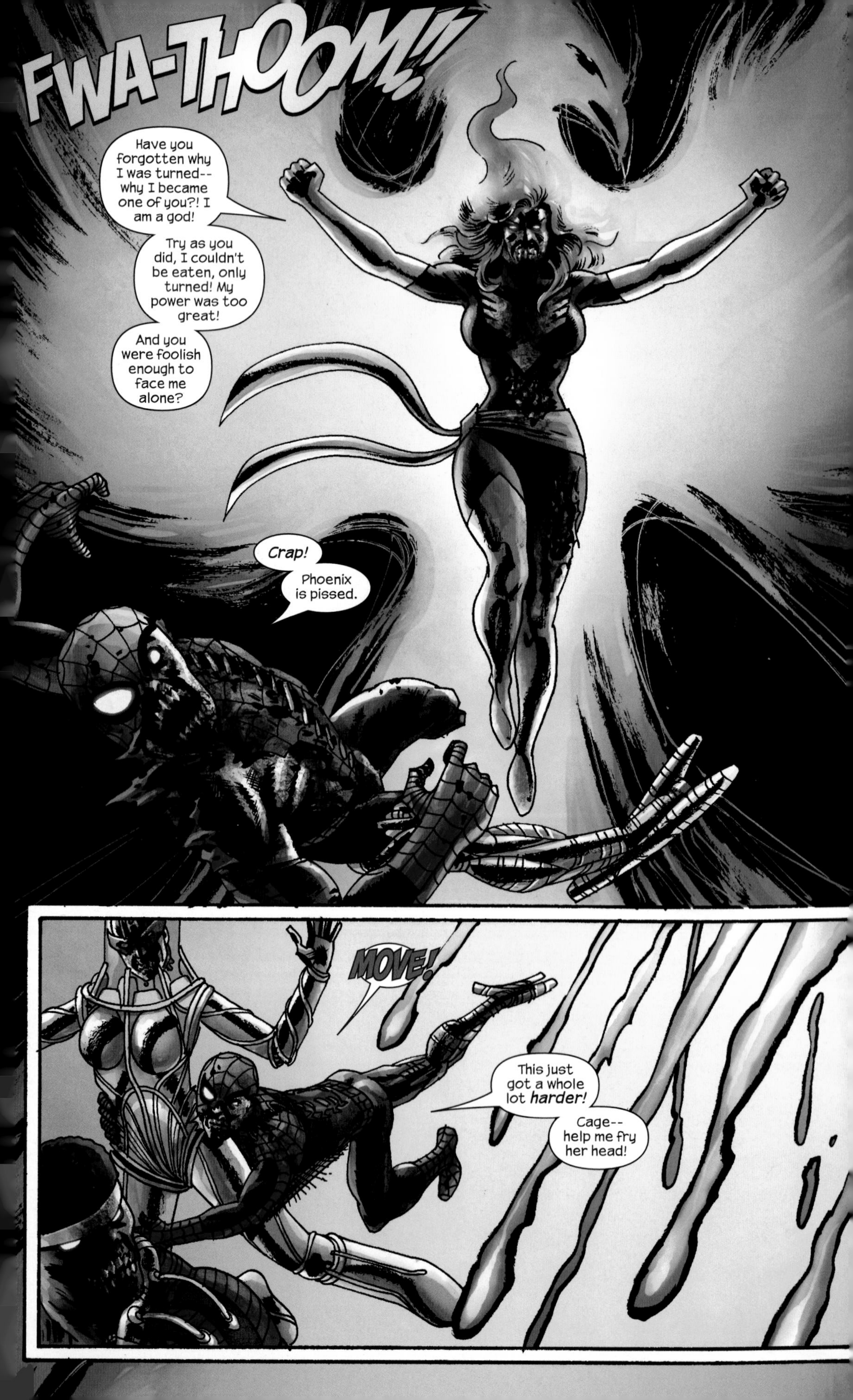
FWA-THOOM!!
Have you forgotten why I was turned-- why I became one of you?! I am a god!
Try as you did, I couldn't be eaten, only turned! My power was too great!
And you were foolish enough to face me alone?
Crap!
Phoenix is pissed.
MOVE!
This just got a whole lot harder!
Cage-- help me fry her head!

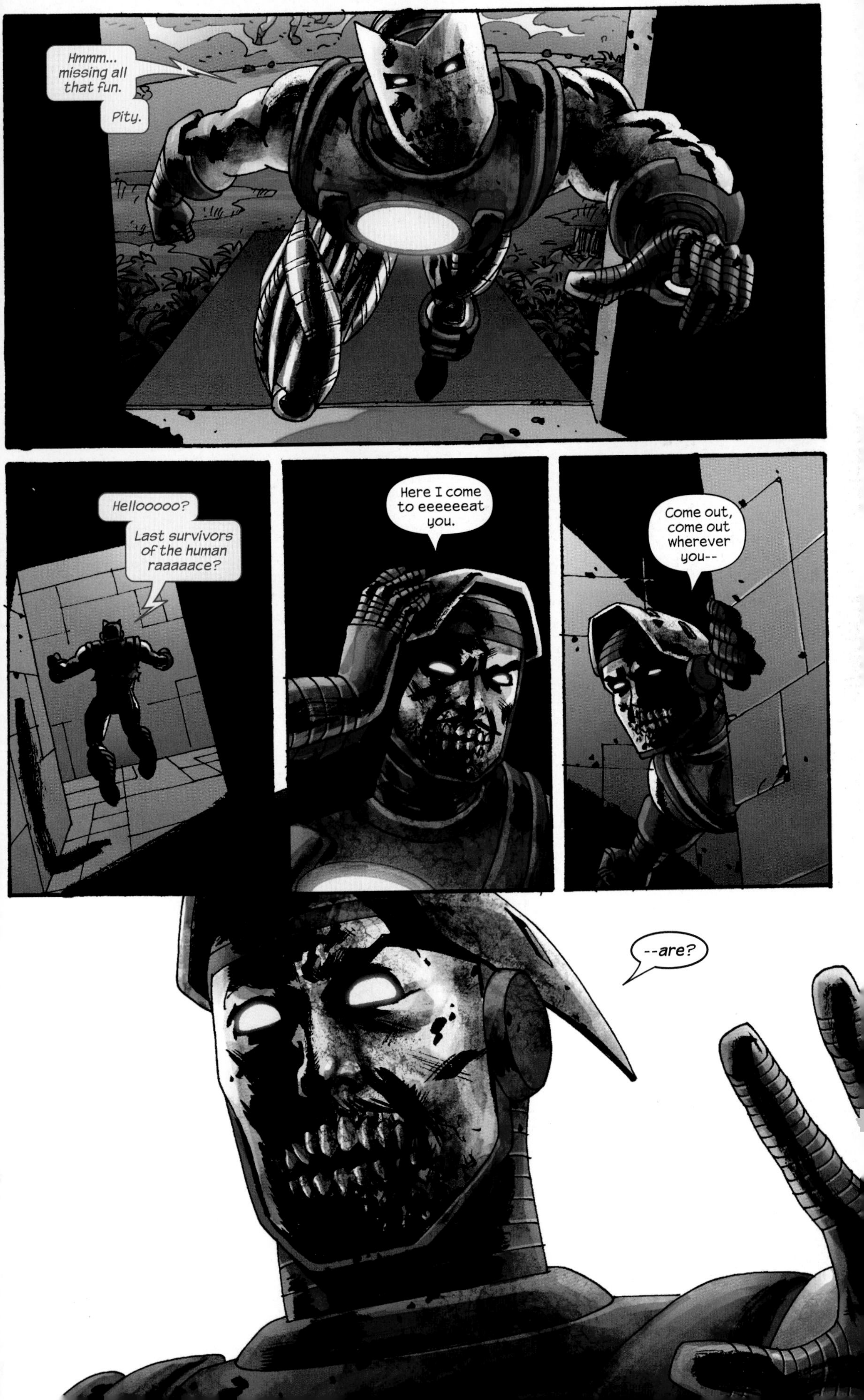
Hmmm... missing all that fun.
Pity.
Hellooooo?
Last survivors of the human raaaaace?
Here I come to eeeeeeat you.
Come out, come out wherever you--
--are?

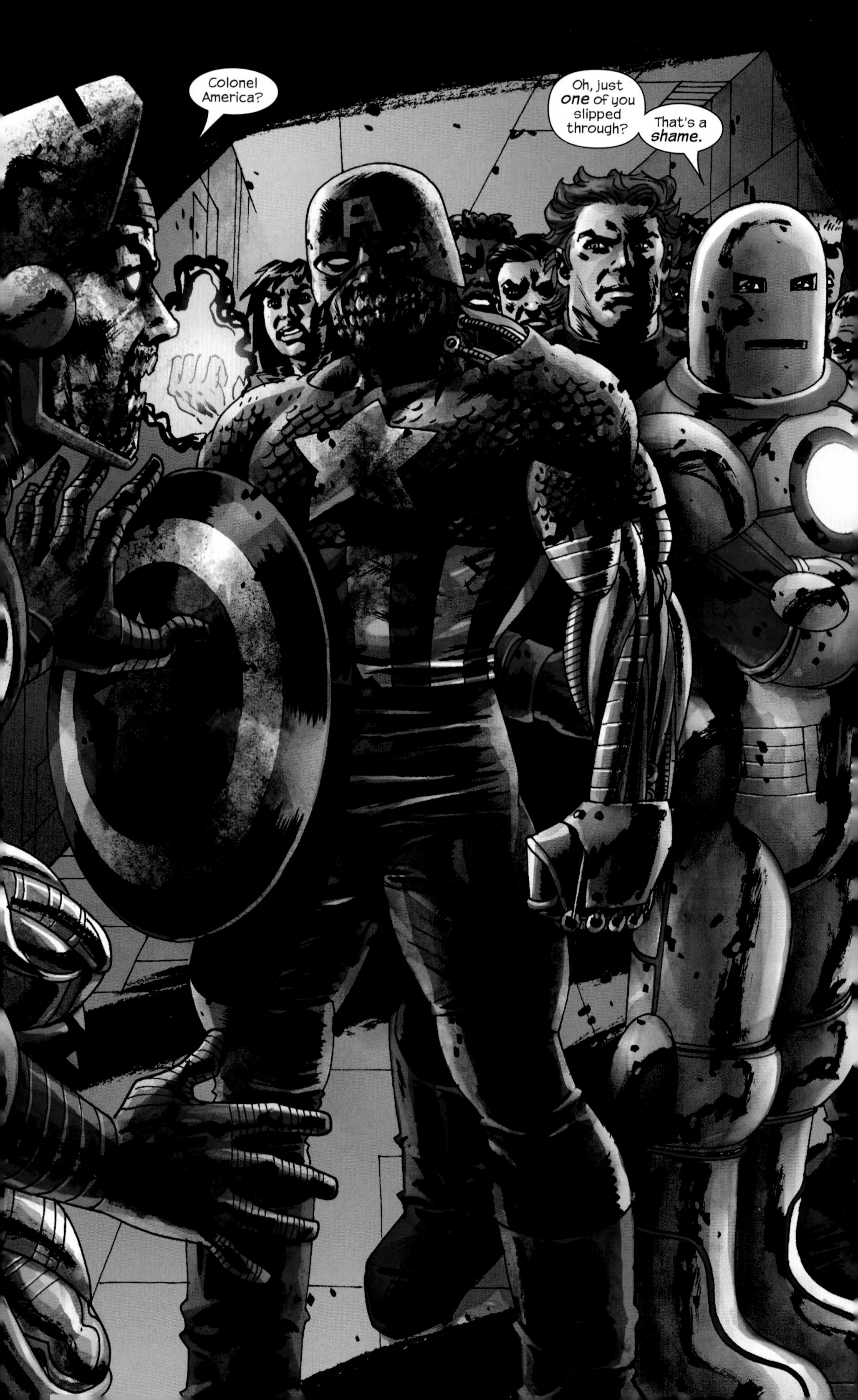
Colonel America?
Oh, just *one* of you slipped through?
That's a *shame*.

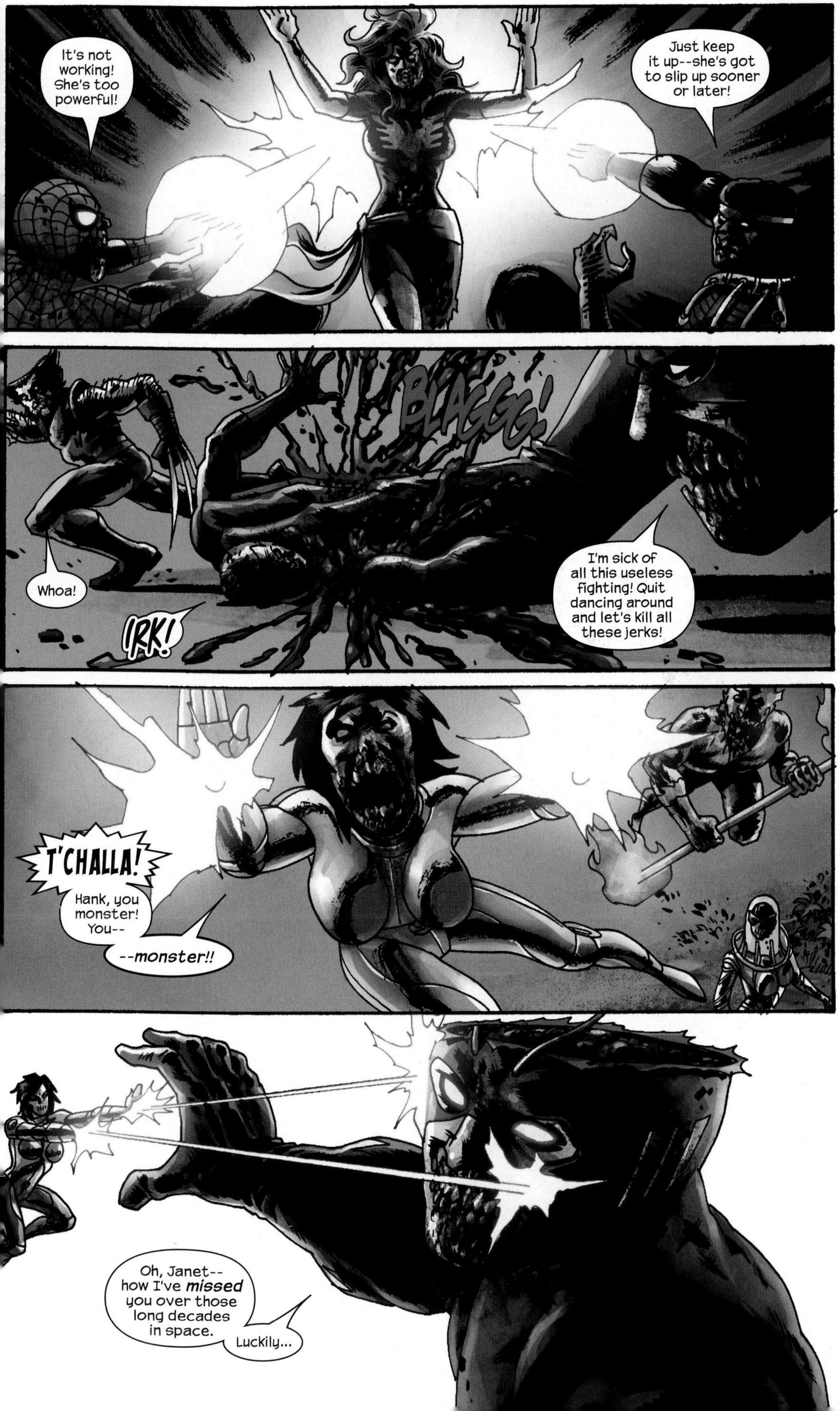
It's not working! She's too powerful!
Just keep it up--she's got to slip up sooner or later!
BLAGGG!
Whoa!
IRK!
I'm sick of all this useless fighting! Quit dancing around and let's kill all these jerks!
T'CHALLA!
Hank, you monster! You--
--monster!!
Oh, Janet-- how I've missed you over those long decades in space.
Luckily...

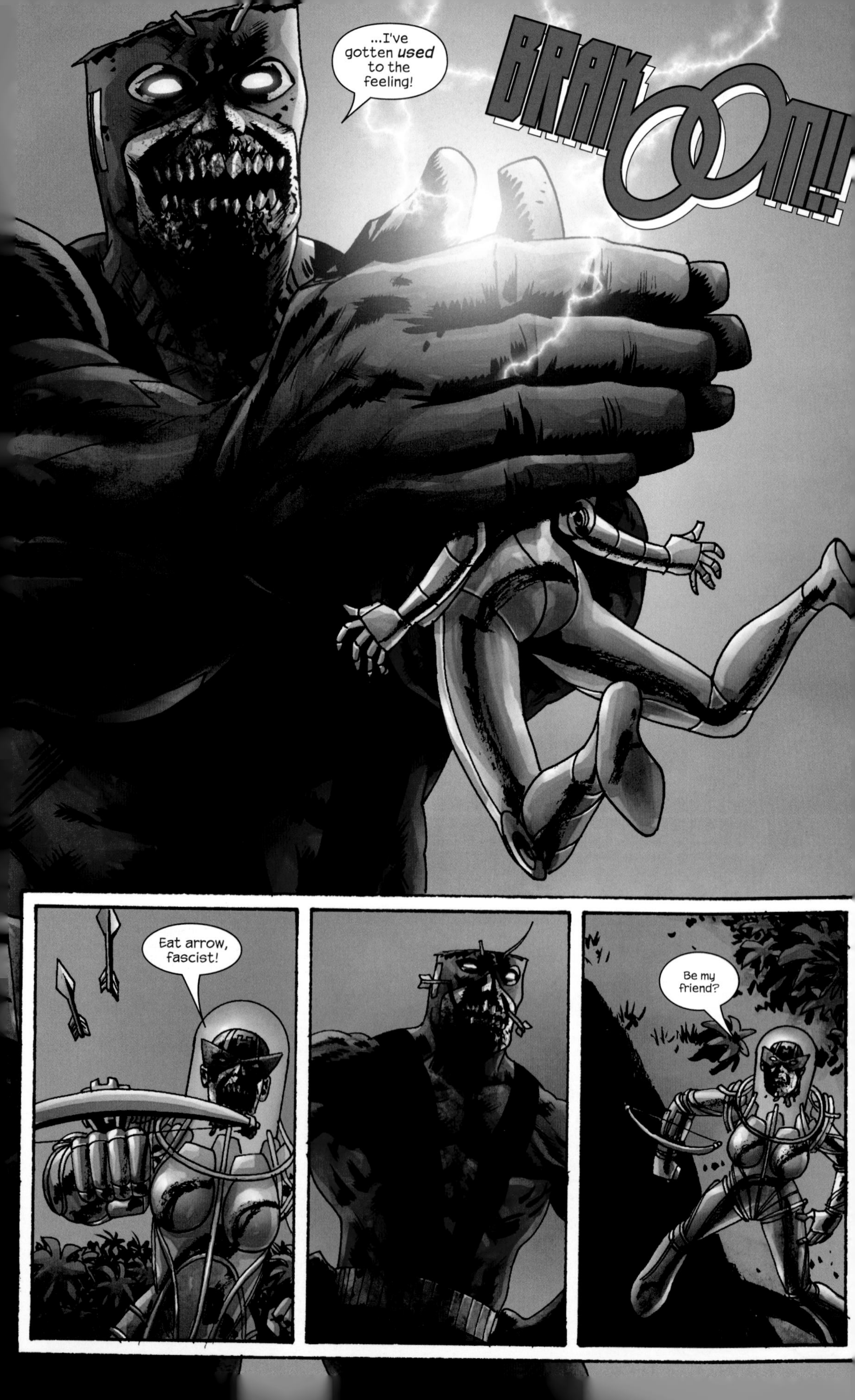
...I've gotten *used* to the feeling!
BRAKOOM!!
Eat arrow, fascist!
Be my friend?

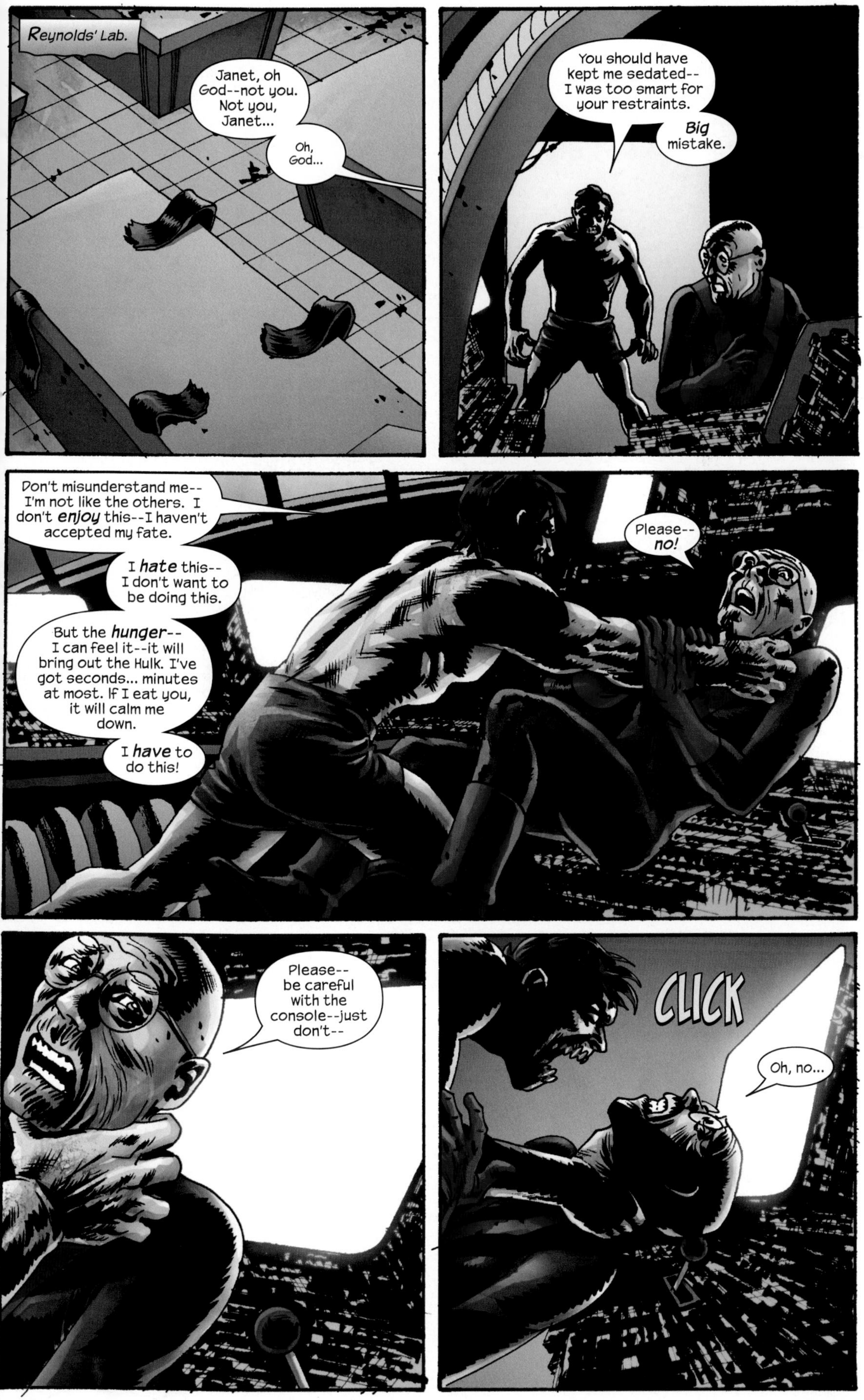
Reynolds' Lab.
Janet, oh God--not you. Not you, Janet...
Oh, God...
You should have kept me sedated-- I was too smart for your restraints.
Big mistake.
Don't misunderstand me-- I'm not like the others. I don't enjoy this--I haven't accepted my fate.
I hate this-- I don't want to be doing this.
But the hunger-- I can feel it--it will bring out the Hulk. I've got seconds... minutes at most. If I eat you, it will calm me down.
I have to do this!
Please-- no!
Please-- be careful with the console--just don't--
CLICK
Oh, no...

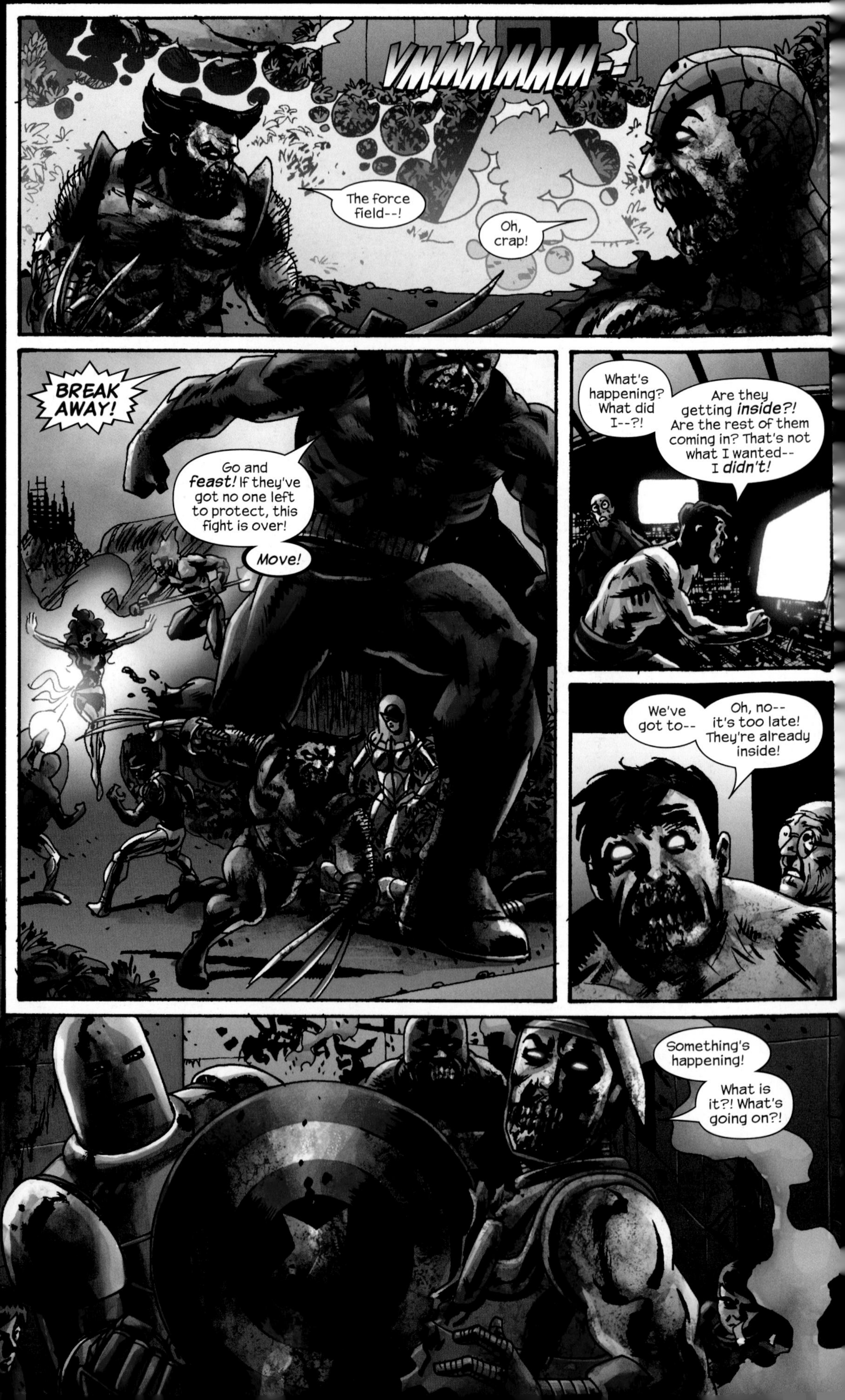
VMMMMMM--!
The force field--!
Oh, crap!
BREAK AWAY!
Go and feast! If they've got no one left to protect, this fight is over!
Move!
What's happening? What did I--?!
Are they getting inside?! Are the rest of them coming in? That's not what I wanted-- I didn't!
We've got to--
Oh, no-- it's too late! They're already inside!
Something's happening!
What is it?! What's going on?!

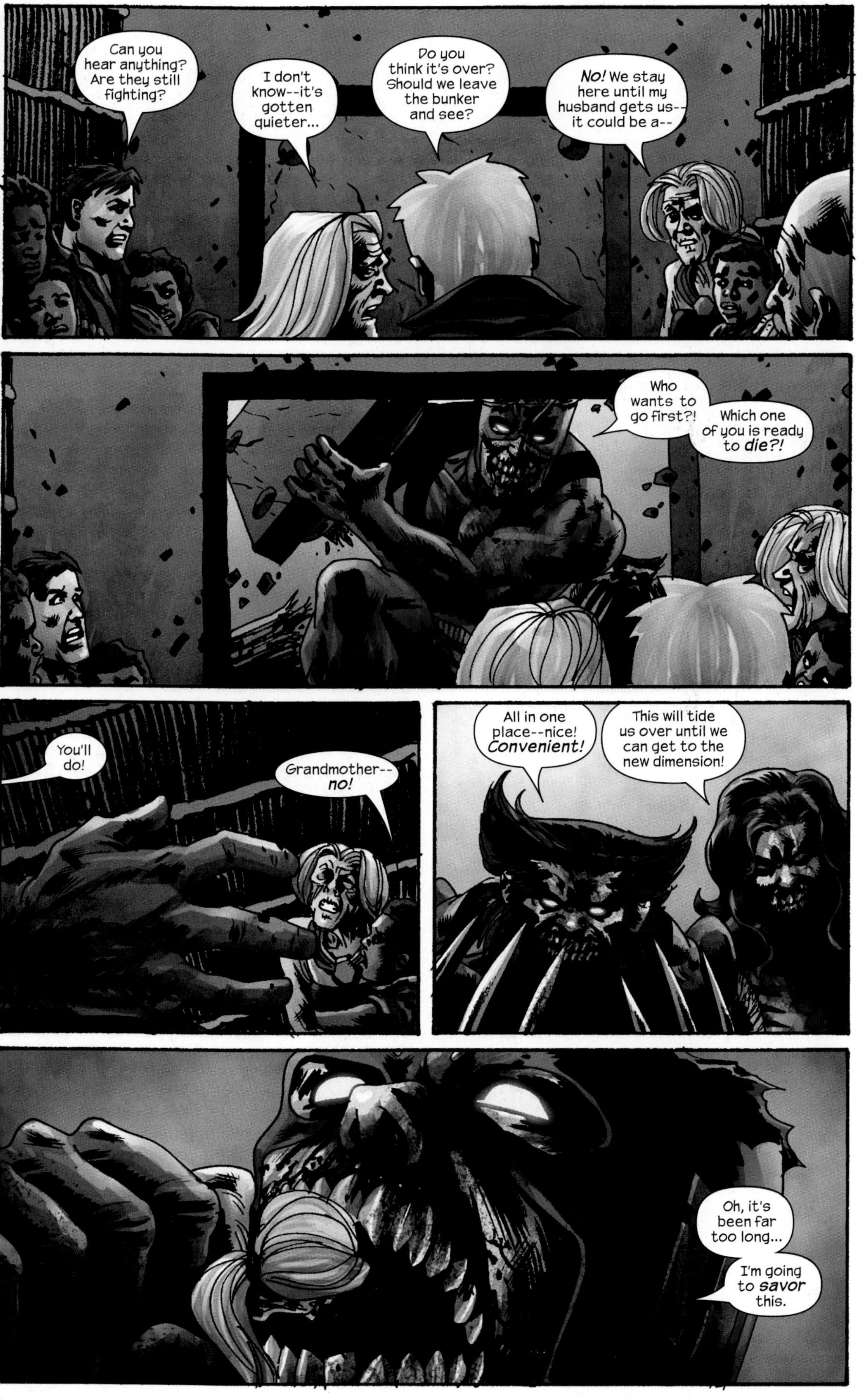

Can you hear anything? Are they still fighting?
I don't know--it's gotten quieter...
Do you think it's over? Should we leave the bunker and see?
No! We stay here until my husband gets us-- it could be a--
Who wants to go first?!
Which one of you is ready to die?!
You'll do!
Grandmother-- no!
All in one place--nice! Convenient!
This will tide us over until we can get to the new dimension!
Oh, it's been far too long...
I'm going to savor this.

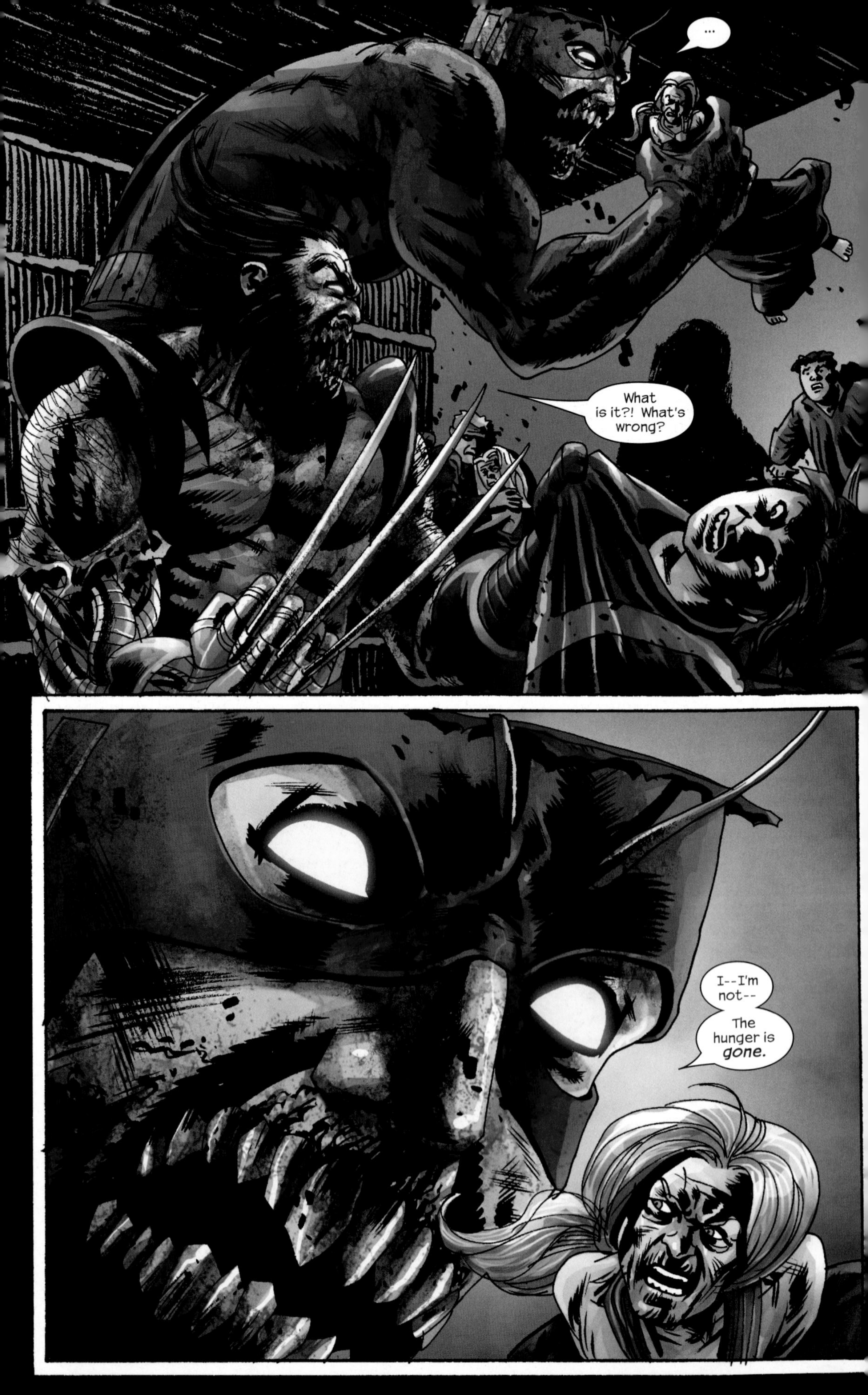
...
What is it?! What's wrong?
I--I'm not--
The hunger is *gone.*

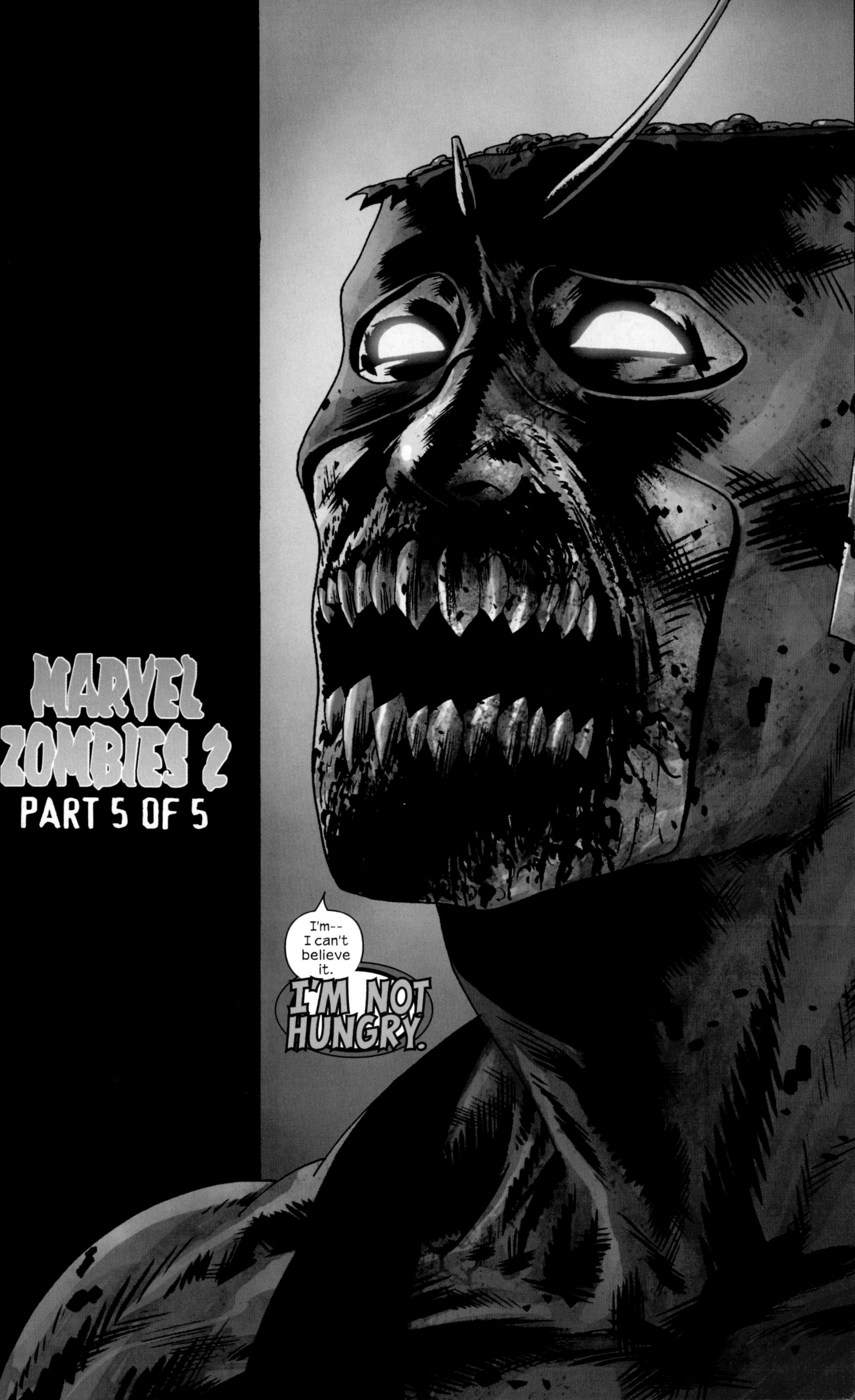
MARVEL ZOMBIES 2
PART 5 OF 5
I'm-- I can't believe it.
I'M NOT HUNGRY.

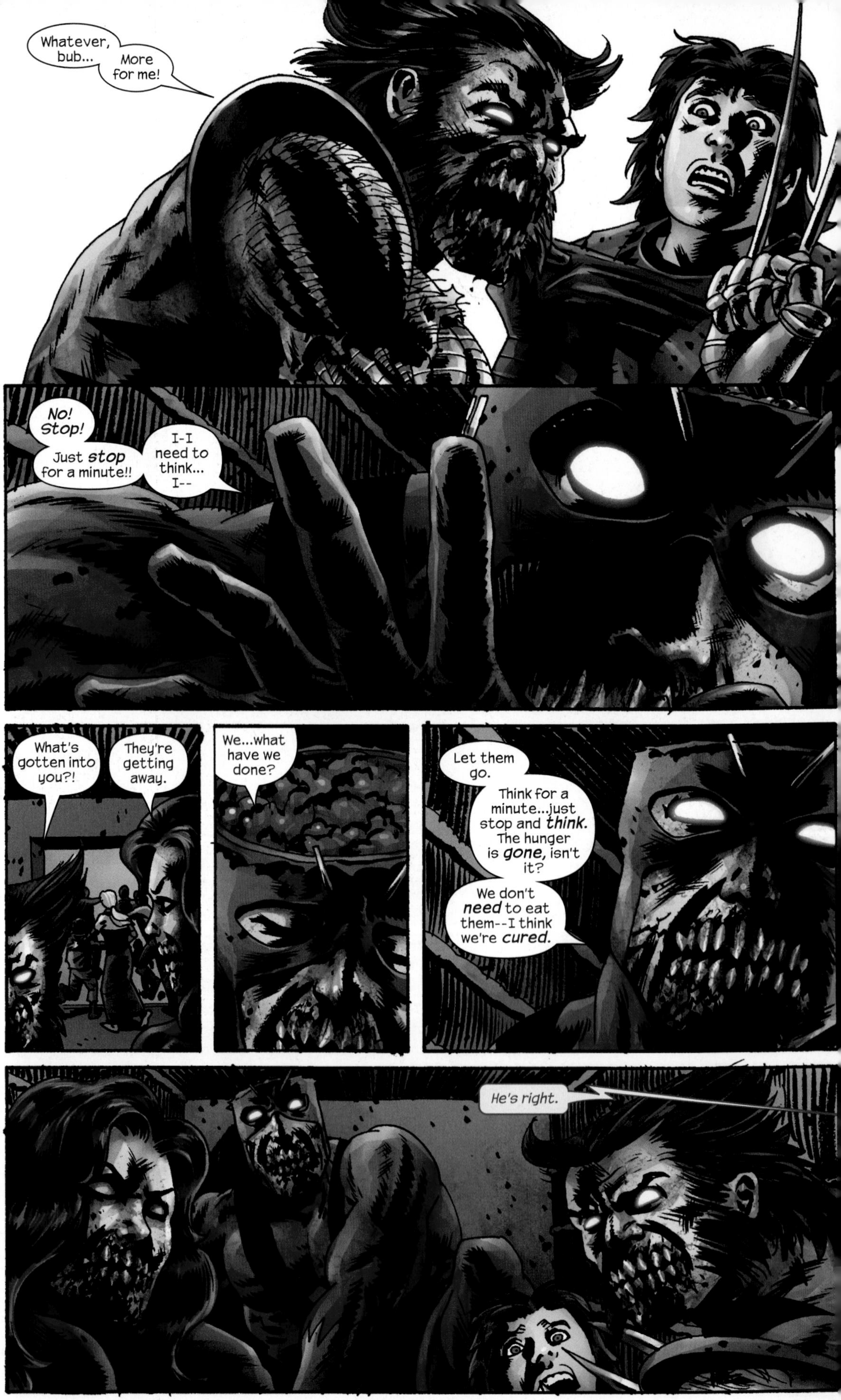
Whatever, bub...
More for me!
No! Stop!
Just stop for a minute!!
I-I need to think... I--
What's gotten into you?!
They're getting away.
We...what have we done?
Let them go.
Think for a minute...just stop and think. The hunger is gone, isn't it?
We don't need to eat them--I think we're cured.
He's right.

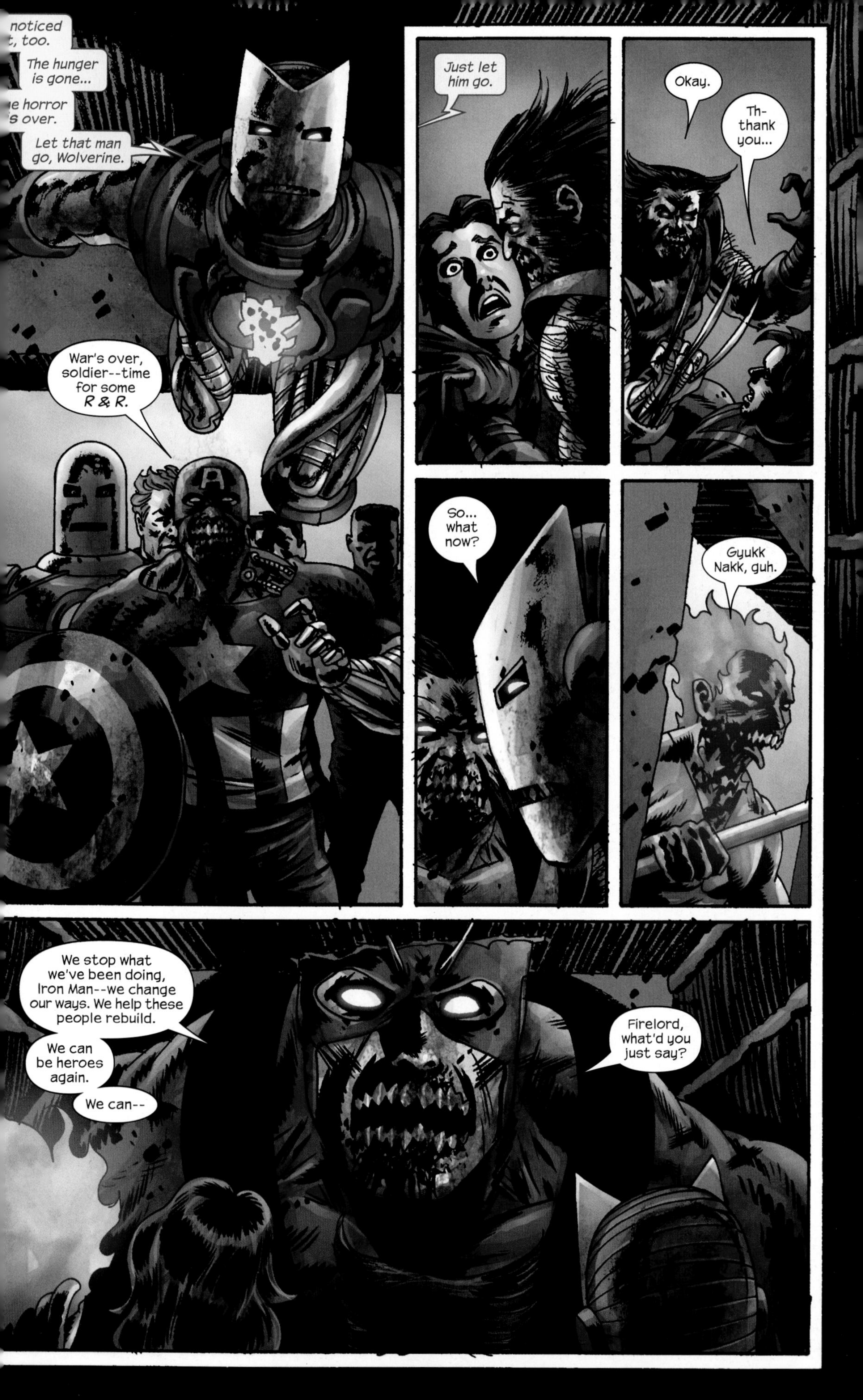
noticed
t, too.
The hunger
is gone...
e horror
's over.
Let that man
go, Wolverine.
War's over,
soldier--time
for some
R & R.
Just let
him go.
Okay.
Th-
thank
you...
So...
what
now?
Gyukk
Nakk, guh.
We stop what
we've been doing,
Iron Man--we change
our ways. We help these
people rebuild.
We can
be heroes
again.
We can--
Firelord,
what'd you
just say?

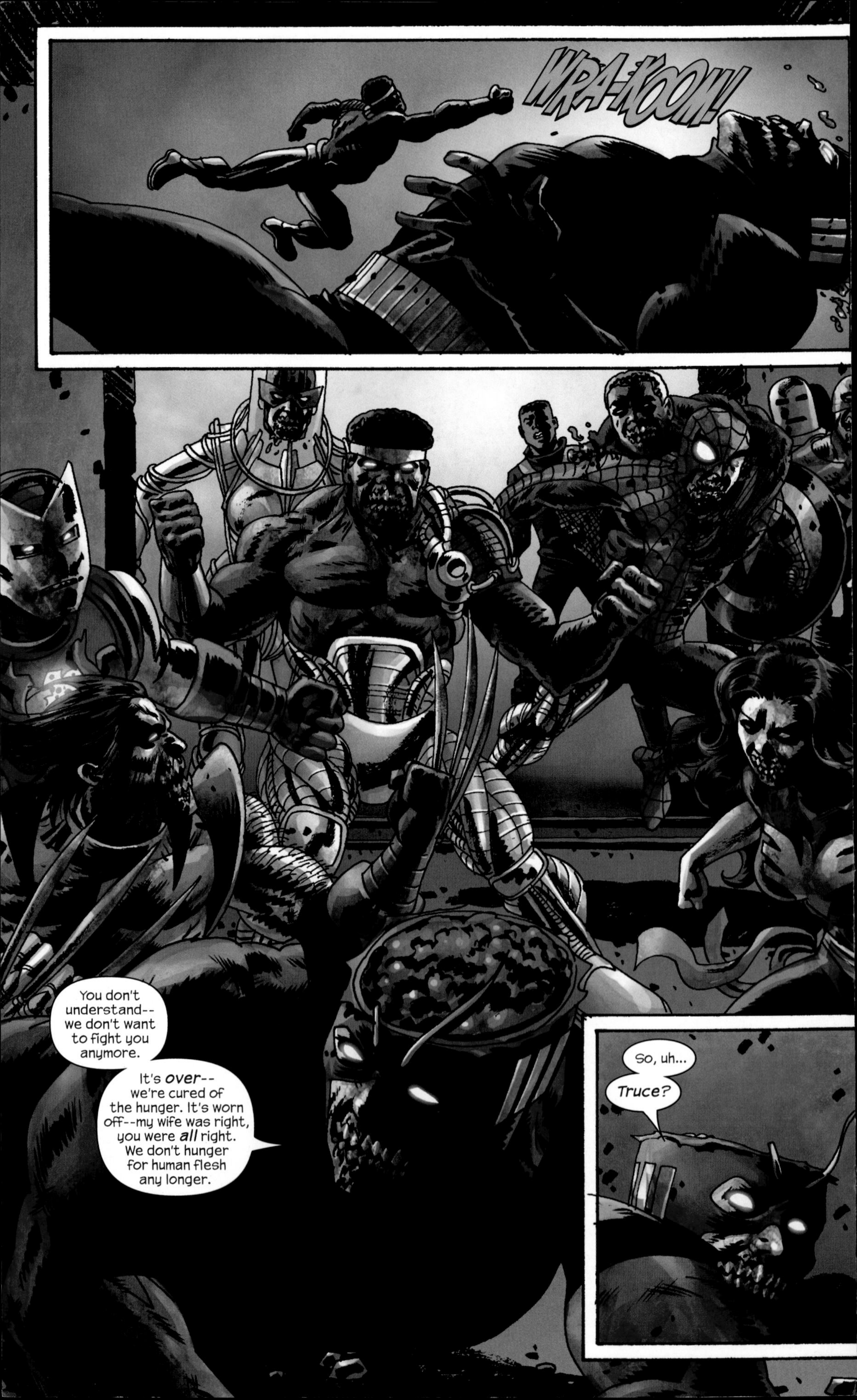
WRA-KOOM!
You don't understand-- we don't want to fight you anymore.
It's over-- we're cured of the hunger. It's worn off--my wife was right, you were all right. We don't hunger for human flesh any longer.
So, uh...
Truce?

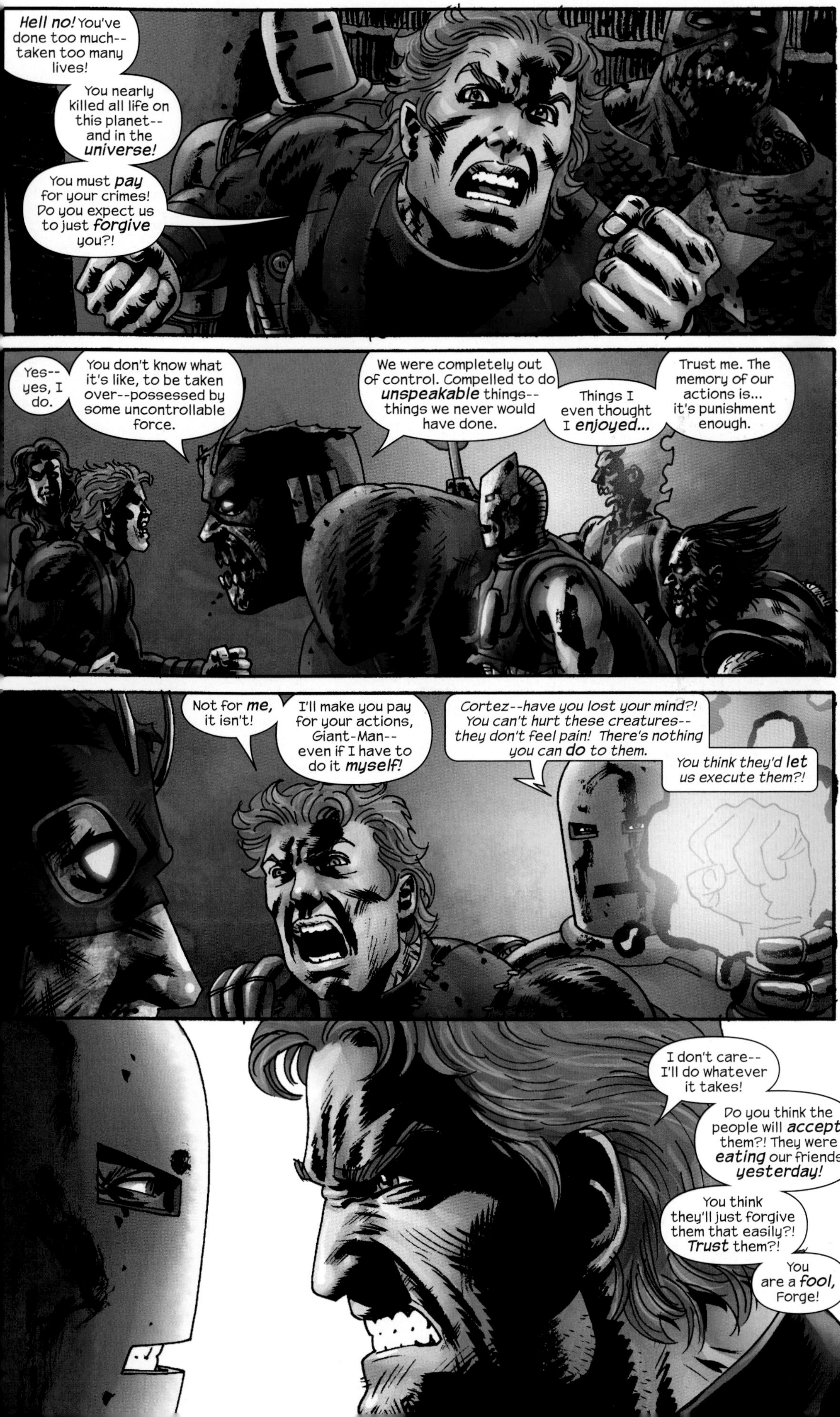
Hell no! You've done too much--taken too many lives!
You nearly killed all life on this planet--and in the universe!
You must pay for your crimes! Do you expect us to just forgive you?!
Yes--yes, I do.
You don't know what it's like, to be taken over--possessed by some uncontrollable force.
We were completely out of control. Compelled to do unspeakable things--things we never would have done.
Things I even thought I enjoyed...
Trust me. The memory of our actions is... it's punishment enough.
Not for me, it isn't!
I'll make you pay for your actions, Giant-Man--even if I have to do it myself!
Cortez--have you lost your mind?! You can't hurt these creatures--they don't feel pain! There's nothing you can do to them.
You think they'd let us execute them?!
I don't care--I'll do whatever it takes!
Do you think the people will accept them?! They were eating our friends yesterday!
You think they'll just forgive them that easily?! Trust them?!
You are a fool, Forge!

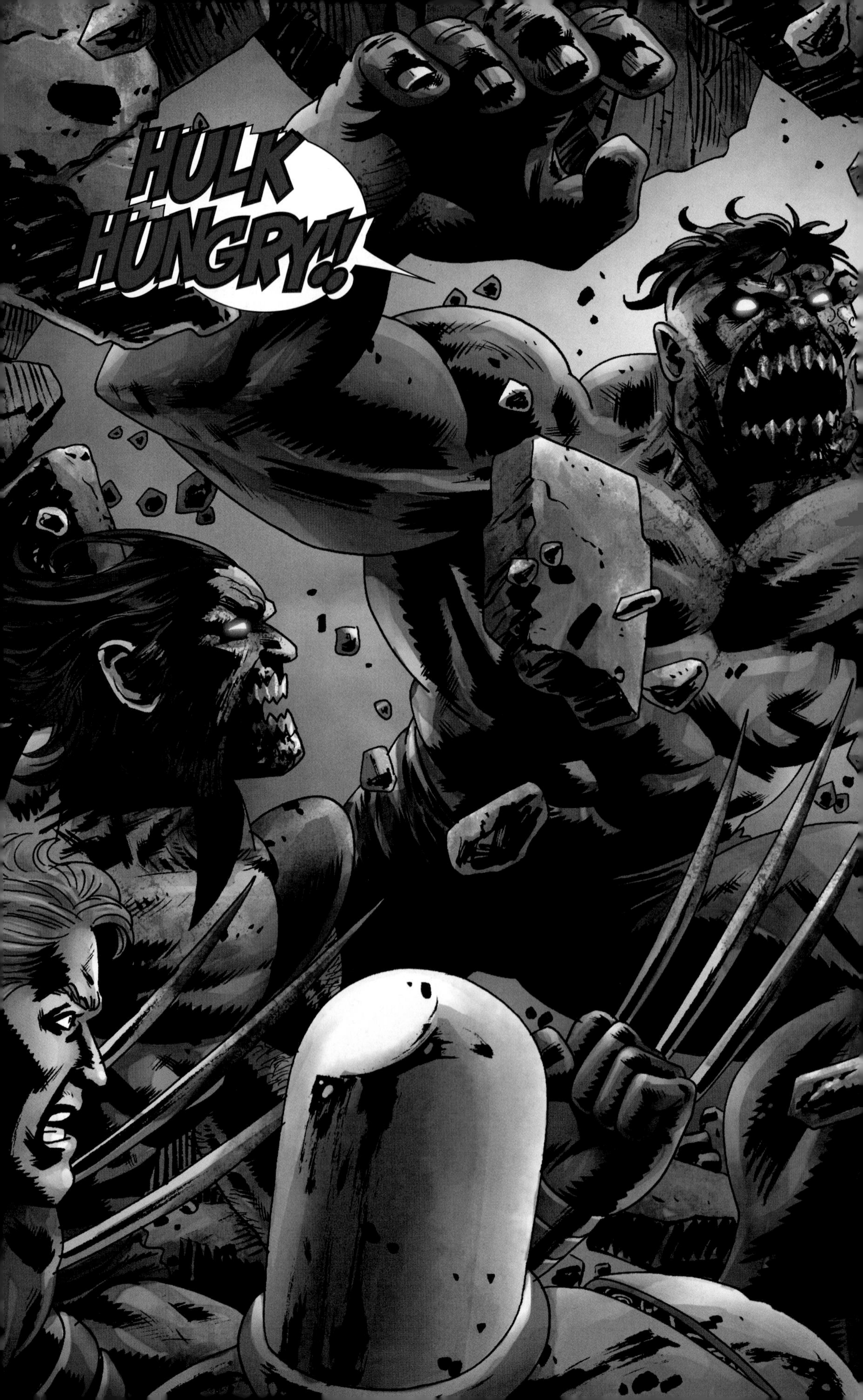
HULK HUNGRY!!

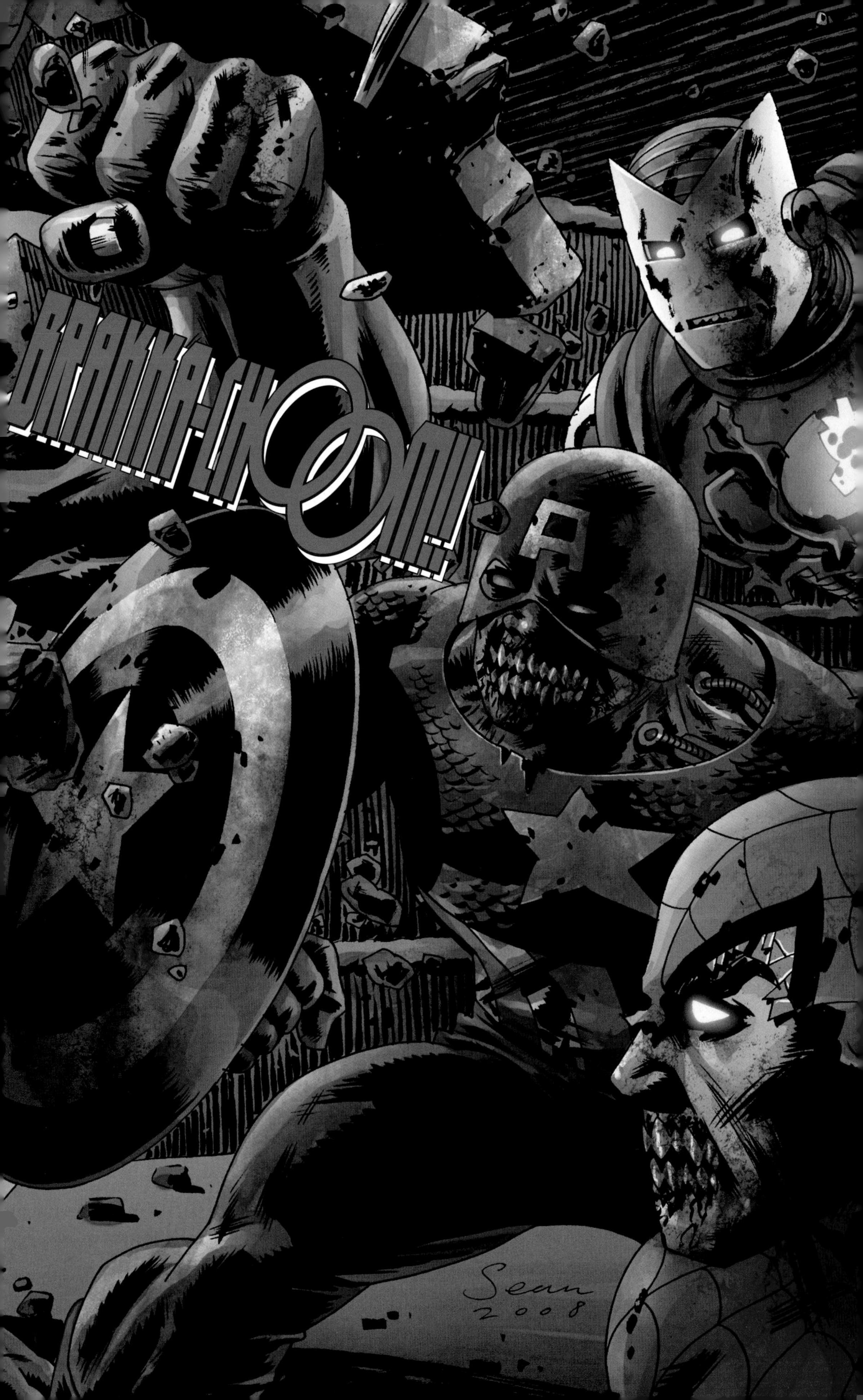
BRAKKA-CHOOOM!!
Sean 2008

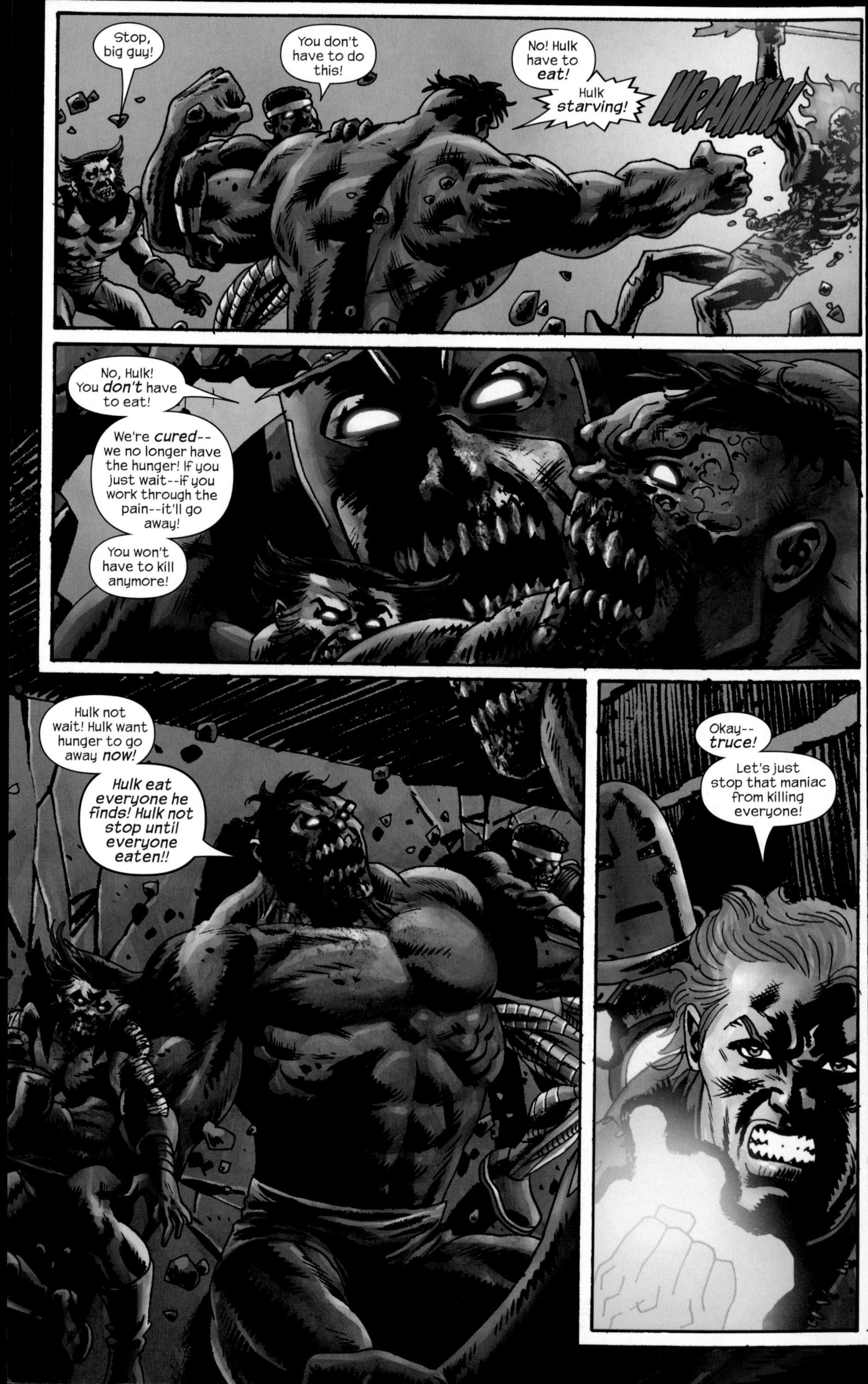
Stop, big guy!
You don't have to do this!
No! Hulk have to eat!
Hulk starving!
WRAMM!
No, Hulk! You don't have to eat!
We're cured--we no longer have the hunger! If you just wait--if you work through the pain--it'll go away!
You won't have to kill anymore!
Hulk not wait! Hulk want hunger to go away now!
Hulk eat everyone he finds! Hulk not stop until everyone eaten!!
Okay--truce!
Let's just stop that maniac from killing everyone!

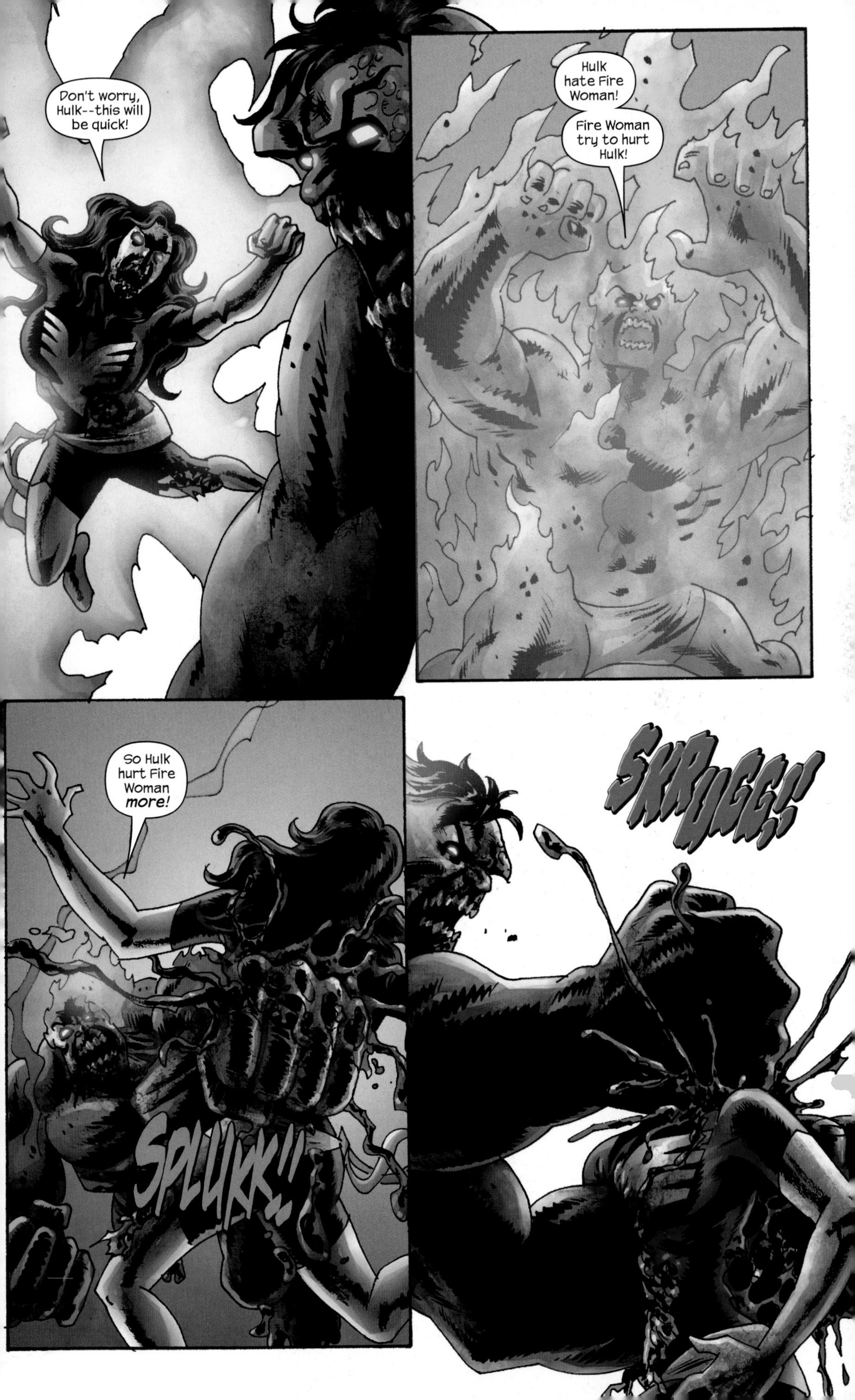
Don't worry, Hulk--this will be quick!
Hulk hate Fire Woman!
Fire Woman try to hurt Hulk!
So Hulk hurt Fire Woman *more!*
SPLURK!!
SKRUGG!!

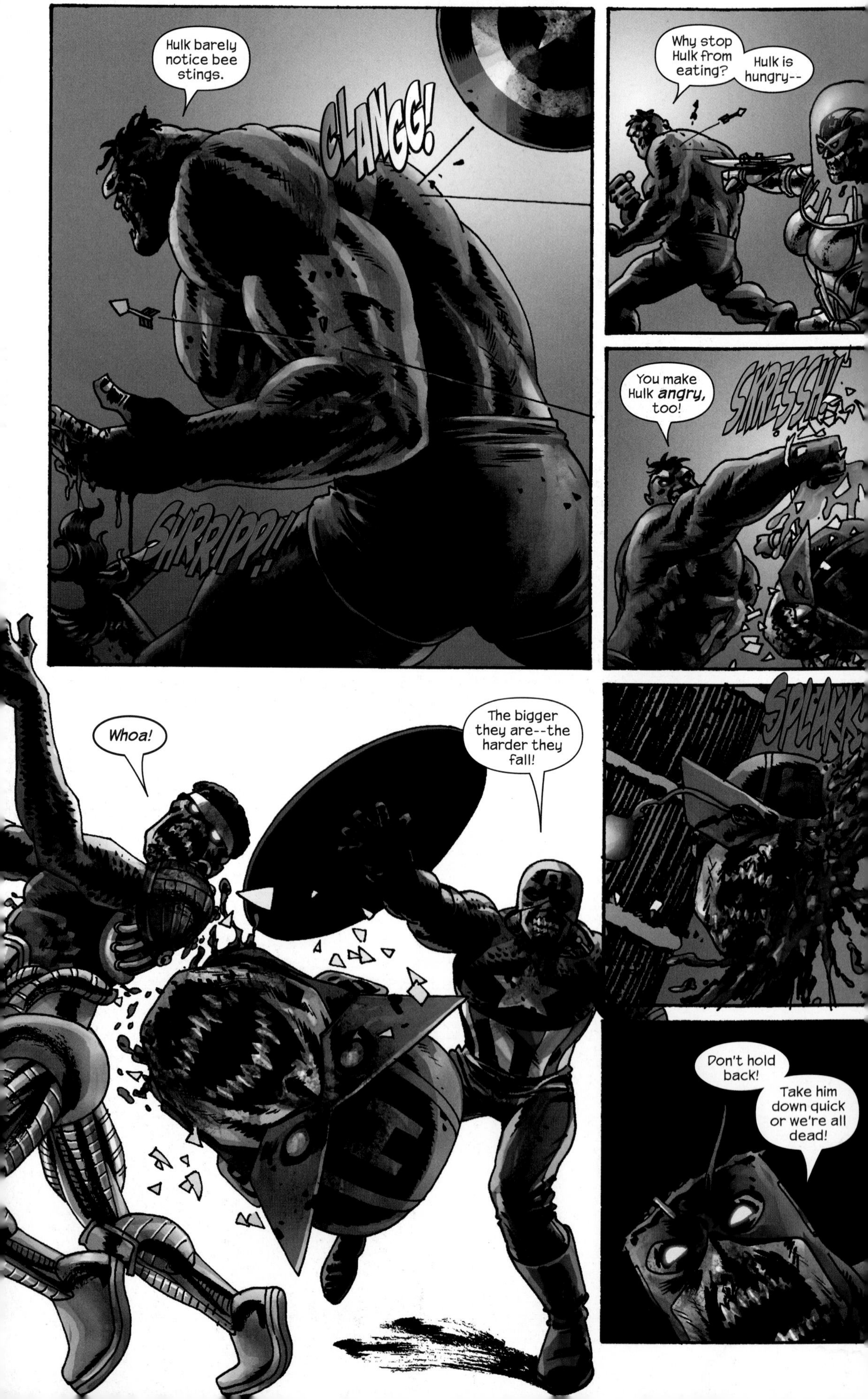

Hulk barely notice bee stings.
CLANGG!
SHRIPP!!
Why stop Hulk from eating?
Hulk is hungry--
You make Hulk *angry,* too!
SKRESSH!
SPLAKK!
Whoa!
The bigger they are--the harder they fall!
Don't hold back!
Take him down quick or we're all dead!

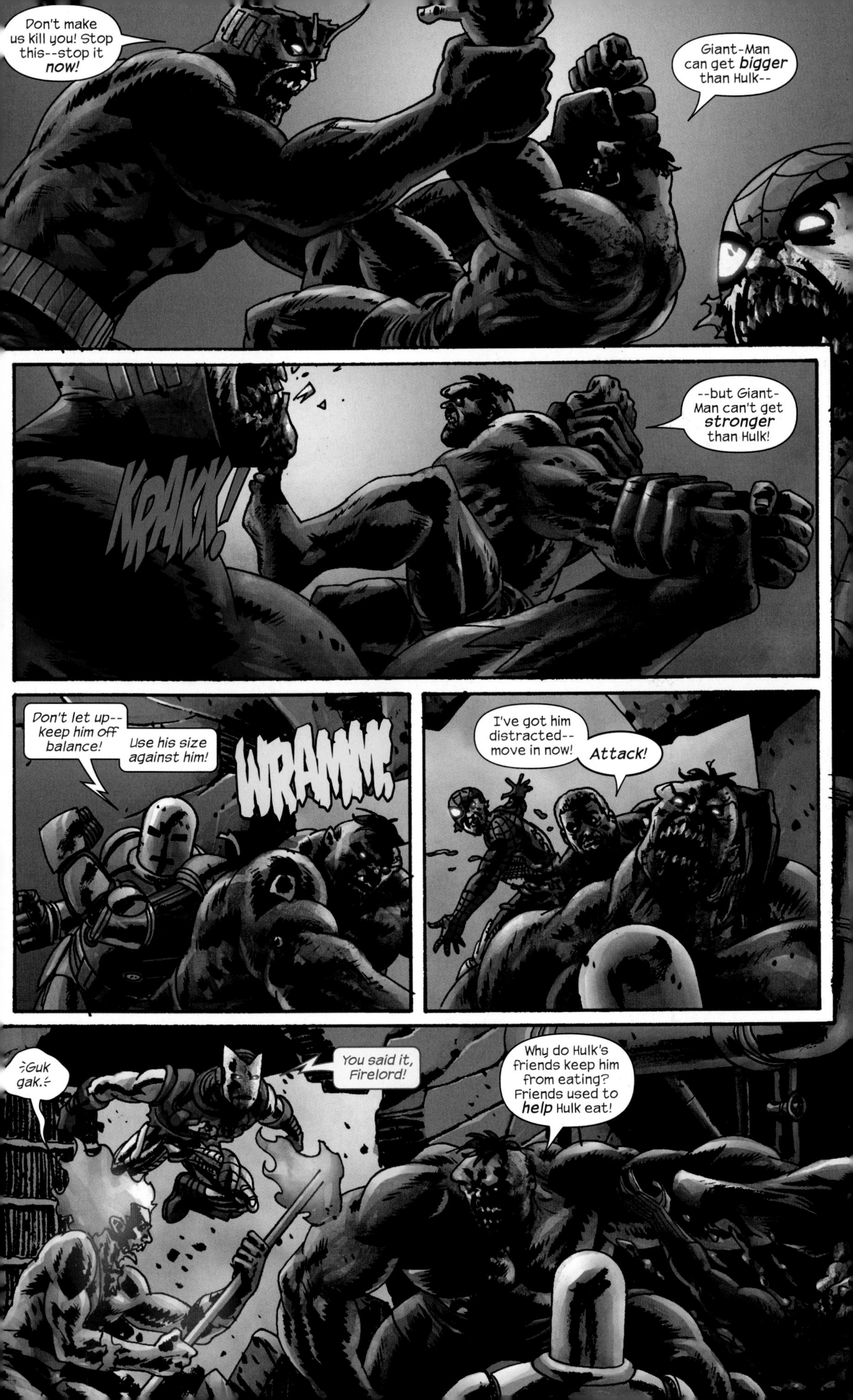
Don't make us kill you! Stop this--stop it now!
Giant-Man can get bigger than Hulk--
--but Giant-Man can't get stronger than Hulk!
KRAKK!
Don't let up--keep him off balance!
Use his size against him!
WRAMM!
I've got him distracted--move in now!
Attack!
Guk gak.
You said it, Firelord!
Why do Hulk's friends keep him from eating? Friends used to help Hulk eat!

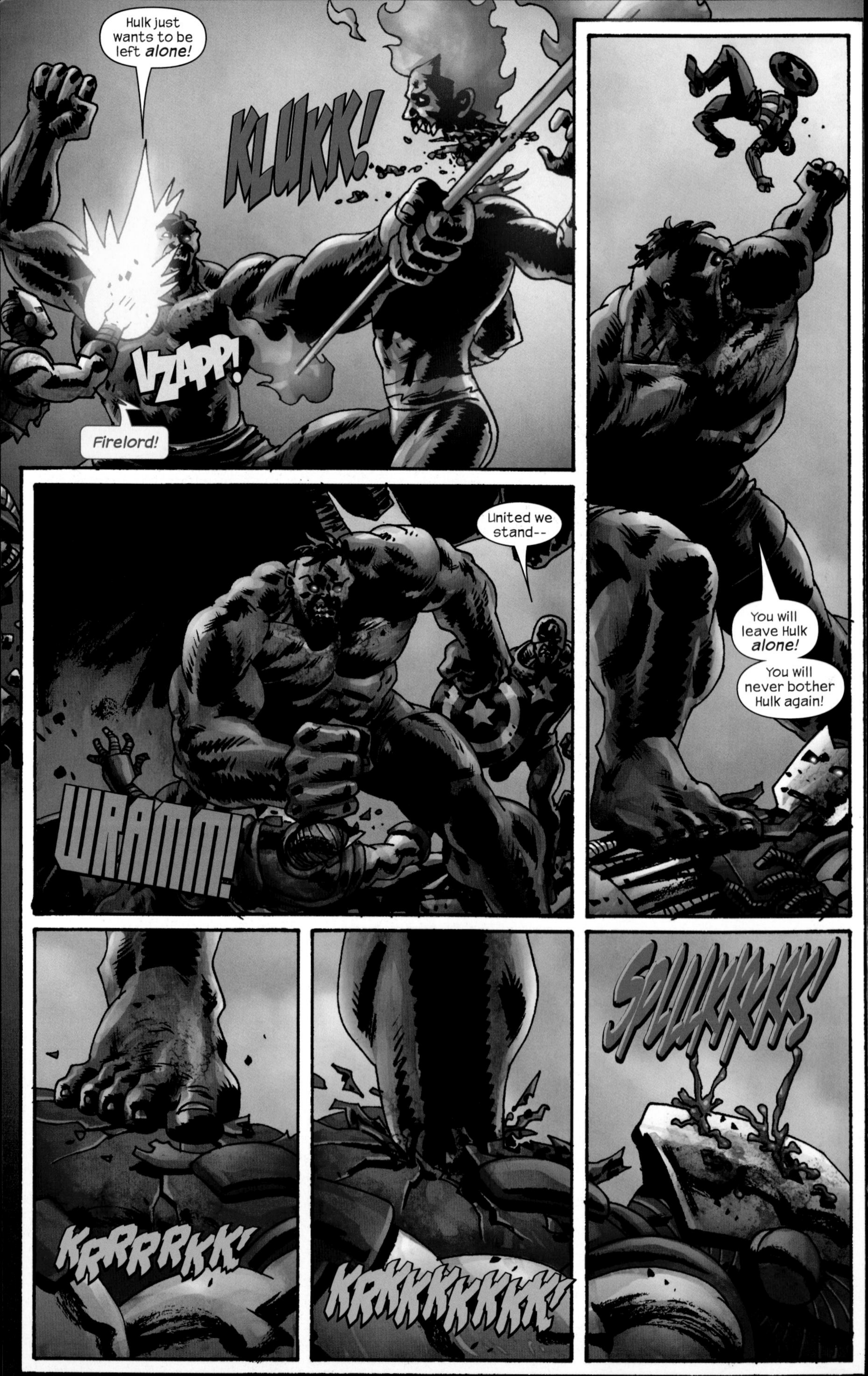
Hulk just wants to be left *alone!*
KLUKK!
VZAPP!
Firelord!
You will leave Hulk *alone!*
You will never bother Hulk again!
United we stand--
WRAMM!
KRRRRKK!
KRKKKKKKK!
SPLUKKKK!

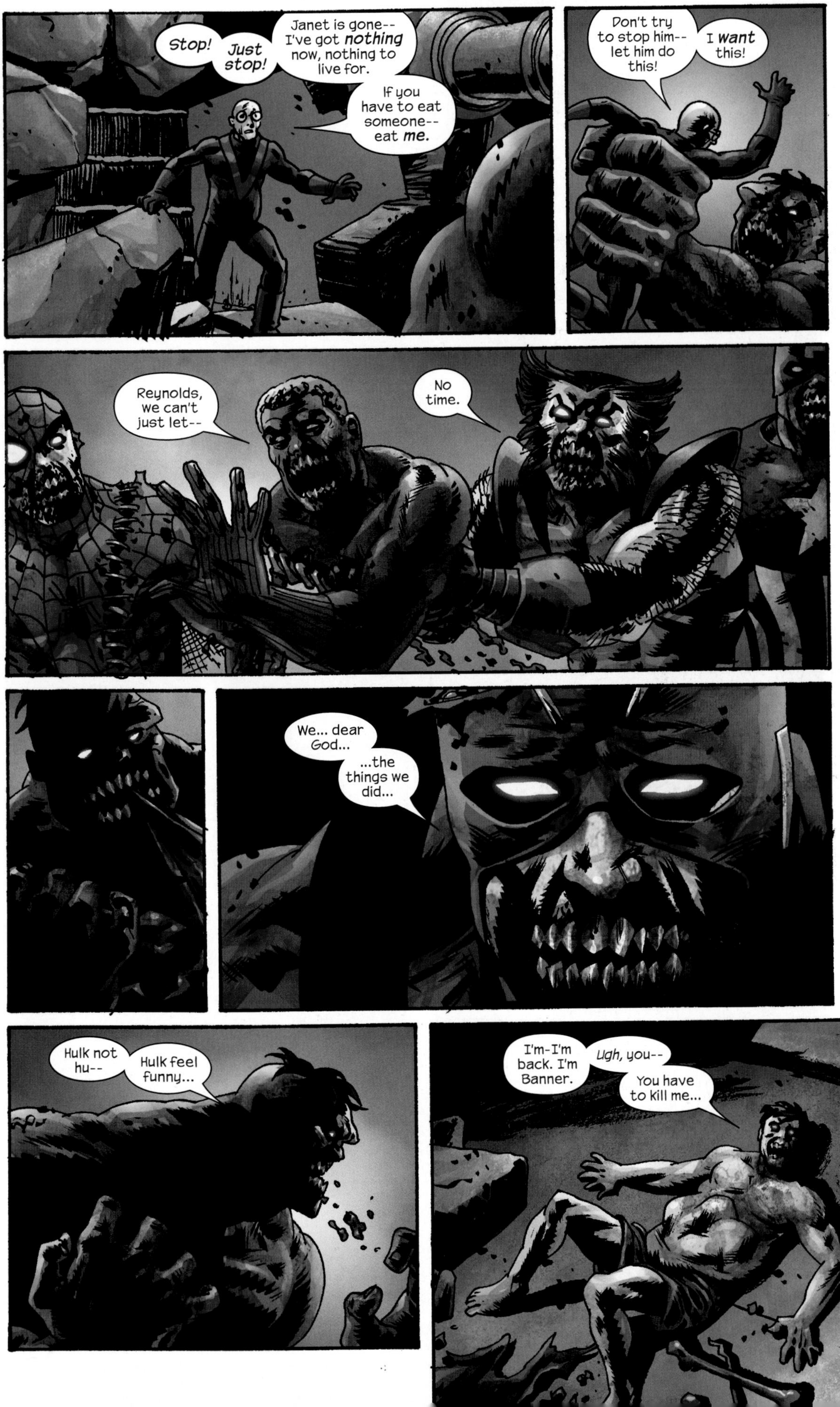
Stop!
Just stop!
Janet is gone-- I've got nothing now, nothing to live for.
If you have to eat someone-- eat me.
Don't try to stop him-- let him do this!
I want this!
Reynolds, we can't just let--
No time.
We... dear God...
...the things we did...
Hulk not hu--
Hulk feel funny...
I'm-I'm back. I'm Banner.
Ugh, you--
You have to kill me...

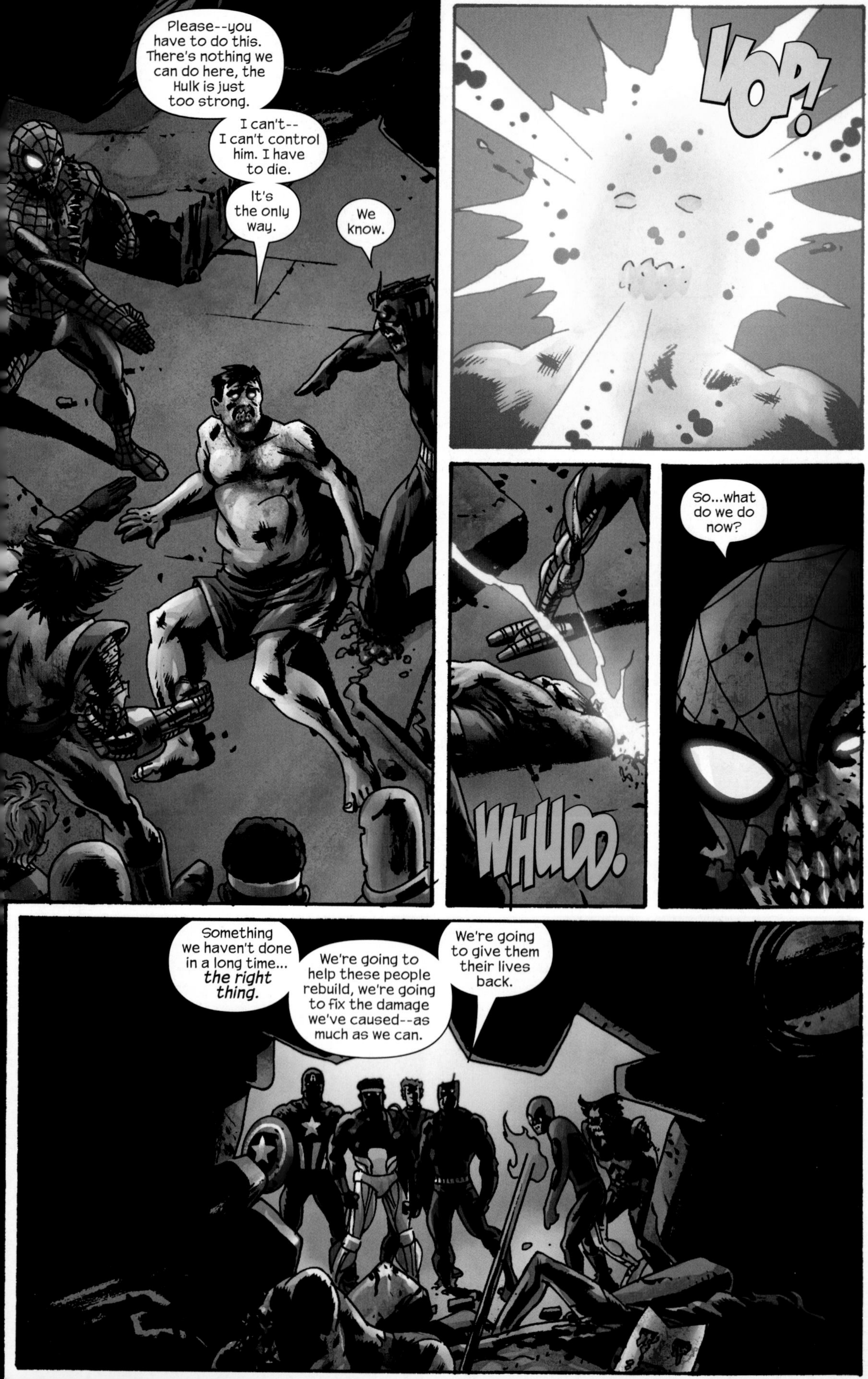
Please--you have to do this. There's nothing we can do here, the Hulk is just too strong.
I can't-- I can't control him. I have to die.
It's the only way.
We know.
VOP!
WHUDD.
So...what do we do now?
Something we haven't done in a long time... *the right thing.*
We're going to help these people rebuild, we're going to fix the damage we've caused--as much as we can.
We're going to give them their lives back.

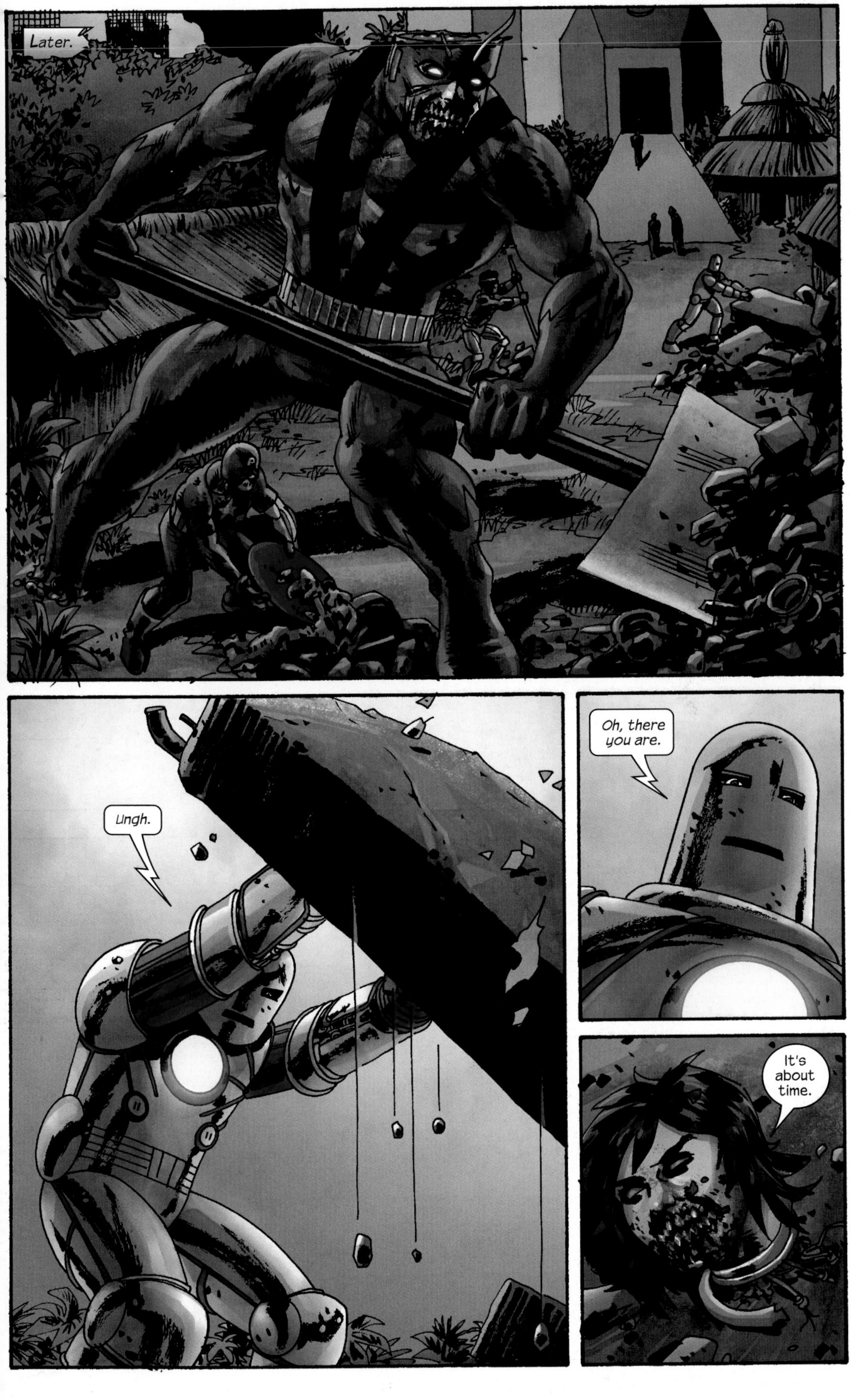

Later.
Ungh.
Oh, there you are.
It's about time.

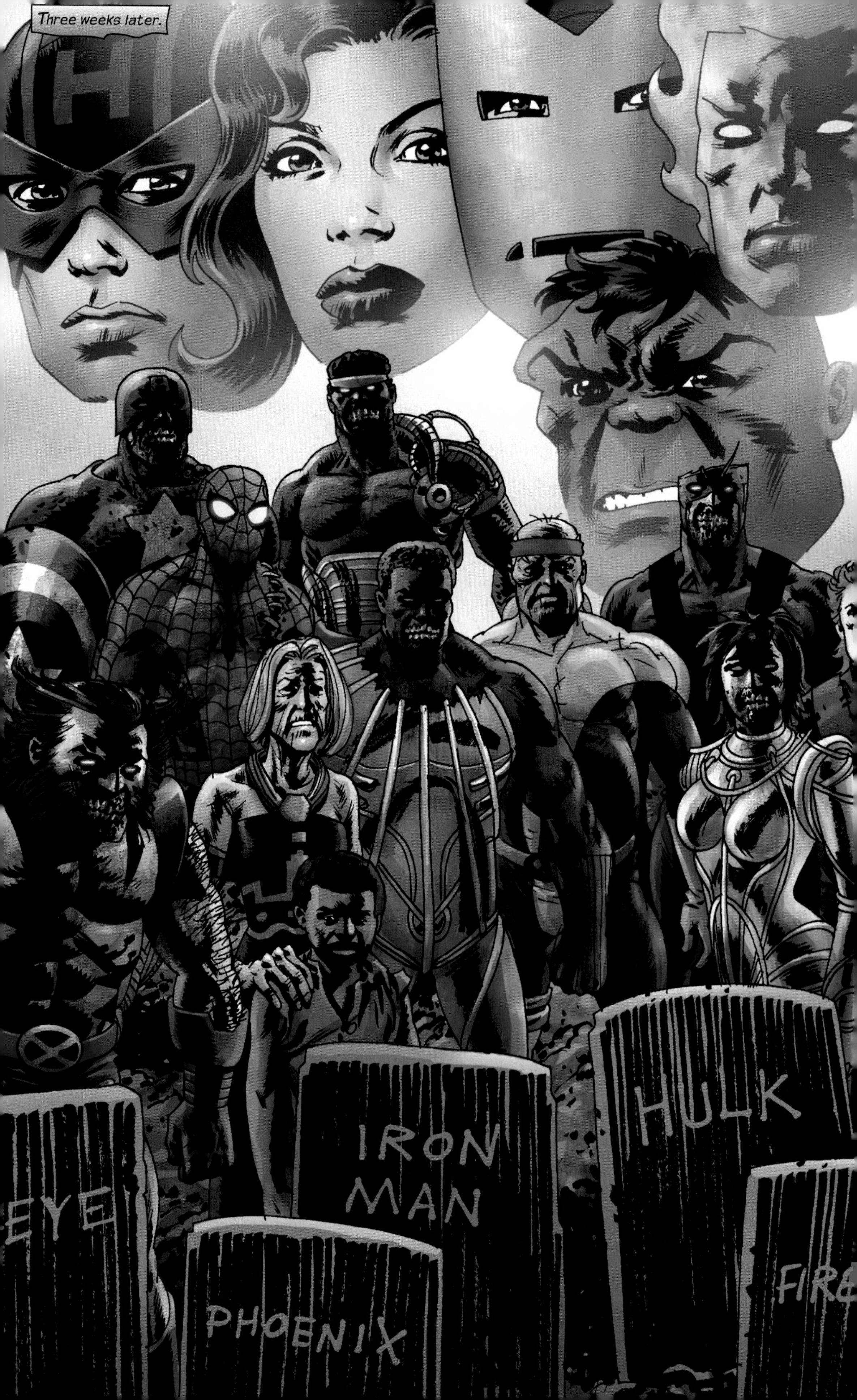
Three weeks later.
EYE
IRON MAN
HULK
PHOENIX
FIRE

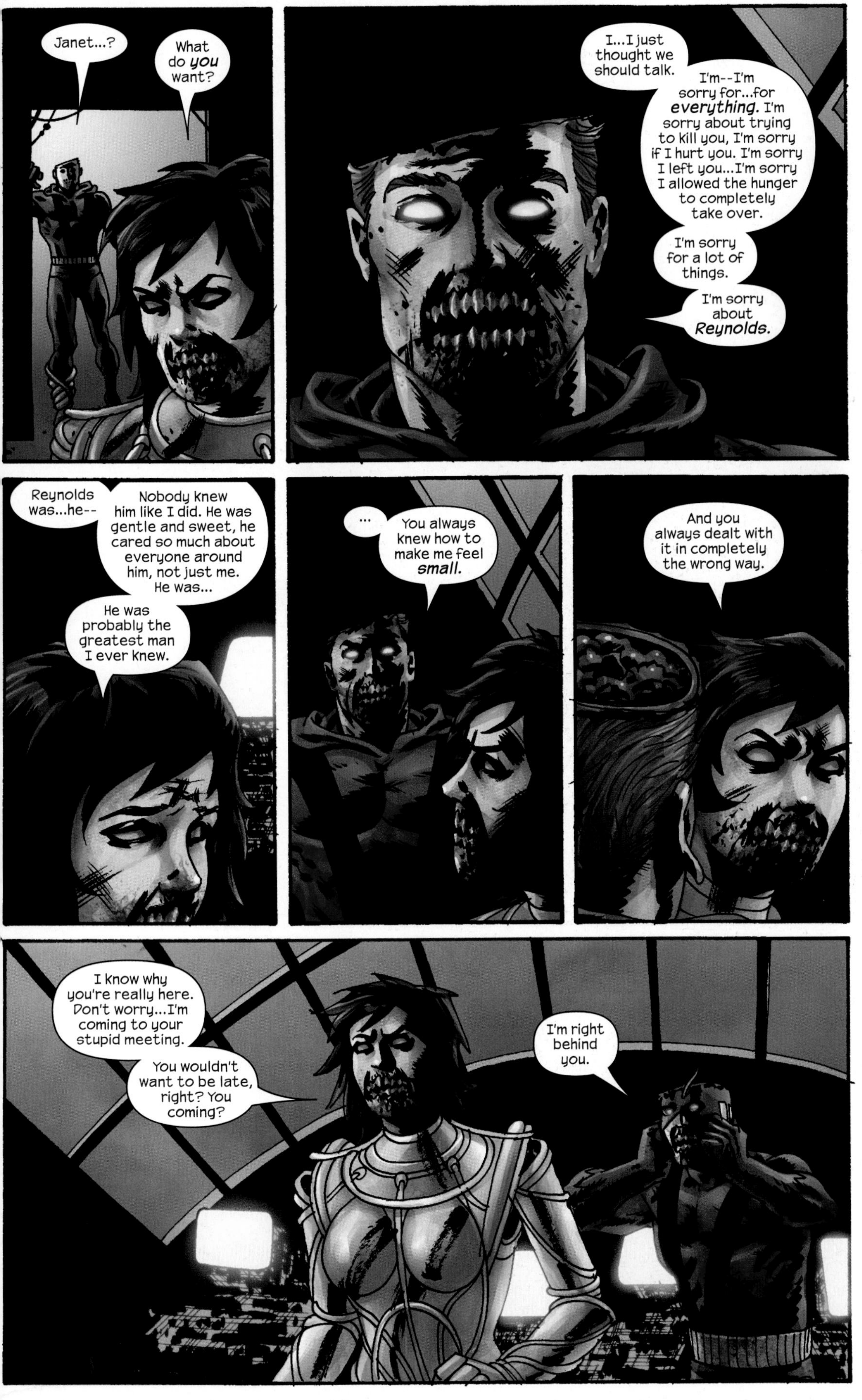
Janet...?
What do *you* want?
I...I just thought we should talk.
I'm--I'm sorry for...for ***everything.*** I'm sorry about trying to kill you, I'm sorry if I hurt you. I'm sorry I left you...I'm sorry I allowed the hunger to completely take over.
I'm sorry for a lot of things.
I'm sorry about ***Reynolds.***
Reynolds was...he--
Nobody knew him like I did. He was gentle and sweet, he cared so much about everyone around him, not just me. He was...
He was probably the greatest man I ever knew.
...
You always knew how to make me feel ***small.***
And you always dealt with it in completely the wrong way.
I know why you're really here. Don't worry...I'm coming to your stupid meeting.
You wouldn't want to be late, right? You coming?
I'm right behind you.

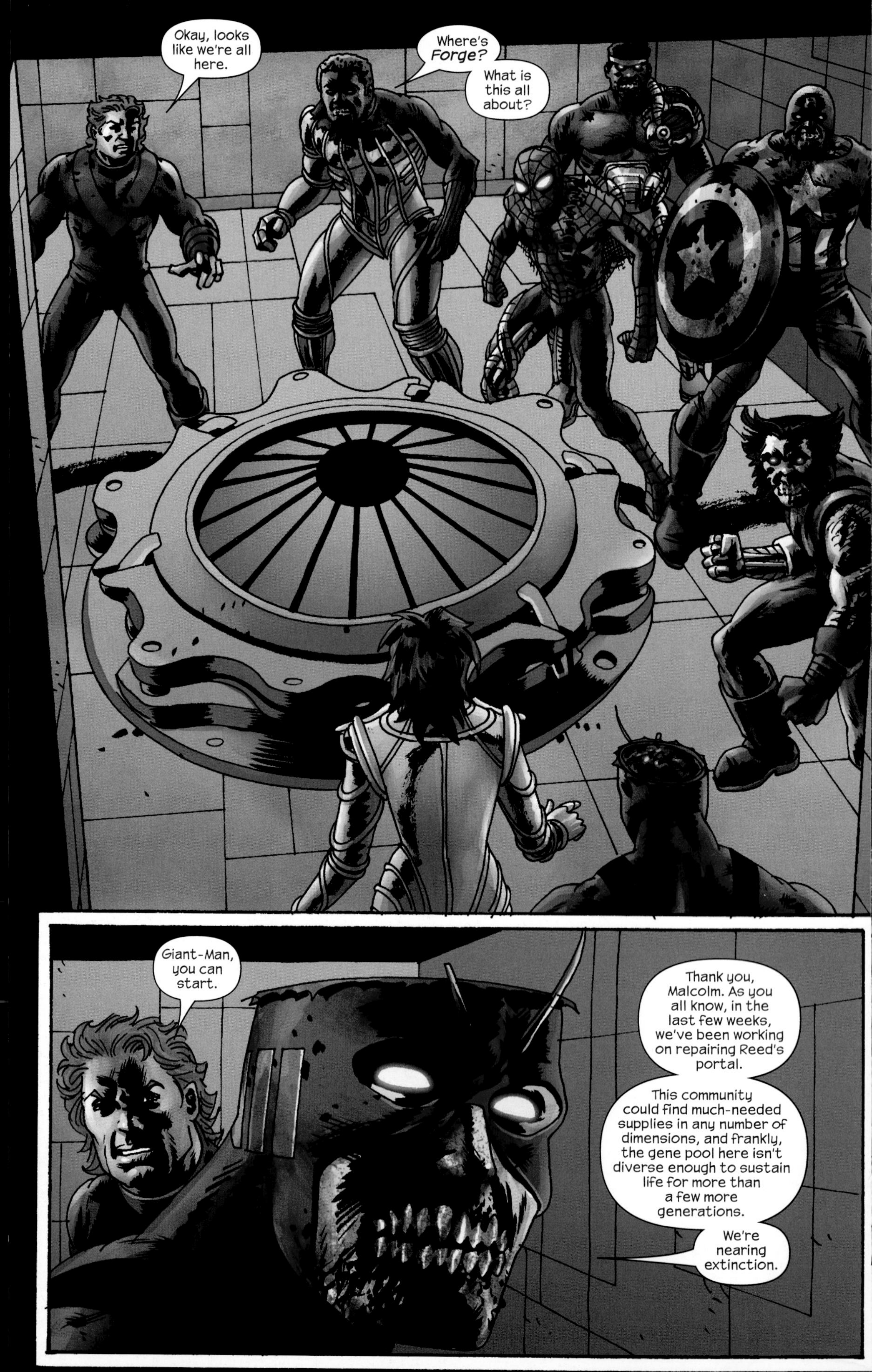
Okay, looks like we're all here.
Where's Forge?
What is this all about?
Giant-Man, you can start.
Thank you, Malcolm. As you all know, in the last few weeks, we've been working on repairing Reed's portal.
This community could find much-needed supplies in any number of dimensions, and frankly, the gene pool here isn't diverse enough to sustain life for more than a few more generations.
We're nearing extinction.

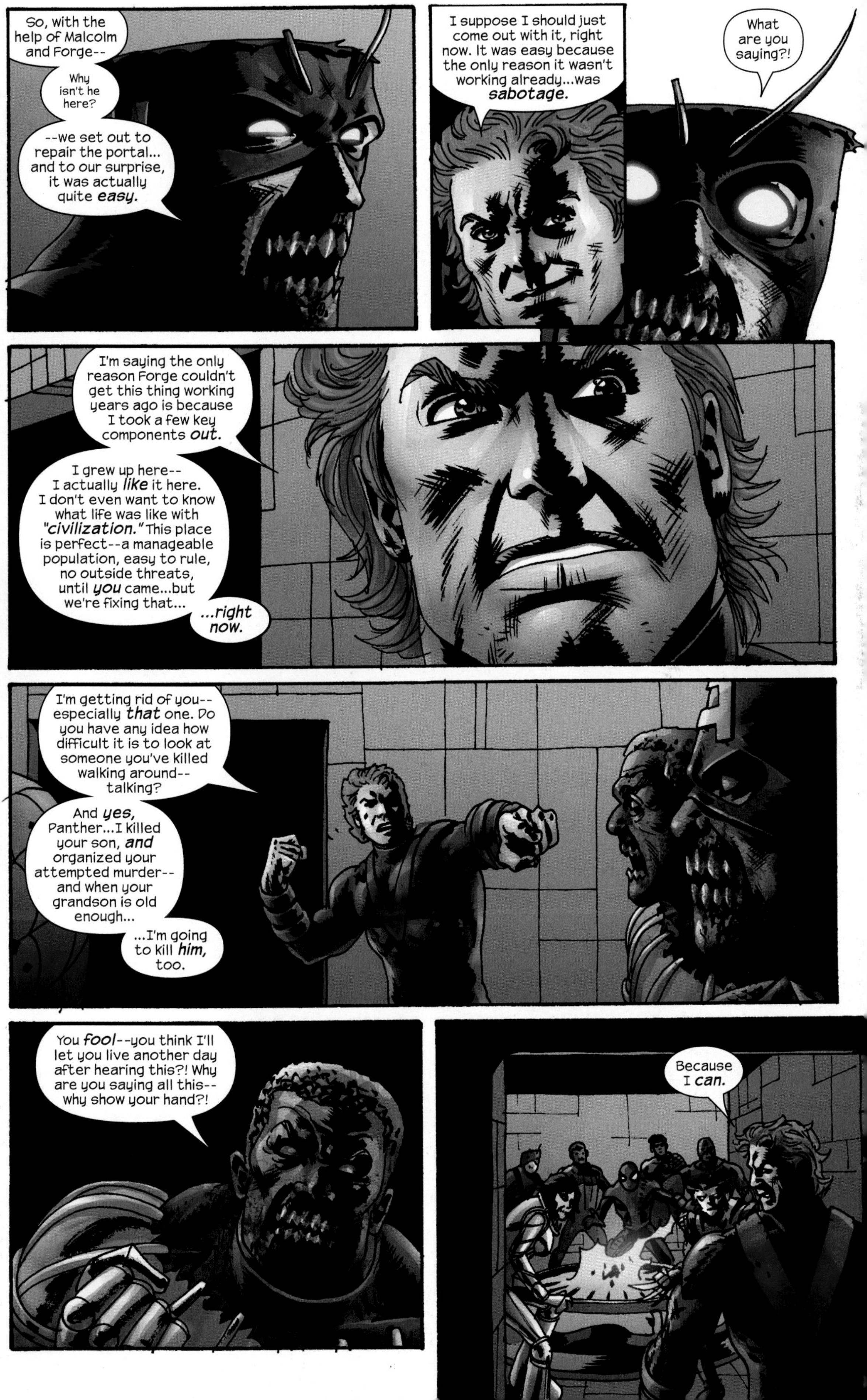
So, with the help of Malcolm and Forge--
Why isn't he here?
--we set out to repair the portal... and to our surprise, it was actually quite easy.
I suppose I should just come out with it, right now. It was easy because the only reason it wasn't working already...was sabotage.
What are you saying?!
I'm saying the only reason Forge couldn't get this thing working years ago is because I took a few key components out.
I grew up here-- I actually like it here. I don't even want to know what life was like with "civilization." This place is perfect--a manageable population, easy to rule, no outside threats, until you came...but we're fixing that...
...right now.
I'm getting rid of you-- especially that one. Do you have any idea how difficult it is to look at someone you've killed walking around-- talking?
And yes, Panther...I killed your son, and organized your attempted murder-- and when your grandson is old enough...
...I'm going to kill him, too.
You fool--you think I'll let you live another day after hearing this?! Why are you saying all this-- why show your hand?!
Because I can.

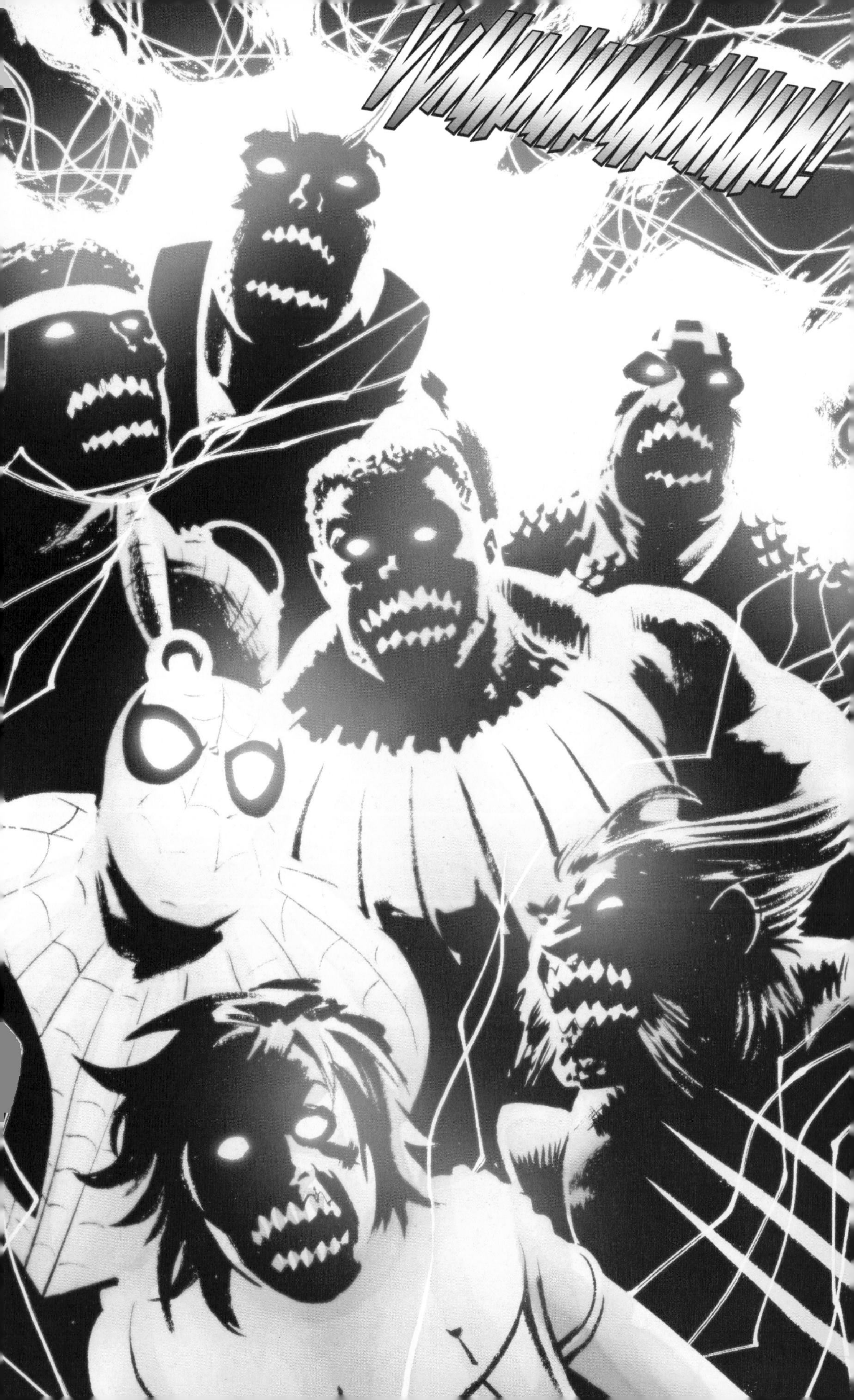

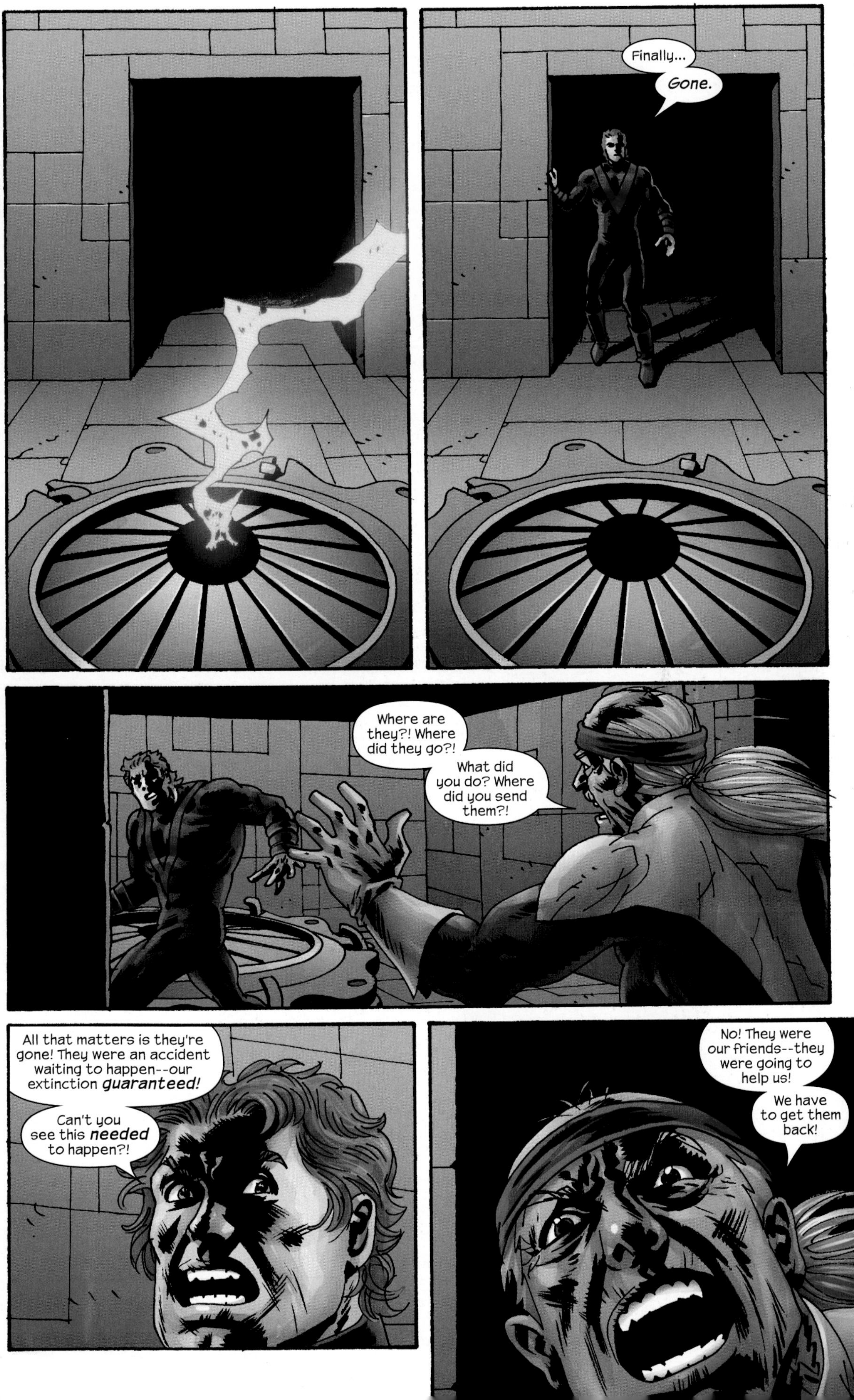
Finally...
Gone.
Where are they?! Where did they go?!
What did you do? Where did you send them?!
All that matters is they're gone! They were an accident waiting to happen--our extinction *guaranteed!*
Can't you see this *needed* to happen?!
No! They were our friends--they were going to help us!
We have to get them back!

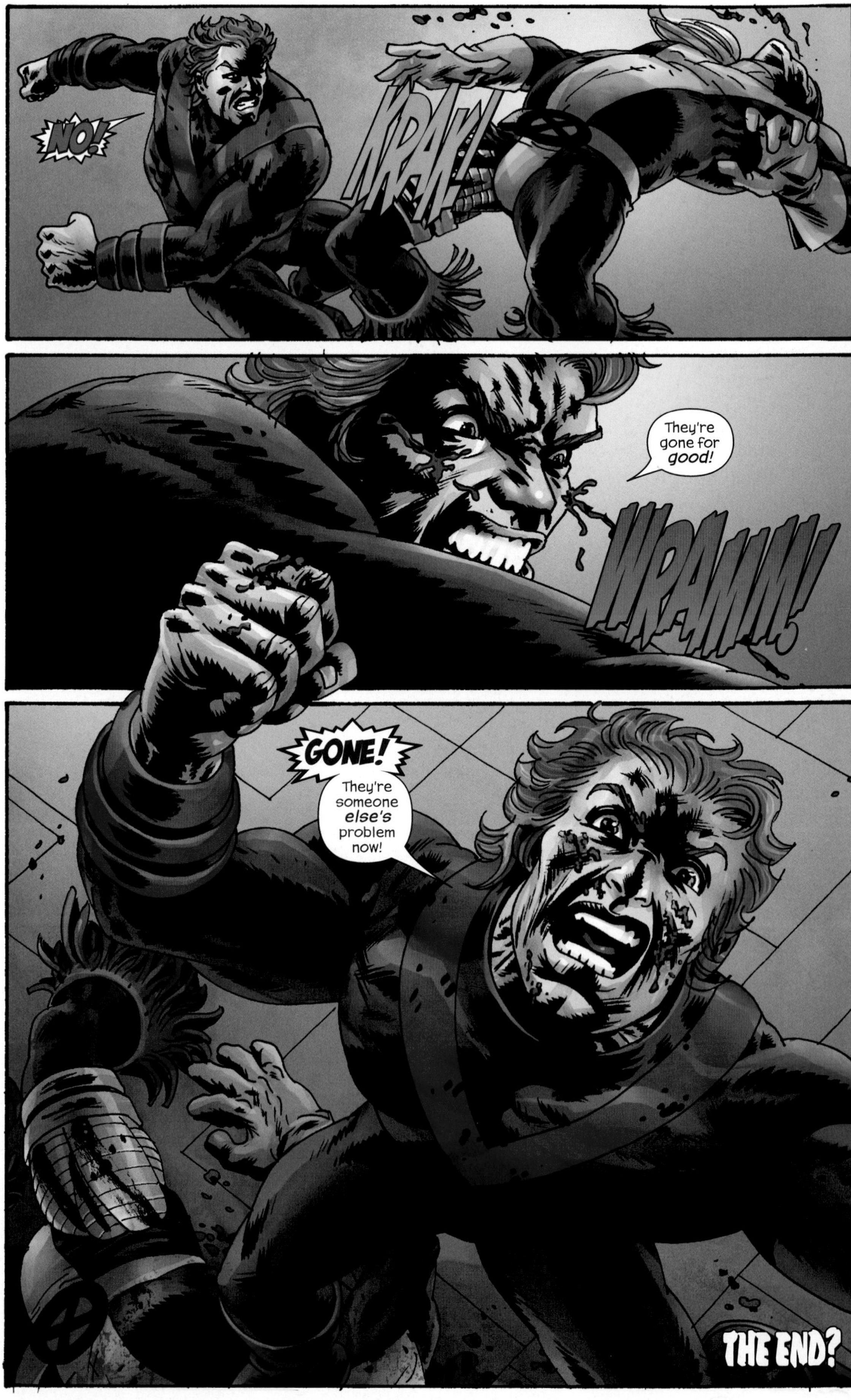
NO!
KRAK!
They're gone for good!
WRAMM!
GONE!
They're someone else's problem now!
THE END?

HARD TO BELIEVE WE'VE HIT THE FINISH LINE FOR THIS, THE SECOND MARVEL ZOMBIES MINI-SERIES, ALREADY. IT SEEMS LIKE JUST YESTERDAY I WAS SITTING DOWN TRYING TO FIGURE OUT HOW TO TURN THIS KOOKY IDEA INTO A STORY. I'D LIKE TO THANK SEAN, JUNE, RUS, RANDY, ARTHUR, BILL, LAUREN, NICOLE, JOHN AND RALPH FOR ALL THEIR CONTRIBUTIONS ON THE TWO MINI-SERIES. I'D ALSO LIKE TO THANK ALL OF YOU, EACH AND EVERY ONE OF YOU, FOR PURCHASING THIS. I HOPE YOU FEEL THE SECOND STORY LIVED UP TO THE FIRST--AND DON'T FORGET...THERE WAS A QUESTION MARK BEHIND "THE END" ON THAT LAST PAGE.

--ROBERT

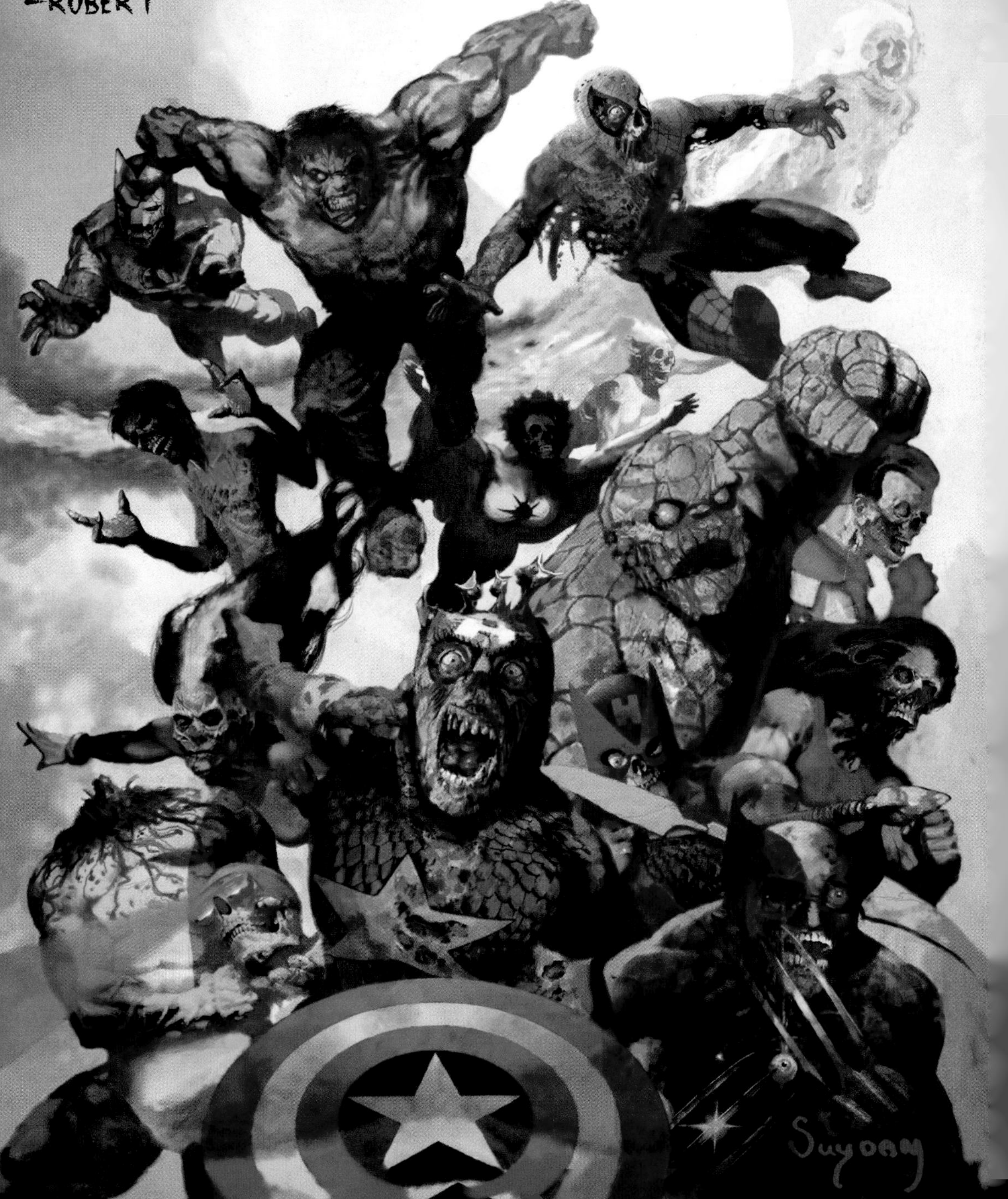

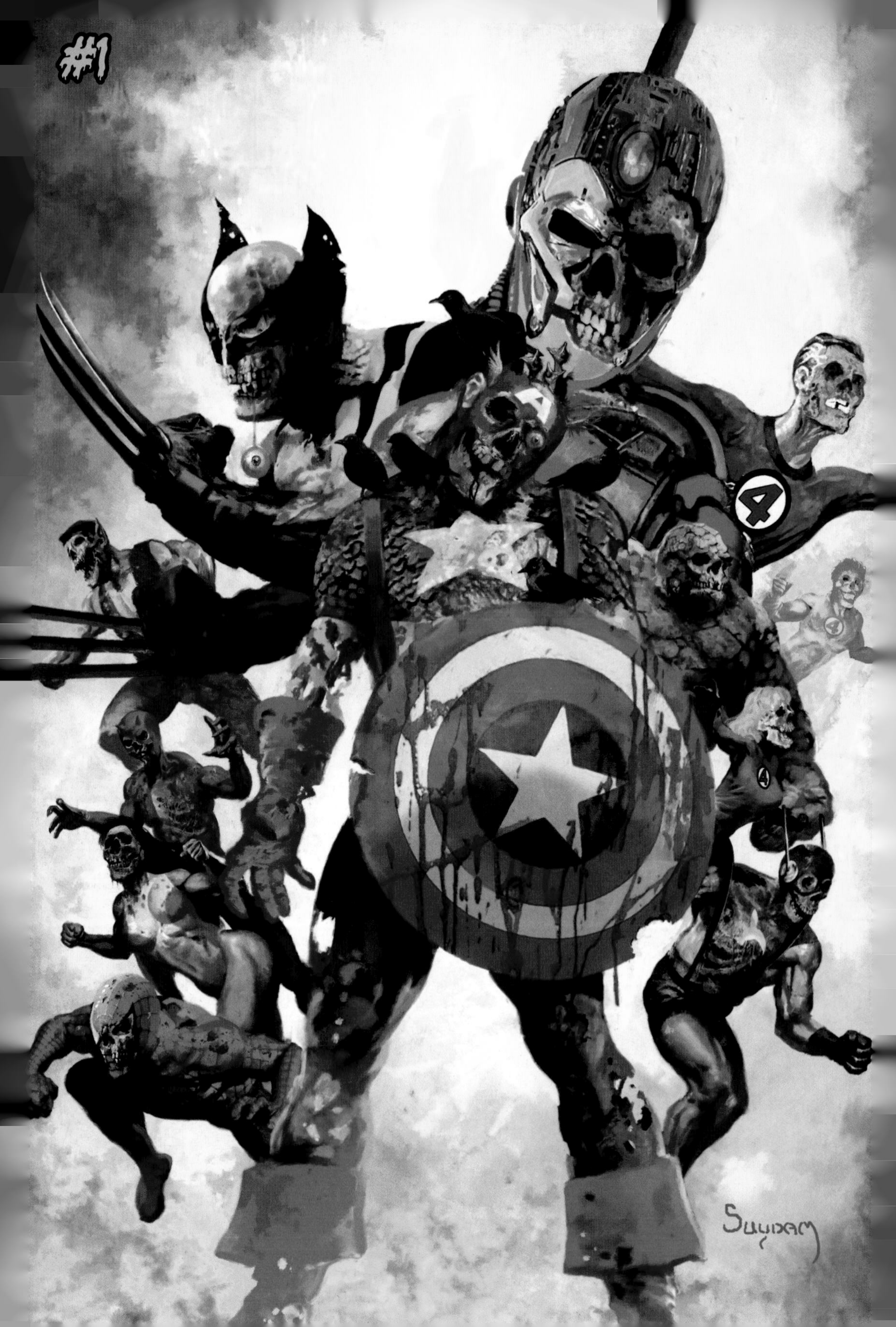
#1
Suydam

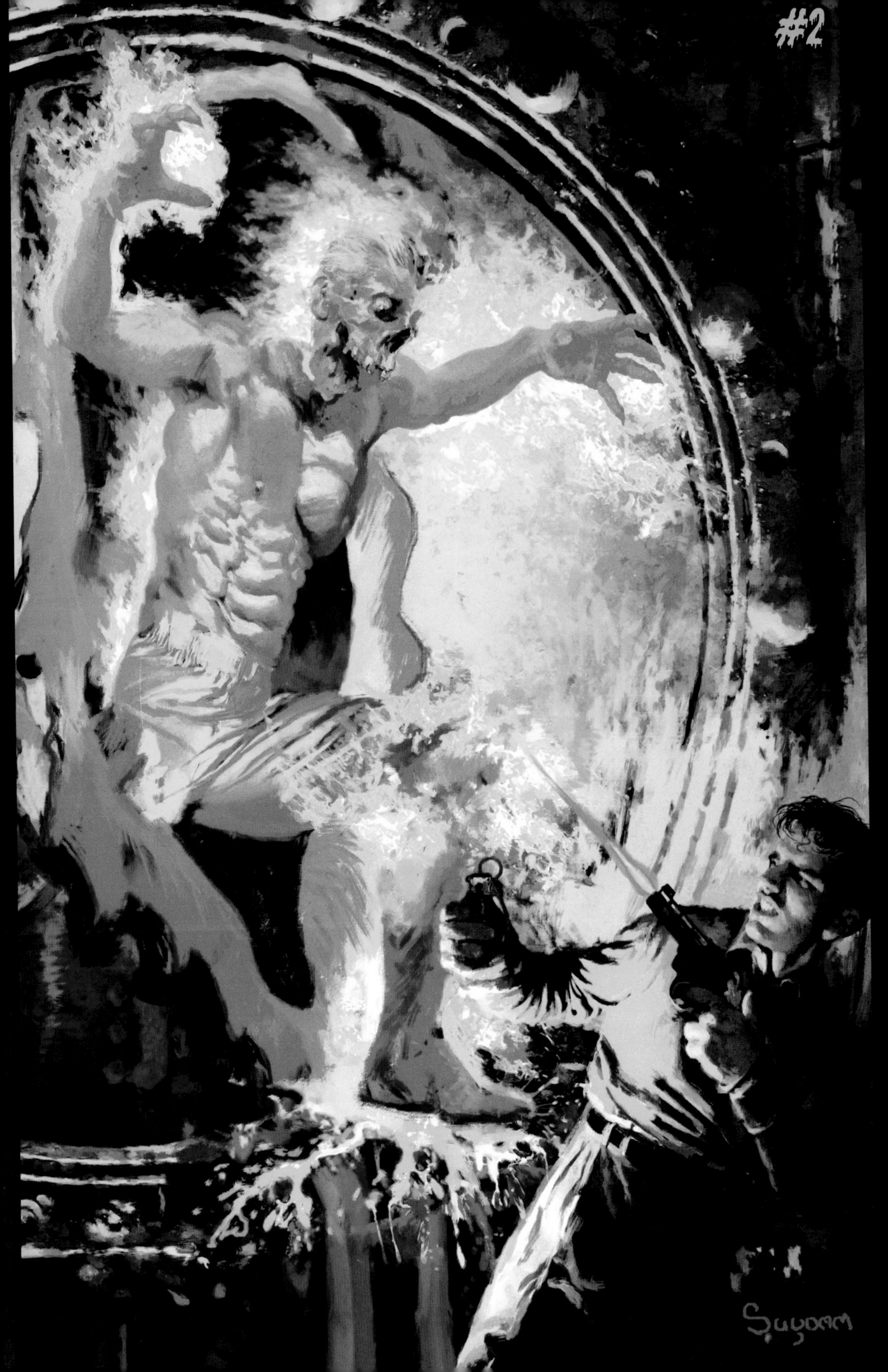
#2
Suydam

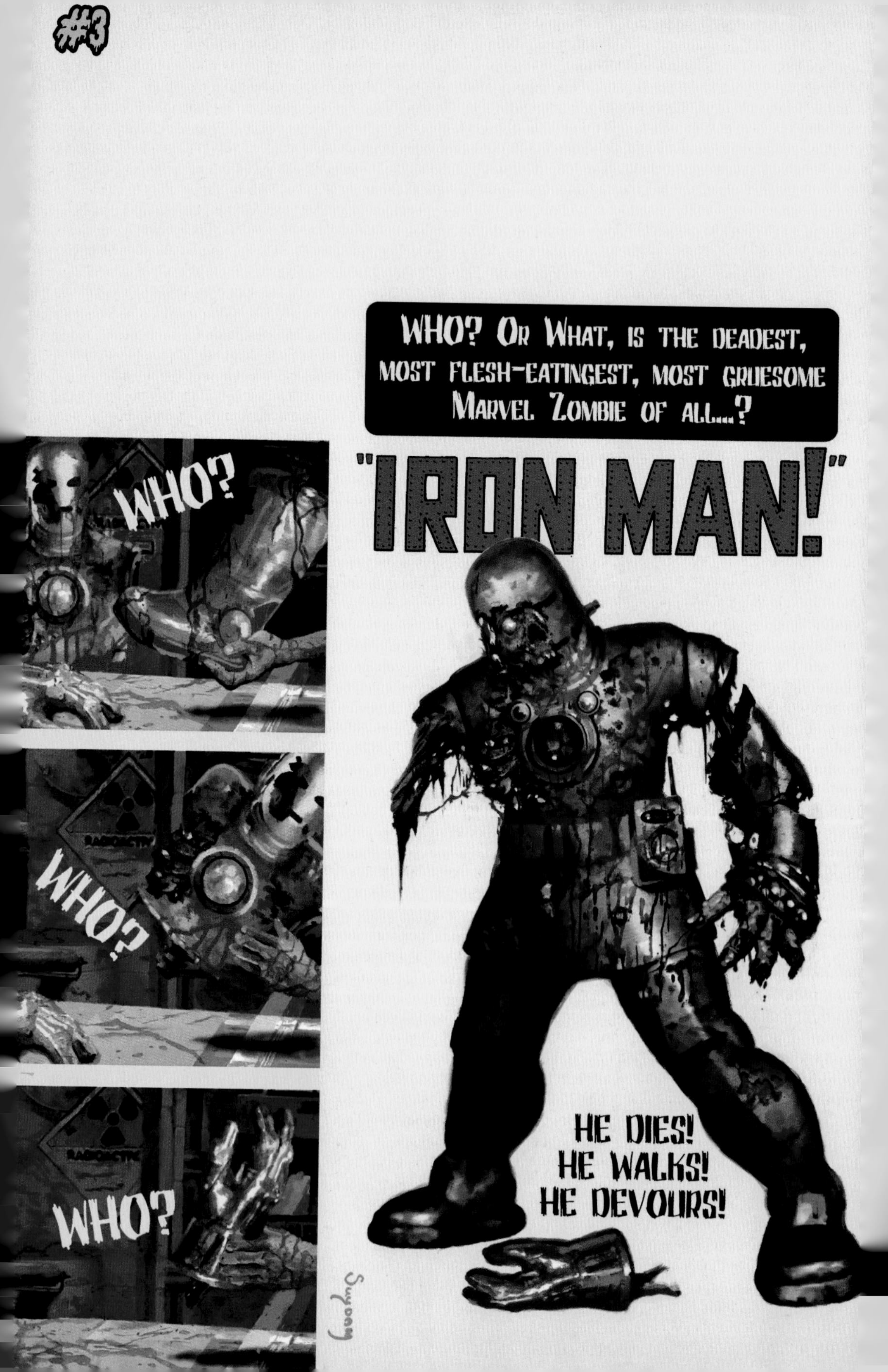
#3
WHO?
WHO?
WHO?
WHO? OR WHAT, IS THE DEADEST, MOST FLESH-EATINGEST, MOST GRUESOME MARVEL ZOMBIE OF ALL...?
"IRON MAN!"
HE DIES!
HE WALKS!
HE DEVOURS!

#4

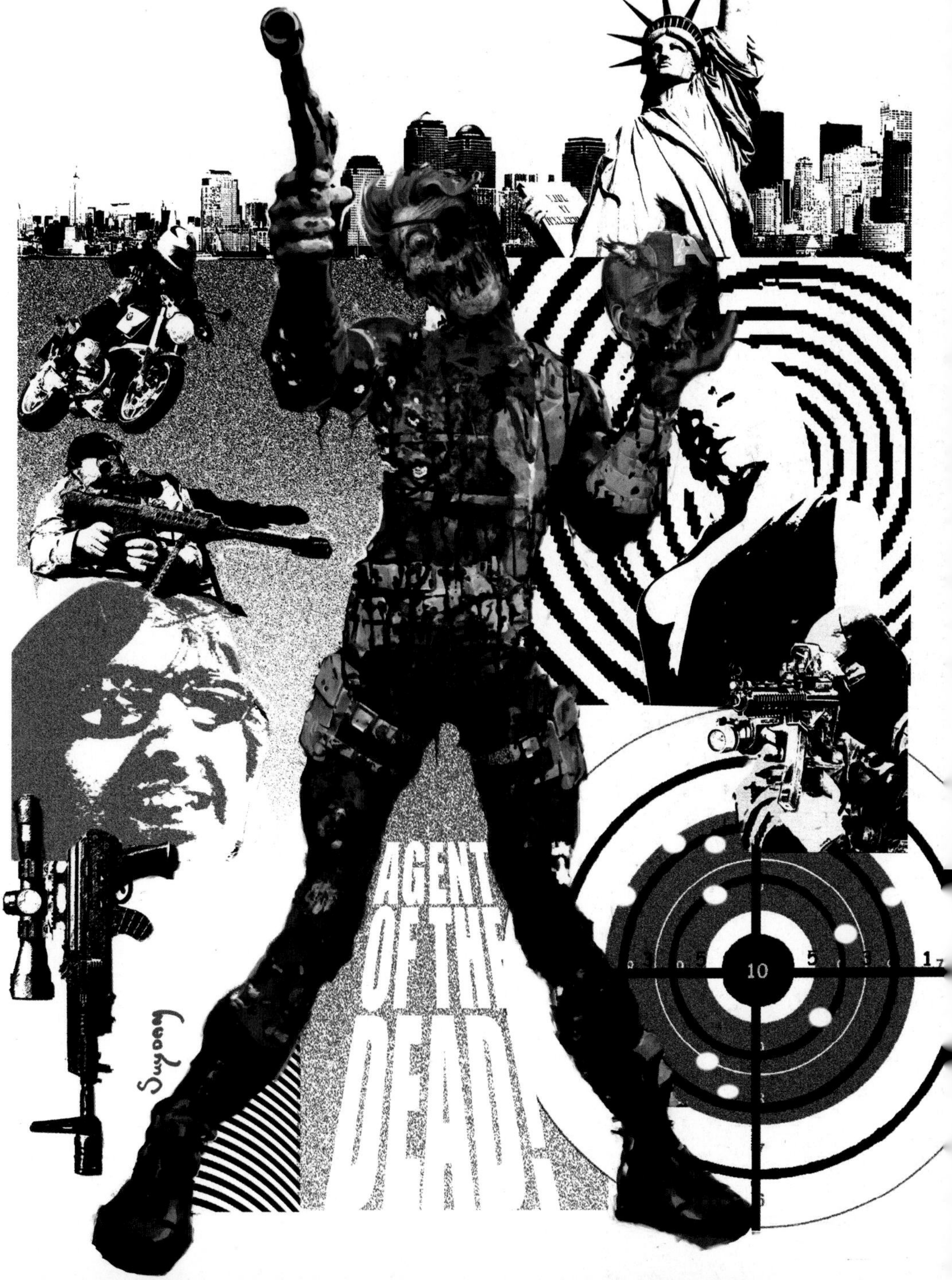
AGENT OF THE DEAD

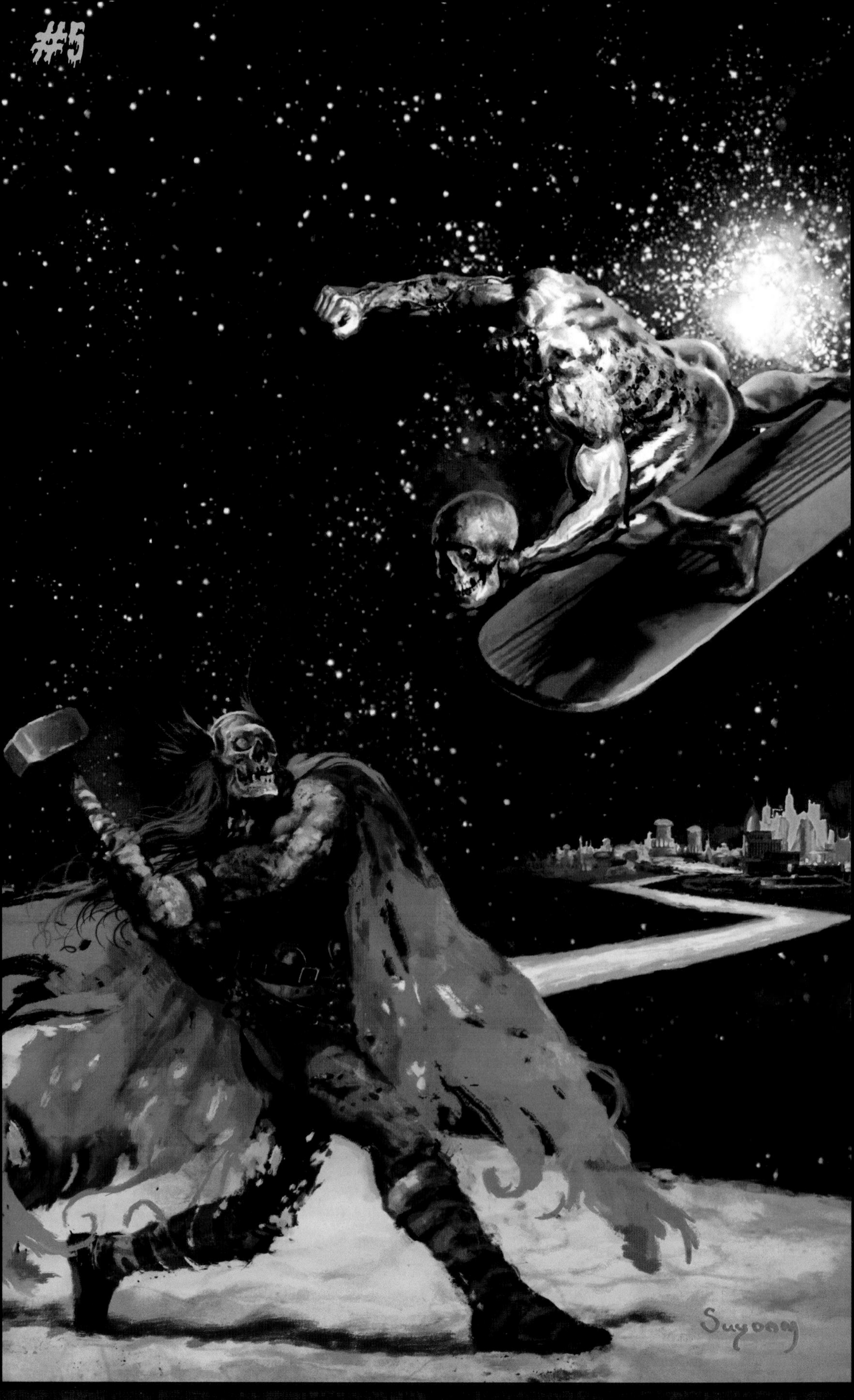
#5
Suydam

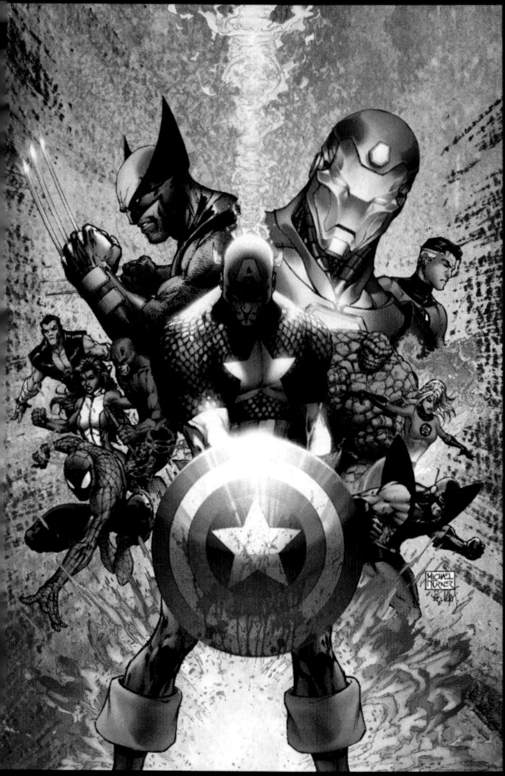

VIL WAR #1 Variant cover by Michael Turner

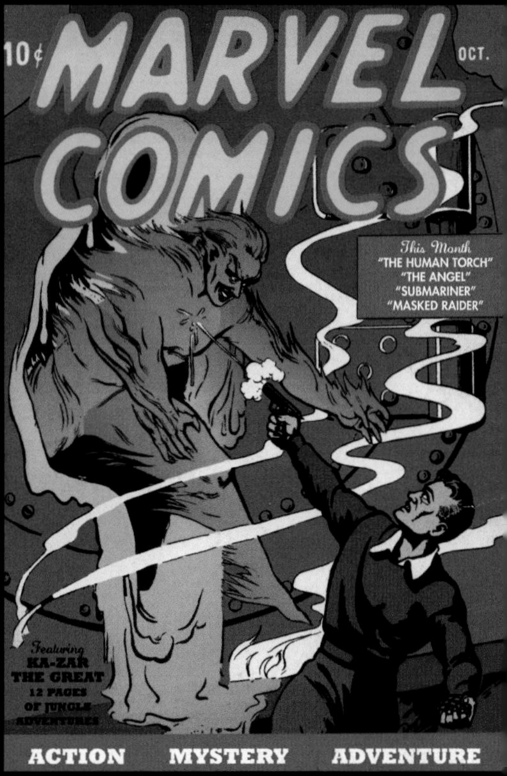
10¢
MARVEL COMICS
OCT.
This Month
"THE HUMAN TORCH"
"THE ANGEL"
"SUBMARINER"
"MASKED RAIDER"
Featuring KA-ZAR THE GREAT 12 PAGES OF JUNGLE ADVENTURES
ACTION MYSTERY ADVENTURE

MARVEL COMICS #1 cover by Frank Paul

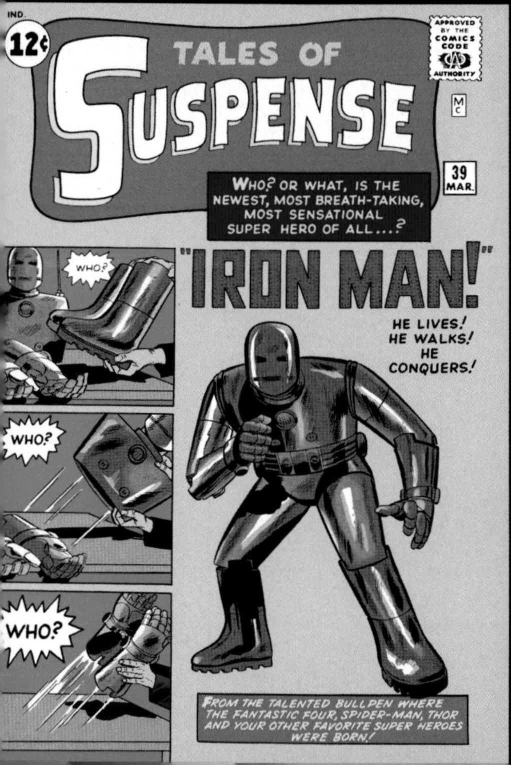
IND.
12¢
TALES OF SUSPENSE
APPROVED BY THE COMICS CODE AUTHORITY
MC
39 MAR.
WHO? OR WHAT, IS THE NEWEST, MOST BREATH-TAKING, MOST SENSATIONAL SUPER HERO OF ALL...?
WHO?
"IRON MAN!"
HE LIVES! HE WALKS! HE CONQUERS!
WHO?
WHO?
FROM THE TALENTED BULLPEN WHERE THE FANTASTIC FOUR, SPIDER-MAN, THOR AND YOUR OTHER FAVORITE SUPER HEROES WERE BORN!

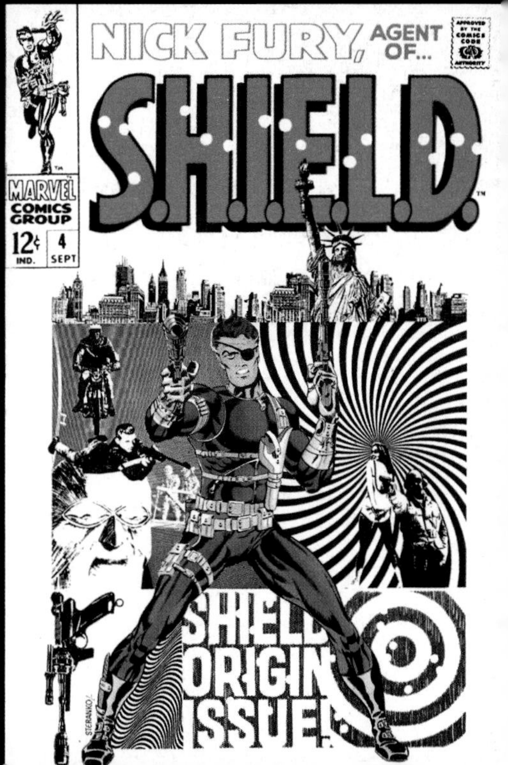
NICK FURY, AGENT OF...
APPROVED BY THE COMICS CODE AUTHORITY
S.H.I.E.L.D.
MARVEL COMICS GROUP
12¢ IND.
4 SEPT
SHIELD ORIGIN ISSUE!

THE SILVER SURFER
25¢ IND.
4 FEB
MARVEL COMICS GROUP

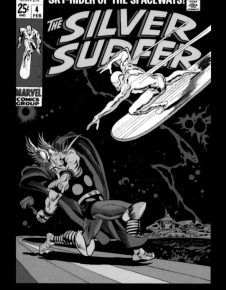

SILVER SURFER #4 cover by John Buscema

ROBERT KIRKMAN

SEAN PHILLIPS

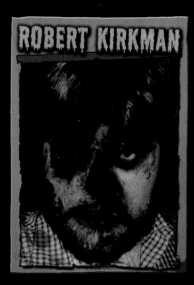

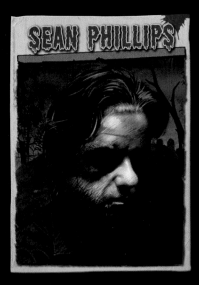

ROBERT KIRKMAN

CURRENTLY WRITING: *Marvel Zombies 2, Ultimate X-Men*, Marvel; *Walking Dead, Invincible*, Image
ZOMBIE CRED: *Marvel Zombies #1-5, Dead Days* one-shot, *Marvel Zombies 2 #1-5*
FAVORITE ZOMBIE MOVIE: *Day of the Dead*... but *Shaun of the Dead* is a close second.
FAVORITE SUYDAM ZOMBIE COVER: *Marvel Zombies #4*, the *X-Men #1* cover. Love that cover to *Dead Days*, though.
FAVORITE COVER NOT YET ZOMBIEFIED: *New Mutants #82*, the first appearance of Cable.

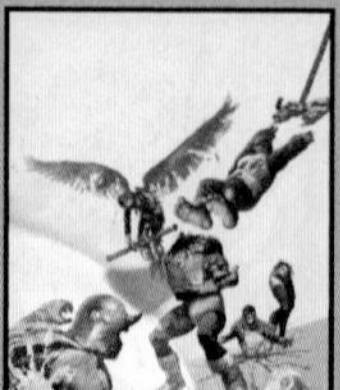

FAVORITE MARVEL ZOMBIE MOMENT: The opening scene of *Marvel Zombies 2* is my current favorite. Sean (Phillips) really knocked that one out of the park.
WHICH MARVEL ZOMBIE WOULD YOU MOST WANT TO BE: Sleepwalker
IF YOU WERE A ZOMBIE,

SEAN PHILLIPS

CURRENTLY DRAWING: *Marvel Zombies 2, Criminal*
ZOMBIE CRED: *Marvel Zombies #1-5, Marvel Zombies/Army of Darkness #4-5, Dead Days* one-shot, *Marvel Zombies 2 #1-5*
FAVORITE ZOMBIE MOVIE: *Shaun of the Dead*
FAVORITE SUYDAM ZOMBIE COVER: *Marvel Zombies HC*, fifth printing, featuring *Mary Jane #2*

FAVORITE MARVEL ZOMBIE MOMENT: Getting that royalty check.
WHICH MARVEL ZOMBIE WOULD YOU MOST WANT TO BE: Hawkeye
IF YOU WERE A ZOMBIE, WHO WOULD YOU MOST WANT TO EAT: No one

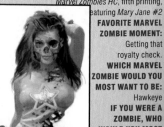